D1605580

AMERICA IN RETREAT

Also by Michael Pembroke

Arthur Phillip: Sailor, Mercenary, Governor, Spy
Trees of History and Romance
Korea: Where the American Century Began

AMERICA IN RETREAT

THE DECLINE OF US LEADERSHIP
FROM WW2 TO COVID-19

MICHAEL
PEMBROKE

ONEWORLD

A Oneworld Book

Published in Great Britain and North America
by Oneworld Publications, 2021

First published by Hardie Grant Books, 2020

ISBN 978-1-78607-987-9
eISBN 978-1-78607-474-4

Typeset in Sabon by Kirby Jones
Printed and bound in Great Britain by Clays Ltd, Elcograf S.p.A.

Oneworld Publications
10 Bloomsbury Street
London WC1B 3SR
England

Stay up to date with the latest books,
special offers, and exclusive content from
Oneworld with our newsletter

Sign up on our website
oneworld-publications.com

MIX
Paper from
responsible sources
FSC® C018072

For Millennials everywhere
and those following

CONTENTS

PREFACE

This book is about our American past and our Asian future – a post-American world that has been emerging for at least a decade; one that has become more evident as the COVID-19 pandemic unfolds and global recession looms. In part, I have developed the theme of my last book, *Korea: Where the American Century Began* (2018). That book was a critique of American military and political excess during the Korean War. I sought to explain how Washington extended the conflict and made things worse; how its overreach on the Korean peninsula established the pattern for the Vietnam conflict and the next seventy years of mostly failed wars and interventions.

Many readers corresponded with me about *Korea* but two elderly men stand out. One was a senior retired military officer, a decorated veteran who had fought in Korea and commanded his men with the fervour of an ecclesiast. In mellow old age, he reflected that 'Only veterans can understand the futility of force for political reasons'. The other had once been a figure of high authority and a pillar of the national and international legal community. Well into his nineties, he wrote to me to say that 'The American Century has been a continuing disaster and demonstrates that we should develop our own strategy'.

A third inspiration was my father, who unexpectedly remarked to me in 2003 that the US-led invasion of Iraq was one of the worst decisions he had ever heard of, and that the Australian and British prime ministers had been 'duchessed'. Time has demonstrated the wisdom of his concerns. The unfolding ineptitude and bloodshed in Iraq caused me to reconsider the role of the United States: whether it was actually making the world a safer or better place; whether it was really a force for good; and whether an American-led 'order' was necessarily the best solution in the rapidly changing world of the twenty-first century.

I was slow to criticise. Conservative institutions have dominated my adult life and shaped my thinking. But this book is written from a unique outlook. I have been engaged by the humanity of the world since childhood. As a boy, I travelled widely and had more opportunities and saw more of the planet than any child could reasonably expect. I was entranced by the gully-gully men of the Suez, mesmerised by the snake charmers of Colombo and ran barefoot in the souk at Aden. I went to school with Muslims, Sikhs and Hindus and was comfortable with turbans and saris, foreign languages and different customs. I lived in colonial Southeast Asia and knew Malays, Indonesians and Chinese. I was, and continue to be, engaged by the diversity and difference of the world, its varied cultures, its conflicting values and its myriad political systems.

The rise of China and the changing world order have been primary motivations for this book. Whatever one's political views, it is not hard to see that something important is happening. Some loud voices in the West seem to suggest that we should return to the 'lunging red arrows of Cold War cartography'. But too few politicians know the history; too many commentators and opinion makers have a short-term focus; and others shape their views through a manifestly moral or political lens. For some, prejudice and racism, xenophobia and paranoia, play a subliminal part. While others cling – with increasing alarmism and instinctive adherence to Washington – to a dangerous, old school, Cold War narrative about authoritarian regimes in general and China in particular.

The world has moved on. In the grand sweep of history, Western dominance has been brief, and the American-led order considerably shorter. China has been the world's top economy for most of the past two millennia. Its time has returned. It will shape all of our futures. Pragmatism, strategic realism and sensitivity, not moral judgment and binary analysis, are a more prudent and profitable response. The West should look to the future, especially in Asia, and treat with reservation the clarion calls of the anti-China enthusiasts. We should be vigilant, of course. But we should also be clear-eyed about the mixed legacy of the United States, wary of the soundness of its judgments and sometimes sceptical of its motivations and interests. And perhaps we should recognise that America's fatal attraction to overreach has itself hastened the changing world order and its own loss of leadership.

Hawthorn Hill,
Mt Wilson
Easter 2020

INTRODUCTION

Why did Simon Chesterman and Michael Byers, writing in the *London Review of Books* two decades ago, say that one might well conclude that the greatest long-term threat to peace is the United States of America – 'undeterred by rules and procedures, driven only by the inconstant winds of its own self-interest'? Why did Lord Christopher Patten, last Governor of Hong Kong and now Chancellor of the University of Oxford, say that 'Around the world, America is seen more and more to contravene the principles it enjoins others to follow'? And why did the 2013 WIN/Gallup International poll, based on a survey of 67,806 respondents in sixty-five countries, record that the United States was 'the greatest threat to peace in the world today'.

Perhaps the starkest recent remarks have been those by Donald Tusk and Thomas Friedman. Tusk, then president of the European Council, said that 'What worries me most is the fact that the rules-based international order is being challenged not by the usual suspects, but by its main architect and guarantor, the US'. And Friedman, respected columnist for *The New York Times*, remarked that 'We are in danger of losing America as an instrument of moral authority and inspiration in the world'.

This book is in part an exploration of the historical basis for those fears and apprehensions; how the high standards and treasured principles set in place after World War II were ignored; how perceptions of self-interest have operated to the exclusion of international laws, norms and conventions; how hubris and hypocrisy replaced idealism; how adherence to the rule of law became selective; and how the authority and leadership of the United States have been diminished. It is also a look into the future – a future dominated by greater Asia in general and China in particular.

This is not a comparative exercise. I have focused on the role and example of the United States, and on the qualities of leadership that must sustain power if it is to generate respect rather than resentment – if it is to be a force for good rather than an incitement to terrorism. Effective and enduring leadership requires restraint, as well as standards of behaviour 'higher than that trodden by the crowd'. This is what Lord Bingham, the greatest English jurist of the modern era, had in mind when he wrote in the context of the debate over the invasion of Iraq and the scandal of Abu Ghraib, that 'We cannot commend our society to others by departing from the fundamental standards which make it worthy of commendation'.

China and Russia are, of course, selective in their adherence to the rule of law but only the United States has routinely endeavoured, frequently with disastrous human consequences, to transform other countries in its own liberal-democratic-capitalist image; or believes (and insists) that its values and way of life are universal; or that it, above all nations, has a responsibility to act in the general interests of humankind and its own security. Only the United States has purported for seventy-five years to be the leader of the 'free world', whatever that outdated phrase may mean today. Andrew Bacevich, the celebrated soldier–historian and *New York Times* bestselling author, describes this combination of beliefs as the 'American credo', summoning the United States 'to lead, save, liberate, and ultimately transform the world'.

The world of the twenty-first century is changing with unforeseen rapidity. And the answer to its complexities and diversities is no longer the American credo. The worldwide COVID-19 crisis has exemplified the uncertainties and highlighted the weaknesses of a world order once led by Washington. The American Century – a phrase coined in 1941 by magazine magnate Henry Luce – may once have had a certain attraction but it now seems strangely redundant, out of kilter with the modern reality. Certainly, there is no shortage of well-informed commentators who suggest that the 'short American Century' has now ended. The lead article in a recent edition of *The Atlantic* magazine stated: 'What is called The American Century was really just a little more than half a century...It began with the second world war and the creative burst that followed...until it expired the day before yesterday.' An American foreign policy goal that was once framed as 'worldwide democracy – victory for all mankind – a worldwide victory for freedom' now seems curiously obsolete, out of sync with the realities of a multi-power, multi-cultural, multi-polar, millennial world. Instead, as was once famously said, the United States runs the risk of becoming – or perhaps has become – 'a world leader that nobody follows and few respect, and a nation drifting dangerously amidst a global chaos it cannot control'.

This book is in four sections. The first section deals with America's exceptionalism and its historical origins. Chapter 1 addresses the outstanding leadership which the United States demonstrated at the end of World War II in the establishment of the international rules and institutions that have become known as the 'rules-based order'. This was the creative burst – without hubris or exceptionalism – in which America demonstrated convincing global authority in pursuit of a better world. Chapter 2 deals with the immediate post-war period, including America's reaction, or overreaction, to Soviet communism; how President Truman changed the world; and how America's leaders quickly succumbed to compromise in pursuit of an ideological conflict that they chose to militarise.

The second section deals with the outcomes of this compromise. Chapter 3 explains some of the most prominent examples of interventionism – in breach of the so-called rules-based order – by the United States. They are by no means exhaustive. It commences with the Italian general elections in 1948 and concludes with the invasion of Iraq in 2003. Chapter 4 examines the powerful criticisms of America's exceptionalism and interventionism by senior figures within the Washington establishment. Their voices are rarely heard and their words rarely read in the modern era. But they are more poignant and relevant today than ever before. They include President Eisenhower, the former general; George Kennan, the intellectual architect of the policy of containment; Senator William Fulbright, the longest-ever serving chairman of the Senate Foreign Relations Committee; and Andrew Bacevich, West Point graduate, Vietnam veteran and *New York Times* bestselling author.

The third section deals with the consequences of exceptionalism and compromise. Chapter 5 addresses America's culture of militarism and its tendency to adopt military solutions in response to international political problems. The defence and national security strategies of the United States are underpinned by the officially endorsed concepts of 'overmatch' and pre-emptive war, and supported by global military presence and global power projection. Chapter 6 explains the increasingly unilateral and dismissive approach of the United States to the United Nations and to international treaties, conventions and institutions. It is a state of affairs that is not unique to the era of Trump, only more overt. International institutions and instruments that were once conceived for the common good are increasingly regarded in Washington as not in the interests of the United States.

The fourth section deals with the future – a new world of increasing connections, greater cooperation and widening collaboration in Asia; one in which China is playing a leading, but not the only role. In contrast to this Asian 'convergence', the United States is sharpening antagonisms, increasing divergence and diminishing its authority. The underlying assumption in Washington is that a nation that competes with the United States for power, influence or economic pre-eminence is an enemy and adversary that threatens American security and prosperity. There is a deep-seated belief in Washington that China is a civilisational threat. And too many commentators condemn China simply for being 'authoritarian' or 'communist' or 'illiberal'. To such superficial analysis, realists such as Dennis Richardson, the former head of the Australian Security and Intelligence Organisation and former Australian ambassador to the United States, would respond: 'So what? Of course. That's China'.

The United States has been a world leader in many areas, but its history since World War II is littered with misconceived international conflicts of dubious utility, questionable legality and unacceptable human tragedy – not to mention an increasing penchant for targeted assassinations and unilateral sanctions. The pattern of American militarism significantly increased after the end of the Cold War and increased again after 2001.

Washington's rejection of the authority of the United Nations and international instruments of collective authority has also increased. As the balance of power shifts, as an Asian order inexorably rises and as the United States lashes out instinctively against any perceived challenge to its authority – especially from China – some question whether an American-led order is necessarily the best solution in a more complex, largely post-Christian world.

The real future is Asia. And it is passing America by. Asia is the most powerful force reshaping the world order today. The Asian-led order encompasses the vast majority of the world's populations. Its economic transformation is changing the global distribution of power. Industrial capitalism, internal stability and global markets are converging in Asia. China has surpassed the United States as the world's largest economy in trading power and purchasing power parity terms; India has become the fastest growing large economy in the world; and Southeast Asia receives more foreign investment than both India and China. Asia in general, and China in particular, has 'the biggest populations and armies, highest savings rates and largest currency reserves'. Modern Asians are building bridges not walls; finding complementarities not differences. While America has wasted trillions of dollars 'flailing about, attacking Iraq, bombing Syria, sanctioning Russia and baiting China' (not to mention Iran), Asian nations have formed powerful common institutions such as the Asian Infrastructure Investment Bank, the Shanghai Cooperation Organisation, the Comprehensive and Progressive Agreement for Trans-Pacific Partnership, the Regional Comprehensive Economic Partnership and the Belt and Road Initiative as instruments of mutual prosperity – from all of which the United States is absent.

PART 1
ORIGINS

CHAPTER 1

EXCEPTIONALISM
Myth & Reality

True Leadership

At the end of World War II, the United States, more than any other country, nurtured the idea of an international community of nations governed by the rule of law. Its leading role in the creation and implementation of the United Nations and the International Military Tribunal at Nuremberg enhanced its post-war moral ascendancy. So did its role in advocating for the Universal Declaration of Human Rights. Although the Nuremberg trials did not address war crimes by anyone on the Allied side, and were criticised by some as victor's justice, they were responsible for the introduction to the world of the concepts of genocide and crimes against humanity. The United Nations and Nuremberg were intertwined. Their establishment was led by the United States and both reflected the highest hopes for humankind.

Those hopes were epitomised in the words and sentiments of the American jurist Robert Jackson, who stepped aside from the Supreme Court to become the United States principal representative and chief prosecutor at Nuremberg. The ancient Bavarian town had been Hitler's venue of choice for Nazi rallies during the 1930s. But in November 1945, amid the old town's rubble and ruin, an intimate wood-panelled courtroom in Nuremberg's Palace of Justice became the venue for 'the greatest trial in history'. German leaders Göring, von Ribbentrop, Speer and twenty-one other accused all appeared in the dock. It has been said that 'Justice was triumphant at Nuremberg. The world is better for it. Nuremberg's impact is universal. Civilization took a giant leap forward'. It is true.

Jackson was hand-picked by President Truman, who had been impressed by a speech Jackson gave about the post-war order on the day after Roosevelt's death in April 1945. In that speech, Jackson envisioned a future United Nations and a future International Court of Justice, explaining that:

> It is not enough that we restore peace...All else will fail
> unless we devise instruments of adjustment, adjudication,
> and conciliation, so reasonable and acceptable to the
> masses of people that future governments will have
> always an honorable alternative to war.

Imagining a future International Court of Justice, he emphasised that:

> ...much hinges on acceptance of the concept of the Court
> as an independent body above obligation to any nation or
> interest.

As a warning to politicians and future American presidents, he reiterated that:

> ...it is futile to think that we can have international courts that will always render the decisions we want to promote our interests. We cannot successfully cooperate with the rest of the world in establishing a reign of law unless we are prepared to have that law sometimes operate against what would be our national advantage.

And as an explanation of the rationale for the necessity of an international court, he added:

> But the worst settlement of international disputes by adjudication or arbitration is likely to be less disastrous to the loser and certainly less destructive to the world than no way of settlement except war.

Six months later, Jackson's celebrated opening speech at Nuremberg was as much political as it was legal. He began by noting America's unique perspective as 'the most dispassionate, for having sustained the least injury, it is perhaps the least animated by vengeance'. He made the connection with the United Nations crystal clear, telling the tribunal – and the world – that both the United Nations and the Nuremberg trial were forces for good, operating in tandem, seeking the same objective:

> This trial is part of the great effort to make the peace more secure. One step in this direction is the United Nations organization, which may take joint political action to prevent war if possible, and joint military action

to insure that any nation which starts a war will lose it. This Charter, and this Trial...constitute another step in the same direction...

Echoing the principles on which the United Nations Charter was based, Jackson contended that the unilateral resort to war was, or should be, illegal, saying, 'Our position is that whatever grievances a nation may have...aggressive warfare is an illegal means for settling those grievances' except when justified by self-defence. He returned to the point a number of times, in language that is memorable for its clarity and directness:

> Any resort to war – to any kind of war – is a resort to means that are inherently criminal. War inevitably is a course of killings, assaults, deprivations of liberty, and destruction of property. An honestly defensive war is, of course, legal and saves those lawfully conducting it from criminality.

There was an attractiveness to Jackson's logic. He reminded the tribunal that it was a crime for one man with his bare knuckles to assault another under the law of all civilised peoples. He therefore asked rhetorically, 'How did it come about that multiplying this crime by a million, and adding firearms to bare knuckles, made it a legally innocent act?' He lamented that this was 'intolerable for an age that called itself civilized', as well as being 'contrary to the teachings of early Christian and international scholars such as Grotius'.

There was no hubris or exceptionalism then. The universal and reciprocal nature of the standards imposed by the tribunal was central to Jackson's appeal:

If certain acts in violation of treaties are crimes, they are crimes whether the United States does them or whether Germany does them, and we are not prepared to lay down a rule of criminal conduct against others which we would not be willing to have invoked against us.

And he reminded the parties that 'We must never forget that the record on which we judge these defendants is the record on which history will judge us tomorrow'.

Jackson's words and sentiments in 1945 reflected an American outlook on the world that shone briefly and brightly after the war: one that represented unquestioned moral leadership. The country was admired for its virtue and envied for its peace-and-plenty economy. At that time it did not claim any privilege, any special dispensation, absolving it from the rules and conventions of international law that applied to other nations. What happened?

The Idea

The idea of exceptionalism took hold in Washington. The concept is, if anything, a twentieth-century phenomenon: faintly traceable to President Woodrow Wilson, coming into its own after World War II and being turbo-charged by the end of the Cold War – the point in history that Francis Fukuyama described with portentous simplicity as the 'end of history'. In modern America, it has become a mantra, cloaked in the language of a 'divine mission to deliver not only success for itself but global salvation'. Jeffrey Sachs has explained that the idea of American exceptionalism is so 'deeply set in American culture and the institutions of foreign policy' that it has become a 'civic religion'. Its adherents contend that the United States has a 'destiny and duty to expand its power and the influence of its institutions and beliefs until they dominate the world'. It is said to be a moral imperative. But to adapt the language of Yuval Noah Harari in *Sapiens*, it is 'an imagined order woven into the tapestry of life'.

A modern rational person, whether religious or not, might be forgiven for questioning the credibility, let alone the wisdom, of any continuing notion that a country could have a divine mission – even a destiny and duty – to do anything. It is a startling presumption, oddly arcane, which does not survive critical analysis. It is reminiscent of the Chinese 'Mandate of Heaven' which, according to ancient theory, was bestowed upon the emperor not to exploit the world but to spread justice and humanity. The French philosopher Bernard-Henri Lévy encapsulated the curious, other-worldly essence of American exceptionalism and its missionary ideal in his recent book *The Empire and the Five Kings*, sub-titled *America's Abdication and the Fate of the World*.

Yet exceptionalism has become so entrenched that American politicians who dare to question it do so at their peril – as President Obama found to his chagrin when he declared that he believed in American exceptionalism 'just as, I suspect, the Brits believe in British exceptionalism and the Greeks believe in Greek exceptionalism'. It should not be forgotten that in an earlier time, the German kaiser once said of Germany that 'God has created us to civilise the world' and Cecil Rhodes contended that the English 'are the first race in the world, and the more of the world we inhabit the better it is for the human race'. These ideas, like exceptionalism, now seem decidedly strange – in equal parts chauvinism, religiosity, ignorance and bombast.

Some people consider the sacred text of American exceptionalism to be the sermon delivered by John Winthrop before the eleven ships of the Massachusetts Bay Company sailed to New England in 1630. Winthrop was an Englishman preaching to Englishmen. He gave the sermon either in the church of the Holy Rood in Southampton or aboard the *Arbella* in the port. And he coined the expression 'city upon a hill' as a way of expressing his desire that the 'plantation' that he and his fellow Puritans were setting out to establish would be an example for other English colonies. The context and significance of Winthrop's sermon were understandable in the circumstances. They hardly justify its description by one patriotic American academic as 'the greatest sermon of the millennium'. Not dissimilar aspirations were expressed, but without the religious fervour, when another English fleet (also of eleven ships) sailed from Southampton in May 1787 to found the colony of New South Wales. Such aspirations were a commonplace of colonial exploration and expansion.

But in 1980 when a deeply emotional Ronald Reagan expropriated Winthrop's language, mangled the name of the ship and placed it and the sermon off the coast of Massachusetts, he elevated the imagery of the 'city upon a hill' and endorsed a lasting mythical vision of the American republic, one that thrilled and energised his political partisans. And George W Bush took the vision to a new level when he declared – with disconcerting sincerity – that 'The ideal of America is the hope of all mankind. That hope still lights the way...And the light shines in the darkness. And the darkness will not overcome it'. Reagan and Bush were not the first American political leaders to use an apt phrase to appeal to an evangelistic national destiny.

Some American historians, searching for provenance, refer to Thomas Jefferson and Abraham Lincoln. The former used the expression 'the world's best hope' in his first inaugural address. And Lincoln captured the popular imagination with his more literary improvement – 'the last, best hope on earth'. But Jefferson was describing his administration, not the United States. There was no sense in which he was referring to the salvation of the world. And Lincoln's 1862 statement was directed to the emancipation of the slaves – in a country that was one of the last redoubts of slavery and the only nation where it was necessary to resort to civil war to bring slavery to an end. In contrast, the British government had refused to countenance the introduction of slavery to the first Australian colony more than seventy years earlier – memorably epitomised in the pronouncement of its founder that 'There can be no slavery in a free land, and consequently no slaves'.

During the nineteenth century another expression – 'manifest destiny' – emerged. But its original purpose and context were to justify westward continental expansion, especially to Texas and Oregon. The author, a newspaper editor, referred to a 'manifest destiny to overspread and to possess the whole of the continent... which Providence has given us for the development of the great experiment of liberty and federated self-government entrusted to us'. It was about agrarian expansionism, although some conflated the idea with romantic nationalism. Contemporary critics suggested that the advocates of manifest destiny were citing divine providence to justify actions that were motivated by chauvinism and commercial self-interest. This was of course true but the phrase had a beguiling attraction and it caught on.

Manifest destiny played no part in the United States' first foray into the Asia-Pacific in 1898, despite its occasional continued invocation as a lodestar. After intervening on a pretext in an insurrection in Cuba and conducting a brief war with Spain, the Philippines became an American colony. During the ensuing years of conflict with the native Filipinos, President McKinley suggested that the colonisation would 'Christianize' the heathens of the Philippines – unaware that they had long ago been converted to Catholicism. But commercial advantage, not benevolence, was the true object; and the prospect of unimaginable riches was the lure. The leading imperialist and Asia expert, Senator Albert Beveridge, told Congress in 1900 that 'The Philippines are ours forever...And just beyond the Philippines are China's illimitable markets...We will not abandon our opportunity in the Orient...The Philippines give us a base at the door of all the East'.

Nor did divine inspiration lie behind the new foreign policy that President Theodore Roosevelt articulated in his State of the Union Address in 1904. That policy asserted that the United States was justified in exercising something called 'international police power' to intervene in the Western Hemisphere to put an end to chronic unrest between the European colonial powers and the countries of Latin America. The policy rested on national and commercial self-interest, not on any genuine sense of missionary responsibility, and was later renounced by Franklin D Roosevelt.

President Woodrow Wilson, who assumed office in 1913, held the firm conviction that the United States was a nation set apart from the rest of the world by its values and principles. He disavowed territorial conquest but not military intervention, declaring – in language that now seems quaint – that the use of force by the United States was only 'for the elevation of the spirit of the human race'. And in words that could have been uttered by George W Bush, he told a joint session of Congress that the entry of the United States into World War I was only to 'make the world safe for democracy'. Wilson would not, however, have countenanced the dominant contemporary view in Washington that state sovereignty can be ignored in the exercise of an American 'responsibility to protect' peoples everywhere from autocratic government.

The end of World War I was the moment 'when America might have led the world', but the moment passed. The United States was the only major Allied power that would not ratify the Treaty of Versailles, part of which was the covenant for the proposed League of Nations. The league's core principle was contained in Article 10, written in language which reflected the last of Wilson's idealistic 'Fourteen Points' that he put forward to Congress in 1918. The commitment was simple: each member was obliged to respect the territorial integrity and political independence of the other states. The sceptics and patriots in Washington asserted that Article 10 was a limitation on the power of the United States government to determine its own affairs. They ensured the defeat of the treaty in the Senate. It was a foretaste of the future. The League of Nations would have failed anyway – Germany, Italy and Japan flagrantly ignored it during the 1930s – but the singular absence of the United States of America was fatal.

Wilson's Republican successors – Harding, Coolidge and Hoover – all perpetuated a policy of high-minded international isolation throughout the 1920s, while simultaneously souring transatlantic relations with angry demands for repayment of Allied war debts. It was like an early version of Trumpism vis-à-vis NATO. When Franklin Delano Roosevelt became president in 1933, he initially continued the isolationist policy and somewhat reluctantly introduced the Neutrality Acts of 1935–39. But in March 1941, the patrician president 'used all his strength, character and cleverness to defeat American isolationism'. In so doing, he overcame 'the first America First movement' and dedicated his administration's foreign policy to the survival of the United Kingdom by any means other than direct military intervention. Roosevelt's signature Lend-Lease program put the almost limitless industrial capacity of the United States at the disposal of the British war effort. The bill submitted to Congress was patriotically numbered HR 1776. It heralded America's return to the world stage and ended its isolationism.

Free food, fuel, ships, aircraft and armaments were distributed to support the British, and later the Russian, war effort. By the end of the war, approximately 11 per cent of the total war expenditure of the United States had been distributed through Lend-Lease while 'five thousand [Allied] sailors died in shipping the aid to Soviet harbors'. The program was so extensive that by 1945, nearly a third of the truck strength of the Soviet Army consisted of American-built Dodge and Studebaker vehicles. Churchill and Stalin were ever grateful for the American generosity. Nikita Khrushchev wrote in his memoirs that Stalin candidly and privately told him that 'if the United States had not helped us, we would not have won the war'.

Despite the magnanimity and beneficence of the United States during and immediately after the war, there was not prevalent then, as there is now, that unique combination of beliefs which, to quote the award-winning former *New York Times* foreign correspondent Stephen Kinzer:

> give Americans a messianic desire to combat evil forces
> in the world, a conviction that applying military power

will allow them to reshape other countries in their image, a certainty that doing so is good for all humanity, and a fervent belief that this is what God wants the United States to do.

To put it in the penetratingly simple language of Yuval Noah Harari, Americans at that time, as distinct from those in the current era, did not espouse a 'moral imperative to bring Third World countries the benefits of democracy and human rights, even if these goods are delivered by cruise missiles and F-16s'.

Roosevelt's Dream

This idea of a moral imperative would only come later, after President Roosevelt. He did not subscribe to any notion of exceptionalism; nor any semblance of the idea that God wants the United States to do his work. During the war years, Roosevelt harboured a dream of a different type – a post-war world in which a viable successor organisation to the League of Nations, in which the United States played a leading part, would regulate the conduct of nations and promote peace and security. Even before the Japanese attack on Pearl Harbor, he was 'encouraging the State Department to thoughts about the post-war order'. In January 1941, Roosevelt's State of the Union address broke from tradition, propounding four fundamental freedoms that people 'everywhere in the world' deserved to enjoy: freedom of speech and worship, freedom from want (a human right to economic security) and freedom from fear of national aggression. The Four Freedoms became part of the personal mission of Eleanor Roosevelt, who ensured that they were incorporated into the preamble to the 1948 Universal Declaration of Human Rights.

In August 1941, four months before the United States entered the war, Roosevelt revealed his intentions for an international organisation. It followed his first secret wartime meeting with Winston Churchill. The meeting's codename was 'Riviera' and the obscure venue was Placentia Bay, Newfoundland. Roosevelt travelled there on the presidential yacht *Potomac* on the pretext of a summer fishing trip. Churchill crossed the North Atlantic on the battleship HMS *Prince of Wales*, stubbornly defying the U-boats of the German Kriegsmarine. The two leaders met on the deck of the USS *Augusta* and then aboard the *Prince of Wales*, where Churchill organised a church service on the quarterdeck for both ships' companies. He selected 'Onward Christian Soldiers' to accompany the service and later explained that he did so because 'we had the right to feel that we are serving a cause for the sake of which a trumpet has sounded from on high'. Churchill wanted support for the war effort; Roosevelt was prepared to oblige but he had broader aspirations.

The joint declaration following the meeting became known as the Atlantic Charter. For Roosevelt, who had served as a junior official in the Wilson administration, it was a tentative step toward the new world order that became his greatest legacy. The declaration expressed agreement to 'the establishment of a wider and permanent system of general security' – anticipating, it would seem, some form of 'united nations'. And it stipulated, as a cardinal principle, respect for 'the right of all peoples to choose the form of government under which they will live'. This would later prove to be problematic to successive American presidents when, for political, moral or ideological reasons, they disapproved of a foreign state's chosen form of government.

Progress toward the new order was episodic but there were significant milestones. In December 1941, a few months after the Atlantic Charter, and not long after the attack on Pearl Harbor, Churchill came to Washington for an extended visit over the Christmas and New Year period. At their conference, this time codenamed 'Arcadia', Roosevelt proposed, and Churchill agreed, that the Allied forces should henceforth be known as the 'United Nations'. It was the first use of the term. And it appealed to Churchill – ever the warrior – because of the lines in Byron's 'Childe Harold's Pilgrimage':

> Here, where the sword united nations drew,
> Our countrymen were warring on that day!

The two men also conceived and drafted a 'Declaration by United Nations', which they signed on New Year's Day 1942 along with the representatives of the Soviet Union and the then nationalist China. The next day, the emissaries of twenty-two other governments signed the declaration. The signatory states committed their support for the 'common program of purposes and principles' embodied in the Atlantic Charter, necessarily including the establishment of a wider and permanent system of general security and the right of all peoples to choose the form of government under which they will live.

There was still a long way to go before the eventual United Nations organisation would come into existence but over the next three years twenty-one more countries signed the declaration. It became more than a badge of solidarity; it metamorphosed into an entry card to the future world body.

Throughout the war years, and at Roosevelt's urging, the State Department planned and prepared for his hoped-for international organisation. And in October 1943, the foreign ministers of the United States, the United Kingdom, the Soviet Union and China met in Moscow and signed a joint declaration on general security. In addition to reiterating their resolve to continue the war against the Axis powers, the Moscow declaration stated:

> That they recognize the necessity of establishing at the earliest practicable date a general international organization, based on the principle of sovereign equality of all peace-loving states, and open to membership by all such states, large and small, for the maintenance of international peace and security.

Roosevelt's idea had moved a step closer to crystallisation. The foreign ministers' declaration in Moscow was followed in November by a leaders' summit in Tehran. The most important issue for discussion was the proposed Allied invasion of France known as Operation Overlord. Stalin had been demanding that pressure on the Red Army be relieved and complained that 'Ten thousand men a day were being sacrificed on the Russian front...' Roosevelt committed to launching the invasion in May 1944. But he was also thinking ahead to his vision of a post-war international body that could provide a check against international aggression and also be a venue for the resolution of disputes. On 1 December 1943, on the last day of the summit, in the president's quarters at the Soviet embassy in Tehran, Roosevelt personally introduced Stalin to the concept of a 'united nations' organisation.

In the late summer of 1944, the representatives and officials of the three major Allied powers and nationalist China attended a planning conference at Dumbarton Oaks, a stately home in Georgetown, Washington DC. The outcome was a draft – referred to as a set of 'proposals' – for what would become the Charter of the United Nations. The proposals included 'the principle of sovereign equality of all peace-loving states' and a commitment to refrain in international relations 'from the threat or use of force' in any manner inconsistent with the purposes of the organisation. Two unresolved issues, one relating to voting in the Security Council and the other relating to the number of Soviet republics to be admitted to membership, were deferred until Roosevelt, Stalin and Churchill would next meet at the Yalta conference in February 1945.

When they did so, they resolved the last of the Soviet objections. A final conference to settle the Charter of the United Nations took place over two months in San Francisco in 1945 as the Pacific war was drawing toward its inevitable conclusion. Delegates, diplomats, officials and a scourge of lawyers from fifty countries reviewed, analysed, parsed and rewrote the 'proposals' made at Dumbarton Oaks. The fifty participating nations consisted of all but one of the forty-seven states – Poland not having a functioning government at that time – who had signed the 1942 'Declaration by United Nations' and had declared war on Germany or Japan, plus four other states invited by the conference. Those four states were two Soviet republics (Ukraine and Byelorussia), Denmark and, despite its Nazi sympathies, Argentina. The San Francisco conference was the culmination of Roosevelt's vision but he died on 12 April, two weeks before it commenced, and never saw his dream come to fruition.

The UN Charter

The representatives of the fifty participating nations signed the Charter of the United Nations on 26 June 1945. The historic concord was based on 'the twin ideas that all countries, including the United States, should agree to be constrained by international law and that they would benefit from doing so'. The most profound change was that each member state agreed to give up its age-old right to resort to war, except in self-defence, and to 'refrain from the threat or use of force' against the territorial integrity or political independence of any state in any manner inconsistent with the purposes of the United Nations. Unilateral resort to war was replaced by collective decision-making in the Security Council on behalf of all member states.

This fundamental commitment was predicated on respect for the 'equal rights and self-determination of peoples' and recognition of 'the sovereign equality of all its members'. German and Japanese aggression may have been front of mind, but the restriction on a country's right to resort to war was intended to be universal, the United States included. Regime change might be a consequence of lawful action authorised by the Security Council but, by itself, it could no longer be a lawful objective of military action by an individual state.

This was groundbreaking. And the charge was led at the time by the United States. The Covenant of the League of Nations had not gone this far. It had discouraged resort to force but did not prohibit it. It was not until the Kellogg–Briand Pact of 1928 that there was any general renunciation of warfare as an option to states as an instrument of national policy. But the making of that pact had not deterred Japan from invading Manchuria,

Italy from invading Abyssinia, Russia from invading Finland, and Germany from invading most of Europe. The Charter of the United Nations – reinforced by structural elements such as the Security Council and the International Court of Justice – was a more compelling attempt to outlaw unilateral aggression. Among other things, each state solemnly undertook to comply with the decisions of the International Court of Justice in any case to which it was a party.

In 1945, the original fifty member states of the United Nations were almost all American allies or supporters. Today the membership has increased to nearly two hundred: one hundred and ninety-three states plus the Vatican City and Palestine, who have observer status. Americans today complain that many member states of the United Nations do not share their values. This is true. It is also unsurprising. It simply reflects a more complex, culturally varied and politically diverse set of international relations. America's values, including its model for society and its system of government, are not universal, no matter how admirable they may be thought to be. This is the point that the Singaporean Prime Minister, Lee Hsien Loong, made so diplomatically and wisely at the Shangri-La Dialogue in 2019:

> To expect every country to adopt the same cultural values
> and political system is neither reasonable nor realistic. In
> fact, humankind's diversity is its strength. There is much
> we can learn from one another, from the differences in
> our values, perspectives, systems and policies.

The modern United Nations, representing multifarious political systems and diverse values, has become a true 'Parliament of

Man' – a phrase to which Roosevelt's successor Harry Truman was initially drawn in its early years, when the organisation more closely reflected American interests. That simple, hopeful and prescient phrase was coined by Alfred, Lord Tennyson in his poem 'Locksley Hall':

> Till the war-drum throbb'd no longer, and the battle
> flags were furled
> In the Parliament of man, the Federation of the world.
>
> There the common sense of most shall hold a fretful
> realm in awe,
> And the kindly earth shall slumber, lapt in universal law.

Unrivalled Authority

At the end of the war, the United States deservedly held unrivalled practical and moral authority in the world. Its late intervention had ensured victory against the Axis powers and brought an end to hostilities in Europe and East Asia. It had led the way in the establishment of the United Nations and the reorganisation of the international financial system. It had a trade surplus, was the world's only major creditor nation, accounted for more than half the world's manufacturing capacity, held two-thirds of total available financial reserves and possessed the world's only stable currency in which global trade was generally denominated.

Not only was the United States Navy larger than all the world's other navies combined but more than 60 per cent of the world's heavy aircraft was American. And the reorganisation of the international financial system in 1944 at the United Nations Monetary and Financial Conference at Bretton Woods, New Hampshire, had legitimised America as the world's economic behemoth. It resulted in the establishment of the International Monetary Fund and the International Bank for Reconstruction and Development (later the World Bank) – in both of which the United States was given predominant board representation and special veto powers over major decisions. The system agreed at Bretton Woods formally entrenched the primacy of the US dollar, gave the United States an immense advantage in international trade and provided it with the opportunity to influence the economies of other countries.

Just as the Roman denarius, the Persian daric and the gold dinar had been dominant during the lengthy periods of hegemonic supremacy of the Roman, Persian and Ottoman empires, so too became the US dollar. The British team at Bretton Woods, led by John Maynard Keynes, sought to avoid this prospect and advocated an alternative system involving an international unit of account between nations known as the 'bancor' as a measure of each country's trade deficit or trade surplus. But American opposition was implacable. The head of its delegation responded bluntly to the British proposal – 'We have been perfectly adamant…absolutely no'. The editor of the *Economist* magazine later wrote that 'Lord Keynes was right… the world will bitterly regret the fact that his arguments were rejected'.

The US Treasury ensured that it would never lose. Its postwar objectives were to maintain economic dominance, increase access to foreign markets, prevent any impediment to its trade and avoid the financial chaos of the interwar years – a period that had seen the collapse of the gold standard, the Great

Depression and the rise of protectionism. The founding of the United Nations and the reform of the international financial system were not purely altruistic. They were also intended to facilitate the creation of a post-war world order that would 'work better for the United States'.

CHAPTER 2

IDEOLOGY
Cold War

Harry Truman

Within a few brief years of the Truman presidency, the Cold War began. Time and circumstance combined to ensure that Truman – a vastly different man to Roosevelt with a more conservative inclination – would have a significant influence on world events. The down-to-earth Truman was hardly prepared for the role that destiny had thrust upon him. He had little in common with Roosevelt, whom he had met only twice during his eighty-two days as vice-president. He was decisive, but freely admitted that he was 'not a deep thinker'. Nor did he share Roosevelt's pragmatism or his knowledge of world affairs, let alone his 'charisma, political suaveness and ability to avoid overall confrontation'. Truman's early influential inner circle included his old Senate mentor, Jimmy Byrnes, from South Carolina, who left school at the age of fourteen to work in a law office. Within a short time, Byrnes was appointed to the role of secretary of state. The somewhat supercilious British Ambassador Lord Halifax probably had him in mind when he referred to the 'Missouri County court-house calibre' of Truman's early entourage.

The new president's relationship with Stalin was poisoned by distrust from the outset. His anti-Russian feelings were as clear as his anti-German feelings. In 1941, during the debates over Lend-Lease after Germany invaded Russia, he was on record as saying: 'If we see that Germany is winning, we ought to help Russia; and if Russia is winning, we ought to help Germany, and in that way let them kill as many as possible...' Truman's outlook was binary and his natural tendency was toward moral certitude: one was either good or inherently evil. He never learned the lesson that the elderly Henry Stimson, the secretary of war who had advised four presidents, tried to teach him:

> The chief lesson that I have learned in a long life is that
> the only way you can make a man trustworthy is to trust
> him; and the surest way to make him untrustworthy is to
> distrust him and show your distrust.

For most of the war, Roosevelt's vice-president of choice – the man who would succeed him in the event of his death in office – had been the high-minded internationalist Henry Wallace. Wallace was the polar opposite of Truman, but party officials increasingly mistrusted his devotion to principles over politics, feared his liberal views and preferred someone more amenable to the party's conservative forces. Wallace fell out of favour partly for his repudiation of Henry Luce's notion of the 'American

Century', first advanced in Luce's *Life* magazine in February 1941. Luce urged Americans, in words that now seem unsettling, to 'exert upon the world the full impact of our influence, for such purposes as we see fit and by such means as we see fit'. Wallace responded with his own 'Century of the Common Man':

> Some have spoken of the 'American Century'. I say...the
> century...which will come of this war – can and must be
> the century of the common man...No nation will have
> the God-given right to exploit other nations...there must
> be neither economic nor military imperialism.

Many in the political establishment thought that Wallace's remarks were a source of concern; and that his ideology was suspect. At the 1944 Democratic National Convention in Chicago, party officials staged a coup and Wallace was demoted, removed from the vice-presidential ticket and replaced by Harry Truman, who was at that time an undistinguished senator from Missouri with a hardscrabble background and a hardline anti-communist attitude. When Roosevelt's new term commenced in January 1945, Truman stepped into the vice-president's shoes and Wallace became secretary of commerce. When Roosevelt died and Truman, as the new president, unleashed his combative attitude toward Soviet Russia, Wallace waged a peace offensive – speaking publicly against the atomic bomb and urging a conciliatory policy toward Soviet Russia. For Truman, who was cut from a different cloth, it was infuriating.

In March 1946 when the visiting and out-of-office Winston Churchill delivered his provocative 'Iron Curtain' speech at Fulton, Missouri, Truman was sitting reverently at his side. Wallace's retort was sobering:

The only kind of competition we want with the Soviets
is to demonstrate that we can raise our standard of
living faster during the next twenty years than Russia...
The only way to defeat Communism in the world is to
do a better and smoother job of maximum production
and optimum distribution...Let's make it a clean race,
a determined race but above all a peaceful race in the
service of humanity.

He added:

Four years ago I repudiated the American Century. Today
I repudiate the Anglo-Saxon century with even greater
vigor...The destiny of the English speaking people is to
serve the world, not dominate it.

Wallace's remarks concerned the British Secret Service, which
was already monitoring him. The intelligence officer covering
Wallace was RAF lieutenant and future novelist Roald Dahl,
whose personal view was that his subject was 'too innocent
and idealistic for this world'. Others at that time disagreed.
In September, Wallace drew an audience of twenty thousand
supporters to Madison Square Garden in New York. His
incendiary speech sealed his fate with party bosses but his
observations on relations with Russia are almost as true today
as they were then. They could equally be about modern China:

We may not like what Russia does in Eastern Europe.
Her type of land reform, industrial expropriation and
suppression of basic liberties offends the great majority
of the people of the United States...But at the same time

we have to recognise that the Balkans are closer to Russia than to us...Russian ideas of social-economic justice are going to govern nearly a third of the world. Our ideas of free-enterprise democracy will govern much of the rest. The two ideas will endeavour to prove which can deliver the most satisfaction to the common man...

The speech went on:

Under friendly peaceful competition the Russian world and the American world will gradually become more alike. The Russians will be forced to grant more and more of the personal freedoms and we shall become more absorbed with the problems of social-economic justice.

Support for Wallace poured in that year, including from Albert Einstein and many others. Einstein wrote that 'Your courageous intervention deserves the gratitude of all who observe the present attitude of our government with grave concern'. Truman could not abide it. His distrust of the Russians was deep-seated. So was his antipathy toward New Deal progressives and the Roosevelt family. After Wallace's Madison Square Garden speech, he decided to fire him. Truman's ranting diary entry that night was an ominous indication of a future America twisted off course by a visceral anti-communism – even before Senator Joe McCarthy had arrived in Washington. After disparaging Wallace as 'a pacifist one hundred percent' who 'has absorbed some of the Commy-Jesuit theory', Truman lumped him in with what he called the 'parlour pinks and soprano voiced men' who were 'a sabotage front for Uncle Joe Stalin'.

Some have said that Wallace's departure from the administration marked 'the last chance to avert the Cold War and nuclear arms race' – but the die had been cast already. With Wallace gone, the Truman administration moved progressively toward an overt policy of confrontation with Soviet Russia. On 24 September 1946, only days after firing Wallace, Truman received the report he had been waiting for from newly appointed White House counsel, Clark Clifford, who had the president's ear. Clifford's hardline report ruled out further efforts to negotiate with the Soviets; insisted that 'The language of military power is the only language' the Soviets understand; and recommended that 'the United States must be prepared to wage atomic and biological warfare' against Soviet Russia. He said his report was 'the kind of black and white analysis that Truman liked'. Clifford later conceded that he had 'no real background' in foreign policy or national security and 'had to learn as I went'. A competing report from the experienced professional intelligence officer, Ludwell Lee Montague, which concluded that Moscow 'would not provoke the next war and could not afford a direct conflict with the United States', sank like a stone.

One of the assumptions in the Clifford report was that any Soviet challenge, even to abstract notions such as the 'position' or 'prestige' of the United States, necessitated an increase in the atomic arsenal, an expansion of the network of foreign military bases and a strengthening of military capabilities. The US adopts the same attitude today, whether the challenge is from China, Russia or elsewhere. Wallace continued to speak against the confrontational direction of US foreign policy. He told a national radio audience that 'Winning the peace is more important than high office' and emphasised that 'we must respect the rights and interests of other peoples, just as we expect them to respect ours'. President Truman did not agree. From the outset of his presidency, and no doubt from well before, Truman believed that the Soviets were expansionist. He led the American public down a path that was increasingly fuelled by anti-communist and anti-Soviet feverishness.

Fear of Communism

An ideological confrontation between communism and capitalism was historically inevitable; a military confrontation was a matter of choice. The origins of communism as a competing ideology to capitalism lay in the social transformations of the late nineteenth century when workers reacted to the miseries of industrialisation and the inequities of capitalism. Social democratic political parties and workers' movements flourished among the smoke stacks and factories of the Victorian era. Some were inspired by the principles of Marxism but 'most of them emphasised reform over revolution, and campaigned for the extension of democracy, workers' rights, and social services accessible to all'. The adherents of Karl Marx, who called themselves 'communists' after the title of his *Communist Manifesto* (1848), represented a variant of socialism, characterised by anti-democratic dogmatism and the advocacy of class-struggle through revolution.

The ideological divide was sharpened by a global economic crisis in the 1890s. The crisis originated with the near insolvency and collapse of Barings Bank, the British bank that was once known as the 'sixth great power'. The destabilising panic and economic depression that followed in Europe and the United States caused high unemployment, massive labour unrest and social upheaval. Workers, young professionals, even some members of the establishment, questioned whether capitalism was finished. Political leaders were assassinated by anarchists across the world, including the President of France (Sadi Carnot), the Prime Minister of Spain (del Castillo), the Empress of Austria (Elizabeth), the King of Italy (Umberto) and the President of the United States (McKinley). Trade union membership skyrocketed and the extreme left was vitalised.

Vladimir Ulyanov – who came to call himself Lenin – emerged in 1895 from this maelstrom as one of the founders of a Marxist group called the Saint Petersburg League of Struggle for the Emancipation of the Working Class. By 1917, he was the leader of the Bolshevik Party which seized power in Saint Petersburg and Moscow and overthrew the provisional government. Their November coup, known as the 'October Revolution' because of the old Russian calendar, resulted in the creation in 1918 of the first Soviet state: the 'Russian Socialist Federative Soviet Republic'. It was an alternative vision to the capitalism that the United States symbolised. By 1922, a federation of Bolshevik-ruled republics known as the Union of Soviet Socialist Republics (USSR) had been carved out from the former Russian Empire.

The Bolshevik revolution fired the imagination and hopes of some men and women outside Russia who were enthused by the possibility of a better world. Many, especially in Europe, questioned the goals of society; their doubts intensified by the collective suicide of the Great War (1914–18). That conflict killed 16 million people, mostly young men in their prime, and left fear, destitution and economic hardship in its wake. Britain introduced food rationing for the first time in its history; the French GDP declined by 40 per cent; the German GDP by much more. An anti-capitalist chorus gathered momentum. The call of the Comintern, the Communist international organisation set up by Lenin in 1919, was heard throughout the world. For some onlookers, Soviet communism seemed a viable alternative to war, privation and colonial oppression. Others turned to nationalist authoritarian movements like fascism and nazism.

In the United States, sheltered from Europe's devastation and destitution, there was debate – much of it alarmist – about the existential threat that communism was thought to pose to values that Americans held dear: religion, individual liberty and self-advancement. The Red Scare in 1919–20 was such a reaction. It led to arrests, deportations, restrictions on freedom of speech and a growing anti-immigration nativism. The methods of the Bolsheviks were brutal and their revolutionary rhetoric was confronting, but the scare was overblown and the threat to the United States largely illusory. Among many colourful critics of Bolshevism, Seattle's mayor Ole Hanson warned of 'free love' as well as other evil consequences:

> ...murder, rape, pillage, arson, free love, poverty, want, starvation, filth, slavery, autocracy, suppression, sorrow and Hell on earth. It is a class government of the unable, the unfit, the untrained; of the scum, of the dregs, of the cruel, and of the failures. Freedom disappears, liberty emigrates, universal suffrage is abolished, progress ceases, manhood and womanhood are destroyed, decency and fair dealing are forgotten...

Others were not so certain. When the stock market crashed in 1929 and the Great Depression caused widespread poverty and ruin, it seemed as if world capitalism was intent on self-destruction. Yale historian Odd Arne Westad, originally from Norway, has pointed out that 'If it had not been for capitalism doing so very badly, Communism would not have won the affection of large numbers'. Many intelligent and dedicated people during the 1930s – unaware of Stalin's rule of terror and subjugation, his paranoia and purges – turned to the social justice ideals of communism as the inspiration for a new model of society.

By 1941, when Soviet Russia and the United States entered World War II, both had been transformed into supercharged empires. The two nations were the embodiment of different approaches to the organisation of society; each represented an extreme version of their respective social model; and 'neither was ever fully replicated elsewhere'. One was based on the market, with all its imperfections and injustices; the other was based on a centralised state-run plan subject to authoritarian control. Russian distrust of capitalism was an historic national tendency – just as instinctive in pre-1917 Imperial Russia as it was in post-1918 Soviet Russia. The advisors to Tsar Nicholas II (1894–1917) denigrated the market as a pollution of Russian values and feared that 'hierarchy, authenticity, empathy and religion, as well as learning and culture, [would be] lost in a frenzied search for material advantage'.

Both empires had a growing sense of mission. While the United States was the most powerful industrial nation in the world, imbued with a sense of uniqueness, mission and abundance, many Russians 'felt their destiny was to forge a dominion from sea to sea, from the Baltic and the Black Sea to the Caspian and the Pacific'. And religion – meaning Evangelical Protestantism in the United States and Russian Orthodoxy in the Soviet Union – played a powerful role in both countries, inspiring the politics of their respective political elites during the Cold War and encouraging a sense that 'they alone were set to fulfil God's plan for and with man'. Russian Orthodox church leaders proclaimed that patriotism and orthodoxy are one. Stalin embraced the Orthodox Church, like Vladimir Putin does today, and presented Russia as a defender of Christian civilisation. After 1941, 'Godless communism' became a myth under Stalin.

Breakdown in Poland

The fact that communism represented an opposing ideology to the capitalist world system did not prevent the pragmatic wartime alliance of the United Kingdom, the United States and Soviet Russia. The three major Allied powers were drawn together by mutual necessity, as a short-term reaction to a global war brought on by mutual enemies. Churchill even formed 'a bit of a sentimental relationship with Stalin as a fellow survivor and victor'. And Stalin was deeply and genuinely saddened by Roosevelt's death, telling US Ambassador Harriman that 'Roosevelt has died but his cause must live on'. But when the war concluded, and Roosevelt and Churchill were no longer at the helm of their countries, the brittle union began to disintegrate. Stalin distrusted the new British and American leaders – Attlee because he represented the right wing of the British Labour movement, who were traditional enemies of communism, and Truman because Soviet intelligence rightly stressed his anti-communism.

Stalin would have preferred the continuation of the alliance, as well as Lend-Lease aid, for a few more years while Russia recovered from its economic and industrial devastation. It had borne the brunt of the war's casualties and the worst of the conflict; suffering far more than the United Kingdom or the United States. Two-thirds of its industrial base had been 'turned into a wasteland'. But Stalin was under no illusions about Russia's longer-term relationship with the West. Before the war was out, he explained to a group of visiting Yugoslavs and Bulgarians:

> The crisis of capitalism has manifested itself in the division of the capitalists into two factions – one fascist, the other democratic. The alliance between ourselves and the democratic faction of capitalism came about because the latter had a stake in preventing Hitler's domination... We are currently allied with the one faction against the other, but in the future we will be against the first faction of capitalists, too.

Trust between the Allies broke down over Poland. After the Yalta conference in February 1945, Stalin believed that he and Roosevelt had an understanding about Poland that respected Soviet Russia's security needs. Churchill and Roosevelt were willing to accept the existing communist government in Warsaw that was controlled by Moscow, while leaving the Polish government in exile in London effectively unrecognised and without power. Roosevelt said, 'It is the best I can do for Poland at this time'. It was a vital issue for Russia, which had been invaded by Germany twice in twenty-five years through Poland and Eastern Europe. Stalin knew that the British and the Americans would extend their form of capitalism into the heart of Europe and he considered it only fair that he should do the same with his system. In April 1945, he told a group of

Yugoslav communists that 'Everyone imposes his own system as far as his army can reach. It cannot be otherwise'.

This was the realpolitik against which the three leaders declared at Yalta that the people of Europe should be allowed 'to create democratic institutions of their own choice'. The declaration was long on principle and short on detail but Churchill and Roosevelt expected Stalin to at least go through the motions of some form of representative elections in Poland and other parts of Eastern Europe occupied by the Red Army. But there was never a realistic prospect of Western-style democracy. The Soviet regime was 'not of that kind'. Some of Truman's most experienced cabinet members understood the Soviet perspective and cautioned him against a hard line. Defence chief Admiral Leahy noted the 'opaque elasticity' of the Yalta agreement and 'the difficulty of alleging bad faith on that basis', adding that 'after the understanding at Yalta', he 'would have been surprised had the Soviets behaved differently than they had'. The veteran secretary of war Henry Stimson told Truman that 'the Russians perhaps were being more realistic than we were in regard to their own security' and added that the American 'understanding of free elections' was shared by very few countries outside Britain and the United States and those under their influence.

This difference of interpretation, of understanding and attitude over Poland, was the source of the breakdown in trust. Truman preferred literalism. He ignored the warnings from senior cabinet members and adopted the language of machismo. When he met with the Soviet foreign minister Molotov only a few weeks after becoming president, he conceded no room for a difference of opinion over Poland; no respect for Soviet security concerns; no recognition of the significance of the concession to Stalin over the Polish government. Truman's belligerent allegations of bad faith and breach of the Yalta agreement were, at the least, undiplomatic. Molotov recalled Truman's 'imperious tone' and 'rather stupid' effort to show 'who was boss'. For his part, Truman saw the encounter in terms of a boxing match, boasting: 'I let him have it. It was the straight one-two to the jaw'. Molotov was affronted; Stalin felt betrayed. The relationship started badly, mired in distrust. It only became worse.

Truman was not capable of grasping a European perspective toward Soviet Russia different from the view in Washington. In fact, in some quarters in Europe, the communists 'carried high the banners of hope'. The hope was for a better society. The communists' blend of anti-fascism, social justice and reflected glory from the courageous Soviet war effort gave them significant popularity. And few Europeans wanted to go back to systems that had created two world wars and a profound economic crisis. In the first post-war European elections, the communists made inroads everywhere. Westad described a European perspective as follows:

> In many parts of Europe the Red Army was seen as the
> real liberator of the continent from Nazi rule. In northern
> Norway...fishermen and their families emerged from
> hiding with banners praising Stalin and the Red Army.
> In Czechoslovakia...people embraced the Soviet soldiers...
> In eastern Europe, many saw the Red Army as a Slav
> army liberating them from German racial oppression...
> even outside their zones of occupation, Stalin and the
> Soviets were hailed as the liberators of the continent...
> Support for Communist parties in western Europe had

> never been greater. Most of the new Communists were
> young people...In their eyes Communism and the Soviet
> example were first and foremost about much-needed
> reform...In spite of the Soviets' bloody past, Communism
> had a model ready for Europe's transformation.

The fallout over Poland in April 1945 was one of Truman's earliest choices. Another choice, two weeks later, was his abrupt termination of Lend-Lease aid to Soviet Russia, only three days after the German surrender. As relations soured and communications became increasingly confrontational, Stalin became more determined to secure his Soviet–European borders through communist regimes supported by Moscow. Red Army control was already in place and it is likely that the Sovietisation of Eastern Europe and the Balkans would have happened in due course but the diplomatic hostility from Washington and London fuelled Stalin's paranoia. And the issue became a fixation for most US policymakers.

Japan & Korea

Even Truman's epochal decision in August 1945 to approve the detonation of atomic bombs over Hiroshima and Nagasaki was motivated in significant measure by his adversarial attitude toward Soviet Russia. Until Roosevelt died, Truman did not know of the atomic bomb and had been unaware of the Manhattan Project. Henry Stimson let him in on the secret after the president's death. A few weeks later, General Groves, the head of the Manhattan Project, explained to Truman that within four months he expected to have 'completed the most terrible weapon ever known in human history, one bomb of which could destroy a whole city'. Groves had firm views about the strategic utility of the bomb. In 1944, he told a shocked Joe Rotblat – later Sir Joseph Rotblat KCMG, CBE, FRS – a British-Polish physicist working on the Manhattan Project, 'You realize of course that the main purpose of this project is to subdue the Russians'. Groves later admitted that 'There was never...any illusion on my part but that Russia was our enemy, and the Project was conducted on that basis'.

Truman was getting the same message from his mentor, Jimmy Byrnes. On the day after Roosevelt's death, Byrnes delphically remarked to Truman that the atomic bomb 'might well put us in a position to dictate our own terms at the end of the war'. He made his position even clearer in late May to a group of concerned scientists who attempted to see Truman to caution him against using the bomb. They were redirected to Byrnes, whose response deeply troubled the physicist Leo Szilard:

> Mr Byrnes did not argue that it was necessary to
> use the bomb against the cities of Japan in order to
> win the war. He knew at that time, as the rest of the
> government knew, that Japan was essentially defeated...
> [he] was much concerned about the spreading of Russian
> influence in Europe; [and insisted] that our possessing
> and demonstrating the bomb *would make Russia more
> manageable in Europe*. [emphasis added]

As the Manhattan Project was coming to fruition, Japanese defeat was a foregone conclusion. When Truman went to Potsdam on 15 July for his first meeting with Churchill and Stalin, the Pacific Strategic Intelligence Summary for that week reported that 'Japan now, officially if not publically, recognizes her defeat...she has turned to the twin aims of (a) reconciling national pride with defeat, and (b) finding the best means of salvaging the wreckage of her ambitions'. Allen Dulles, who later became head of the Central Intelligence Agency (CIA), reminisced several decades later, 'I went to Potsdam and reported there...on what I had learned from Tokyo – they desired to surrender if they could retain the Emperor and the constitution as a basis for maintaining discipline and order...' Truman knew this. He characterised an intercepted Japanese cable which stated that unconditional surrender was the only obstacle to peace as 'the telegram from the Jap emperor asking for peace'.

But Truman wanted more than peace with Japan. He regarded the atomic bomb as a crucial diplomatic tool against Soviet Russia. He had even pushed the start of the Potsdam summit back two weeks in the hope that the bomb would be successfully tested before he began negotiations with Stalin. Oppenheimer gave evidence of the 'incredible pressure to get it done before the Potsdam meeting'. The news of the explosion of the first atomic bomb at Trinity, New Mexico, came through on 16 July. It transformed Truman's attitude at Potsdam. And the change was obvious to Stimson and Churchill. The former wrote, 'The President was tremendously pepped up...and spoke to me of it again and again. He said it gave him an entirely new feeling of confidence'. The latter remarked that Truman 'was a changed man. He told the Russians just where they got on and off and generally bossed the whole meeting'.

Truman and Byrnes were jubilant about the position in which they found themselves but seemingly heedless of the impending human tragedy they would unleash by targeting civilian non-combatants. One of their objectives was the earliest possible use of the atomic bomb in Japan in order to subdue Soviet pretensions. If the atomic bomb hastened a Japanese surrender, Soviet Russia would not need to enter the war against Japan, as Roosevelt had requested at Yalta; or be entitled to the territorial concessions in north-east Asia that he had promised. Byrnes acknowledged that he and the president were 'hoping for time, believing that after [the] atomic bomb, Japan will surrender and Russia *will not get in so much on the kill*' (emphasis added). Truman wrote to himself: 'Believe Japs will fold up before Russia comes in. I am sure they will when Manhattan appears over their homeland'. It was transparent. Churchill observed that 'It is quite clear that the United States do not at the present time desire Russian participation in the war against Japan'.

Stalin knew what was going on and expedited the Soviet Army's advance into Manchuria. The first atomic bomb was detonated over Hiroshima on 6 August; the second, for good measure, over Nagasaki on 9 August. Between those dates, around midnight on 8 August, the Soviet invasion commenced. It was three months, almost to the hour, after the end of the war against Germany. By the time of the announcement of Japan's surrender on 15 August, the Soviet Army was all over Manchuria and the first elements of the 25th Army had entered north-east Korea. A fortnight later, they had completed occupation as far south as Pyongyang. Truman's initial hopes of limiting Soviet territorial gains in north-east Asia were frustrated. But there was another way.

On 10 August, on the day after Nagasaki, and two days after the Soviet invasion, Truman decided with his wartime policy committee, the State-War-Navy Coordinating Committee

(SWNCC), that the Korean peninsula should be partitioned and occupied by US military forces. Freshly returned from Potsdam, Truman was ebullient after having been visited by King George VI on 2 August aboard the USS *Augusta*. He disembarked at Newport five days later. One historian noted drily, 'the fate of the Korean peninsula suddenly became of interest to the Americans'. Neither the Korean people nor any Allied power was consulted. Working from a lift-out map in a 1942 *National Geographic* magazine, two young colonels from the State Department selected the 38th parallel as the line of partition. Truman confirmed the selection a few days later. When the proposal was put to Stalin, he acceded to it – to the relief of Washington.

The three events – the detonation of atomic bombs over Hiroshima and Nagasaki on 6 and 9 August and the decision to partition and occupy Korea on 10 August – had more in common than it might have seemed: more to do with Soviet Russia than Japan. The military necessity for detonating the atomic bombs is questionable – despite the adamantine views of Truman supporters – but its political and psychological advantage against Soviet Russia was not.

Senior military men were later critical of Truman's decision: 'Six of the United States' seven star officers who received their final star in World War II...rejected the idea that atomic bombs were needed to end the war'. They included General MacArthur, the second-highest-ranking active-duty officer in the United States Army, who considered the bomb 'completely unnecessary from a military point of view'; Admiral Leahy, the Chairman of the Joint Chiefs, who complained that the 'Japanese were already defeated and ready to surrender...[it] was of no material assistance in our war against Japan'; Air

Force General Curtis LeMay, who said that 'Even without the atomic bomb and the Russian entry into the war, Japan would have surrendered in two weeks...The atomic bomb had nothing to do with the end of the war'; Admiral Halsey, commander of the US Third Fleet, who said, 'The first atomic bomb was an unnecessary experiment...It was a mistake to ever drop it...the Japs had put out a lot of peace feelers'; and General Eisenhower, who told *Newsweek* magazine that 'I was against it on two counts. First, the Japanese were ready to surrender and it wasn't necessary to hit them with that awful thing. Second, I hated to see our country be the first to use such a weapon'.

Some of these senior military leaders also harboured profound moral concerns. Admiral Leahy felt strongly. On the day of the Hiroshima explosion, he told his secretary: 'Dorothy, we will regret this day. The United States will suffer, for war is not to be waged on women and children'. For Eisenhower, it was a family affair. Both he and his brother Milton had deep misgivings. Milton wrote that 'Hiroshima and Nagasaki will forever be on the conscience of the American people'. There were some other surprising opponents, including John Foster Dulles, the virulent anti-communist who later became Eisenhower's secretary of state, and Henry Luce. Both were devoutly religious.

Truman took his own course and achieved his political and psychological objective. Nuclear jubilation in Washington was matched by nuclear foreboding in Moscow. The physicist Yuli Khariton recalled that 'The whole Soviet government interpreted [Hiroshima] as atomic blackmail against the USSR, as a threat to unleash a new, even more terrible and devastating war'. Marshal Zhukov, Stalin's most senior military commander, who had a good relationship with then

General Eisenhower, was haunted by the apparently gratuitous nature of the bombings. He reflected years later that 'It was clear already then that the US Government intended to use the atomic weapon for the purpose of achieving its Imperialist goals from a position of strength...'

President Truman had no qualms. When he heard the news of the Hiroshima explosion while dining on the USS *Augusta* on the way back from the Potsdam conference, he jumped up and exclaimed, 'This is the greatest thing in history'. When the nuclear scientist Oppenheimer later expressed remorse, saying, 'Mr President, I feel that I have blood on my hands'. Truman told Dean Acheson, his renowned and longest-serving secretary of state, that he never wanted to see Oppenheimer in his office again; that he was a 'cry-baby scientist' and that 'this kind of snivelling makes me sick'.

Doctrine & Distrust

Truman's antipathy to Soviet Russia hardened further in 1946 and the war drums beat louder. Churchill delivered his 'Iron Curtain' declamation; George Kennan, then the American chargé d'affaires in Moscow, despatched his famous 'Long Telegram', which resonated in Washington for the wrong reasons; Wallace departed from the administration; and Truman received the Clifford report telling him that the language of military power was the only language the Soviets understood. Churchill, Kennan and Clifford all used hyperbolic language to describe Soviet Russia's political and subversive aims but Kennan in particular never ceased to regret how his words were misinterpreted and seized upon to militarise the containment of Soviet Russia. And in the alternative world of American domestic politics, the Republicans accused Truman of being too soft on Stalin and the communists and took control of both houses of Congress in the mid-term elections. Looking back on the Cold War years, Dean Acheson conceded that it 'may be true' that 'we overreacted to Stalin, which in turn caused him to overreact to policies of the United States'. The overreaction changed the world.

By 1947 Truman felt that the situation called for bold leadership. He had been 'looking for a means by which to confront the Soviets'. When the British asked for assistance in Greece, he found it. The Greek civil war had flared and Truman insisted that 'the very existence of the Greek state is today threatened by several thousand armed men, led by Communists, who defy the government's authority'. And he was convinced that the Soviets were planning to take control of the Turkish Straits in order to assist the communists in Greece. In March, he asked a joint session of Congress for $400 million (almost $4.5 billion today) to provide economic and military assistance to Greece and Turkey. In language that was 'grandiose and sweeping', he intimated that Western civilisation was imperilled and he coupled the request for funds with an open-ended promise to 'support free peoples who are resisting subjugation by armed minorities or by outside pressures' – wherever they were. This single sentence became the Truman Doctrine. Kennan thought the commitment was unwise, excessive and unrealistic. Bernard Baruch, Roosevelt's trusted advisor, described the speech as 'tantamount to a declaration of...ideological or religious war'.

In June the Marshall Plan was unveiled. Truman said his new doctrine and the Marshall Plan were 'two halves of the same walnut'. He wanted to inhibit the expansion of Soviet Russia and the influence of communism in Western Europe and establish the leadership and power of the United States in the region. The president asked Congress for an unprecedented grant for European reconstruction. The stated objective was to prevent Europe being overwhelmed by economic disintegration, social dislocation and political collapse. The unstated objective – the sine qua non of the Marshall Plan – was to reduce sympathy for communism by securing political and popular support for liberal democracy as the governing European ideology.

Stalin responded to the Marshall Plan by propounding an alternative version known as the Molotov Plan and making it clear to all Eastern European governments that acceptance of American assistance would be regarded as an anti-Soviet act. And in September, he resurrected the Communist International, the Comintern, which had been dissolved during the war as a gesture of goodwill. Its new name was the Cominform (Communist Information Bureau) and its mission was to repel the expansion of anti-communism in the aftermath of World War II. At the inaugural meeting of the Cominform, Stalin's deputy for issues of ideology, Andrei Zhdanov, made clear Stalin's thinking about the Truman administration's antagonism, referring among other things, to the 'crusade against Communism proclaimed by America's ruling circle'.

He was not wrong. Washington chose to militarise the ideological differences between itself and Moscow. By November 1947, the Joint Chiefs had prepared, and Truman had approved, the first complete war plan against Soviet Russia. It was known as 'Plan Broiler' and envisaged thirty-four atomic bombs being dropped on twenty-four Soviet target cities. But as Steven Pinker, the influential Harvard professor and author of *Enlightenment Now*, pointed out, Soviet archives have not revealed 'any serious plans for unprovoked aggression against Western Europe, not to mention a first strike against the United States'. He continued: 'That means that the intricate weaponry and strategic doctrines for nuclear deterrence during the Cold War...were deterring an attack that the Soviets had no interest in launching in the first place'.

Nonetheless, 1948 brought an even harder edge to the Cold War. Stalin chose security and ideological rectitude. And the potential for limited cooperation with the United States and the United Kingdom diminished significantly. In February, the coup by Czech communists with Soviet assistance seemed to signal a final rupture. Czechoslovakia had been the last remaining democracy in Eastern Europe and the reaction to its loss in Washington was dread and despair. A few weeks after the coup, General Lucius Clay, the US military governor of Germany who had never served a day in combat, added to the sense of anxiety by cabling Washington that war might come 'with dramatic suddenness'. Some thought that containment of Soviet influence was no longer sufficient. The National Security Council called for a 'worldwide counter-offensive' against Soviet Russia. The Pentagon lobbied for a substantial increase in its military budget. And a grim President Truman gave a nationwide radio address. Almost alone in the administration, George Kennan, the architect of containment, urged restraint. He wrote in his memoirs that the military and intelligence fraternity had 'overreacted in the most deplorable way' and that a 'real war scare ensued'. In a few years, Truman would marginalise him.

In June the National Security Council, with presidential approval, authorised the CIA to conduct a much expanded program of covert political, economic and paramilitary operations, including subversion against hostile states and assistance to underground resistance movements, guerrillas and refugee liberation groups. Even 'the seemingly benign Marshall Plan provided a cover for subversion. Half of the 10 per cent of the money allocated for administrative costs was siphoned off to fund [CIA] covert operations'. And some of the diverted Marshall Plan money went to support a right-wing guerrilla army in Ukraine called 'Nightingale', which had been established by the Wehrmacht.

In the same month, the Berlin Blockade commenced. Its immediate cause was the decision by the United States and the United Kingdom, without informing the Soviets, to introduce a new deutschmark in their occupation zones. The purpose of the currency reform was to wrest economic control of Berlin from Soviet Russia and facilitate the introduction of the Marshall Plan. Stalin complained, with some justification, that the move would wreck the East German economy and responded by cutting off all surface traffic (road, rail and canal) into West Berlin. Truman's initial reaction was to opt for a show of force and despatch sixty atomic capable B-29s to British and German bases. A stalemate ensued for the next twelve months as Allied aircraft were permitted to bring supplies into Berlin's Tempelhof Airport without Soviet interdiction.

Matters escalated further in 1949, but not before the North Atlantic Treaty Organisation (NATO) was established in April and the Berlin Blockade ended in May. In September, the world – and the American public in particular – were shocked by the announcement that Soviet Russia had successfully tested an atomic bomb. And on 1 October, at the Gate of Heavenly Peace in Beijing, Mao Zedong proclaimed the coming into existence of the People's Republic of China. The long Chinese civil war between the communists led by Mao and Chiang Kai-shek's nationalists, who had been armed and funded by the United States, ended in defeat for the nationalists. *The New York Times* described it as 'a vast tragedy of unforeseeable consequences for the Western World'.

The convergence of events caused many Americans to believe that they were on the verge of World War III in a binary conflict between communism and the 'free world'. The United States and Soviet Russia stood at the edge of a precipice. They were the world's unparalleled superpowers, with each having universalist pretensions. And both had a 'demonstrated capacity for undoubted cruelty' in their treatment of humankind – in the one case the 'nuclear extermination of cities' and in the other 'millions sent to labor camps' and worse. President Truman might have done well to recall the wartime words of the philosopher and religious historian Christopher Dawson: 'As soon as men decide that all means are permitted to fight evil, then their good becomes indistinguishable from the evil that they set out to destroy'. George Kennan, the advocate of restraint, had expressed a similar sentiment when he warned the Truman administration that 'the greatest danger that can befall us in coping with this problem of Soviet communism, is that we shall allow ourselves to become like those with whom we are coping'. Kennan never struck a chord with Truman.

Instead, successive administrations ignored the rules and precepts on which the United States had once so conclusively demonstrated world leadership. As one commentator noted, 'Not only did the United States play a crucial role in writing the new rules for the international community, but it almost immediately began breaking them'. By 1954, at a National

Security Council meeting headed by President Eisenhower, a senior cabinet member could make the following statement without disagreement, protest or objection from anyone in the room:

> Whatever we may choose to say in public about ideas and idealism among ourselves, we've got to be a great deal more practical and materialistic...We should stop talking so much about democracy...[and] support dictatorships of the right if their policies are pro-American.

PART 2
OUTCOMES

CHAPTER 3

COMPROMISE
Coups & Interventions

The CIA

The anxiety caused by the Cold War, and the compromise of moral principle that it induced in Washington, resulted in tragic consequences for America and the world. A pattern of interventionism, inspired by moral and military overreach, became ingrained and institutionalised. The United States went far further than simply supporting 'dictatorships of the right'. Successive administrations conducted or attempted one operation after another to destabilise and overthrow foreign governments, assassinate foreign leaders or invade foreign countries. Nothing strikes at the heart of state sovereignty quite as much. Nothing is quite so antithetical to the principles on which the post-World War II rules-based order was intended to be based. Inevitably, the operations were counterproductive in the long term. All were unlawful under the Charter of the

United Nations – whose provisions President George HW Bush once labelled 'the sacred principles'.

According to *The Washington Post*, there were seventy-two attempts by the United States to change other nations' governments from 1947 to 1989. And according to historian Monica Duffy Toft, from 1992 to 2017, when the United States was effectively unrestrained by superpower competition, the number of American military interventions of all types increased fourfold. Many of the operations were covert and have been, and continue to be, conducted by the CIA.

The CIA is no ordinary intelligence organisation. It came into existence in 1947 as part of the historic reform introduced by the National Security Act, which created the current massive American military establishment, including most notably, a war council known as the National Security Council. The CIA's predecessor was the Office of Strategic Services (OSS), created in 1941 and partly modelled on the British Special Operations Executive (SOE). Both the SOE and the OSS conducted wartime espionage and sabotage, especially in occupied France; both were established to operate in an environment of total war, against enemies with whom each of their countries was in a declared state of war; and both were dissolved when the war concluded. An American military historian identified the essential difference: 'Whereas the target of US paramilitary activity in World War II was an army of occupation, the target in the post-war period had become a political ideology'.

The CIA was not originally proposed to be a sabotage and subversion organisation able to operate covertly with para-military forces contrary to the laws of foreign countries. Nor was it intended to be a replica of the wartime OSS. Its primary task – and the only one expressly stipulated in the National

Security Act – was intelligence gathering and dissemination, namely 'to correlate and evaluate intelligence relating to the national security, and provide for the appropriate dissemination of such intelligence within the Government'. The Senate Select Committee, known as the Church Committee, which conducted a searching review of the CIA's activities in 1975, could find 'no evidence in the debates, committee reports, or legislative history of the Act to show that Congress intended specifically to authorize covert operations'. The principal drafter of the CIA's powers has confirmed that covert operations were 'never considered'.

But the tide of Cold War anxiety was unstoppable and the law was made to fit the facts. Some hardliners sought refuge in a catch-all provision of the act that authorised the CIA to perform 'such other functions and duties related to intelligence'. It was a barely arguable proposition but it did not matter. Pragmatism ruled, and continues to do so to this day. The first director of the CIA, Admiral Hillenkoetter, was opposed to the idea of a clandestine service conducting covert operations in foreign countries during peacetime, but the hardliners, including Secretary of Defense James Forrestal and influential former senior OSS officers, were determined. They argued for a covert capability to be deployed against the spread of communism. The debate was short lived. According to one account, the advice of CIA general counsel was: 'If the President or the National Security Council directs us to do a certain action, and Congress funds it, you've got no problem. Who is there left to object?' The situation has continued unchanged for over seventy years. One military commentator has observed, 'It is perhaps ironic to note that to this day, the CIA has no *legislative* authority to conduct covert activity'.

From its uncertain birth at the beginning of the Cold War, the CIA rapidly became a juggernaut. Allen Dulles, its director under President Eisenhower, decided that it 'must reach into every corner of the world'. It became a form of intelligence agency almost unique among democratic nations – with its own fully armed, fully weaponised, private army able to carry out secret ground, air and maritime paramilitary operations on the basis of 'plausible deniability', without the scrutiny that applies to military operations. Plausible deniability means what it says. The accountability that applies to conventional military operations does not apply to the covert activities of the CIA, which are required by the National Security Council to 'be so planned and executed that any US government responsibility for them is not evident to unauthorized persons and that if uncovered, the US government can plausibly disclaim any responsibility for them'. This requires the use of special funds, namely 'moneys for which no voucher is submitted to the General Accounting Office, to be employed in instances where the use of vouchered funds would divulge information prejudicial to the public interest'. Covert operations are off the books.

From the outset, the agency conducted its activities as if the United States were in a permanent state of war – except it was peacetime. Elections were interfered with, governments were overthrown, democratically elected leaders were assassinated and military incursions took place in foreign states without the sanction of the United Nations. The principle of collective security enshrined in the United Nations Charter was defied; respect for the sovereignty of foreign nations was overlooked; and the rules of international law were ignored. All of these activities were authorised at the highest level – by presidents, national security advisors and CIA directors. Some of the clearest and most damning include: Iran (1953), Guatemala (1954), Vietnam (1963), Chile (1973) and Iraq (2003) but there have been many more. Whatever else they were, they were not victories for democracy or the 'rules-based order'. One former CIA director, currently President Trump's secretary of state, revealed to a Texas university audience in 2019: 'We lied, we cheated, we stole. We had entire training courses'. He then added: 'It reminds you of the glory of the American experiment'.

The CIA's initial 'enemy' was an ideology. Communism was pursued in any country – friend or foe – wherever it might exist or be entertained. Non-communist governments were targeted if they were considered not pro-American or were thought to be left-wing or left-leaning or vulnerable to communism – all the more so if their actions were perceived to threaten the commercial or security interests of the United States. It did not matter that those actions were the result of a lawful constitutional process by a sovereign state. Nor did the operations stop after the Cold War. There was always an 'enemy', whether peacetime or not, and the regime-change operations and destabilisation continued. We will not know for many years, but some in the Turkish government contend that the CIA was instrumental in the failed coup attempt in July 2016. And some in Beijing allege that the CIA was behind the unrest in Hong Kong in 2019.

While most agency operatives were enthusiasts, others became deeply disillusioned. Nearly four decades after the CIA was established, a group of former officers, known as the Association for Responsible Dissent, complained that the CIA's covert operations were counterproductive to the security of the United States. They warned of the dangers, worried about the consequences and denounced:

...US covert operations that killed, wounded and terrorized millions of people whose countries were not at war with the United States, nor possessed the capabilities to do remarkable physical hurt to the United States, who themselves bore the United States no ill will nor cared greatly about the issues of 'communism' or 'capitalism'.

They were voices in the wilderness, like that of Sherman Kent, the legendary CIA intelligence analyst. Kent was so troubled by what seemed like a Faustian bargain that he wrote in despair:

[To send] clandestine operatives into a foreign country against which the United States is not at war and instruct these agents to carry out 'black' operations, not only runs counter to the principles upon which our country was founded but also those for which we recently fought a war.

Few shared Sherman Kent's reservations and the CIA went to work. Its first major operation in a foreign country was a covert campaign to influence the 1948 Italian general elections. It was a watershed in the development of the foreign policy of the United States and launched the CIA on a path of ever more interventions. The operation was carried out with such gusto that it makes anything done by Russia in the 2016 US presidential elections look half-hearted, but more sophisticated. The *Economist* magazine reported that in Italy, 'America took off the gloves for the first time'. It was the beginning of a 'perilous new policy' by the United States. In the famous phrase of the American writer Chalmers Johnson, it has resulted in 'blowback'.

A long-classified CIA report, entitled 'Consequences of Communist Accession to Power in Italy by Legal Means', made clear that a communist accession to power in Italy 'by *popular suffrage and legal procedure*' was unacceptable to the United States (emphasis added). The paradoxical conclusion, only three years after the United Nations Charter, was that unlawful means should be used to prevent a lawful result in a sovereign country. The estimate of funds utilised secretly by the CIA to influence the Italian elections is $10–$30 million. It worked. The 'cash operation' ensured that the Christian Democrats succeeded at the election even though the communists were the largest party organisation in Italy; as they were in France.

For John Foster Dulles, the future Republican secretary of state, and older brother of the future director of the CIA, it was a turning point. He concluded that the victory in Italy showed that hardline anti-communism could succeed. Enthused by success, he called for 'further American intervention abroad'. It was not long before he got his wish – in Tehran.

Iran 1953

Neither the Iranian government in 1953 nor its prime minister, Mohammad Mossadegh, was communist. Mossadegh was a fierce nationalist who believed passionately in democracy, abhorred communist doctrine and excluded the communist party (the Tudeh) from his government. His priority was to temper the despotic shah's role and increase the power of the elected government. *Time* magazine named Mossadegh 'Man of the Year' in January 1952, choosing him ahead of Churchill, MacArthur, Truman and Eisenhower. Yet in August 1953, the United States chose to overthrow Mossadegh's democratically elected government of Iran. The CIA-led operation, known as 'Operation Ajax', was authorised by Foster Dulles and approved by President Eisenhower. Its consequences are still playing out today.

The troubling coup had its origin in an internal dispute between the Iranian government and the British-owned Anglo–Persian Oil Company. It should have been none of America's business. The British company enjoyed the benefits of a grossly unequal concession granted in 1901 that exempted it from income tax and customs duties and obliged it to pay only a fraction of its profits as royalties. For decades there had been fruitless attempts to renegotiate the concession on a more equitable basis. By 1951, popular Iranian demands for nationalisation of the oil industry had dramatically intensified. In response to the public clamour, both houses of the Iranian parliament, the Majlis, voted in March in favour of nationalisation, with due compensation. Mossadegh came to power riding this wave.

As it happened, the nationalisation of critical industries was a key feature of governmental decision-making in many democratic countries at that time. The parliaments of the United Kingdom, France, Canada, India, Australia and New Zealand, as well as the Swedish Riksdag, all passed legislation after the war, with varying success, attempting to nationalise some or other of their banks, transport infrastructure, health services and utility companies. Despite having recently nationalised its own coal and steel industries, the British government was outraged at the decision of the Iranian Majlis. When an appeal to the International Court of Justice was unsuccessful, the British Foreign Office considered bribing Mossadegh, assassinating him or launching a military invasion. But on learning of these intrigues, Mossadegh ordered the closure of the British embassy and the expulsion of its employees and intelligence agents.

Without agents in the country, the Foreign Office turned to the United States, suggesting that turmoil in Iran would lead to communism. For Foster Dulles, it was an opportunity for which he had been waiting. He was easily persuaded. He noted that 'if [Mossadegh] were to be assassinated or removed from power, a political vacuum might occur in Iran and the communists might easily take over'. It was a bizarre triple hypothetical: if... might...might. The only one planning to create turmoil was the CIA, with British assistance. The subsequent operation was led by Kermit Roosevelt, the grandson of President Theodore Roosevelt. Its objective was unequivocal. The title of the long-classified CIA report was 'Overthrow of Premier Mossadeq of Iran, November 1952 – August 1953'.

The CIA plan called for Iranian opinion leaders to be paid substantial sums to 'create, extend and enhance public hostility and distrust and fear of Mossadegh and his government'. Using a network of Iranian agents and spending lavish amounts of CIA money, Roosevelt set Iran aflame. An artificial wave of anti-Mossadegh protest and dirty tricks was created. Influential Iranians were bribed and blandished with secret funds with the object of corrupting the democratic process and destroying Mossadegh's support. The outcome was that some 'members of parliament withdrew their support from Mossadegh and denounced him with wild charges. Religious leaders gave sermons calling him an atheist, a Jew and an infidel. Newspapers were filled with articles and cartoons depicting him as everything from a homosexual to an agent of British imperialism'.

The shah, Mohammad Reza Pahlavi, was taken into the CIA's confidence. Kermit Roosevelt prevailed upon him to sign in advance a secret royal decree, known as a *firman*, dismissing Mossadegh from office and appointing a General Zahedi as the new prime minister. Zahedi was the CIA's man. The shah was reluctant to sign but agreed on condition that he could fly immediately to his retreat on the Caspian Sea. The *firman* was to be held in escrow until the final moment.

In the week leading up to the coup, a plague of orchestrated violence descended on Tehran. In some cases, Iranians were paid to pose as Tudeh members attacking Islamic preachers or the advisors of the shah. In other cases, 'Gangs of thugs ran wildly through the streets, breaking shop windows, firing guns into mosques, beating passers by and shouting "Long live Mossadegh and Communism". Other thugs, claiming allegiance to the self-exiled shah, attacked the first ones'. The leaders of the opposing factions were both working for the CIA.

On 19 August 1953, the day chosen for the coup, thousands of paid demonstrators rampaged through the streets demanding Mossadegh's resignation, seized Radio Tehran and set fire to the offices of a pro-government newspaper. At midday, 'military and police units, whose commanders Roosevelt had bribed' joined the fray, storming the foreign ministry, the central police station and the headquarters of the army's general staff. Amid the chaos, General Zahedi was driven to Radio Tehran clutching the absent shah's *firman* and announced that he was now the lawful prime minister. Mossadegh was arrested. The shah flew back to Tehran, accompanied by Allen Dulles, the head of the CIA and brother of the secretary of state. Foster Dulles stayed in Washington and kept President Eisenhower informed.

The coup entrenched the autocratic shah and replaced the democratic government with a royal dictatorship firmly aligned and indebted to the United States. Several dozen military and student leaders who had been closely associated with Mossadegh were executed; Mossadegh was tried and convicted of treason and kept under house arrest until he died years later; a secret police force called Savak, which became infamous for its brutality, was created to secure the shah's hold on power; and a group of American companies acquired a substantial interest in Iran's oil assets as part of a renegotiated deal that replaced the old Anglo-Iranian Oil Company concession. The deal ensured Western control of Iran's petroleum resources and shut out Soviet Russia. The shah remained beholden to the United States for the next twenty-six years and ensured that Iran was a strategic Middle East ally of Washington. In 1979, popular resentment erupted in revolution, anti-American vitriol and animosity that continues to this day. It had been simmering since 1953.

Half a century after the coup, an Iranian diplomat observed:

> It is a reasonable argument that but for the [CIA] coup, Iran would be a mature democracy. So traumatic was the coup's legacy that when the Shah finally departed in 1979, many Iranians feared a repetition of 1953, which was one of the motivations for the student seizure of the US embassy. The hostage crisis, in turn, precipitated the Iraqi invasion of Iran, while the [Islamic] revolution itself played a part in the Soviet decision to invade Afghanistan. A lot of history, in short, flowed from a single week in Tehran...

By 'violently pushing Iran off the path to democracy in 1953, the United States created a whirlpool of instability from which undreamed-of threats emerged years later'. One recent commentator, writing in the *Foreign Affairs* magazine, described the US-led overthrow of Prime Minister Mossadegh and his democratic government as 'the original sin':

> The overthrow of Mosaddeq was the original sin of the U.S.-Iranian relationship, and Iranian anger at the coup was later compounded by U.S. and Israeli support for Mohammad Reza Shah Pahlavi, whose repressive policies and inept attempts at modernization undermined popular support for his regime. The shah's intimate relationship with the United States tainted both parties in the eyes of Iranians, contributing to the resentment that resulted in the Islamic Revolution of 1979.

Guatemala 1954

Less than a year after the overthrow of Mossadegh, the CIA orchestrated the overthrow of the democratic government of Guatemala. It had little to do with communism and much to do with American commercial interests. The powerful United Fruit Company, an American corporation that was Guatemala's largest landholder and private employer, had grown accustomed to conducting its business in Guatemala 'free of such annoyances as taxes and labor regulations'. And it had many powerful connections in Washington – including both Dulles brothers and Henry Cabot Lodge, the staunch Republican strongman and ambassador to the United Nations. Under President Arévalo, the Guatemalan national assembly established the country's first social security system, guaranteed the rights of trade unions, fixed a forty-eight hour working week and levied a modest tax on large landholders. These developments troubled the United Fruit Company.

When Arévalo's elected successor Jacobo Arbenz became president, the company was even more troubled, not because Arbenz was a professed communist (which he was not), but because his fundamental objectives included 'converting Guatemala from a predominantly feudal economy into a modern capitalist state; and [making] this transformation in a way that will raise the standard of living of the great mass of our people to the highest level'. When the Guatemalan government compulsorily resumed 234,000 acres of uncultivated land belonging to the United Fruit Company at Tiquisate, it ignited a frenzy. Supporters of the company, including prominent members of the United States Congress, engaged in a blizzard of denunciation, alleging that 'In Guatemala, the Reds are in control and they are trying to spread their influence'. They contended that 'Guatemala's democratic leaders had become subservient to the Kremlin's design for world conquest and were turning their country into a Soviet beachhead'.

The Reds were not in control in Guatemala. And nothing could have been further from the truth. Arbenz's government had the support of the miniscule Guatemalan Communist Party but that party only held four seats in the sixty-one-member national assembly. The government bought arms from Czechoslovakia but Soviet Russia had no military, economic, or even diplomatic relations with Guatemala and no delegation of Guatemalans had ever visited Russia. Unfortunately, Foster Dulles and Eisenhower had an almost theological certainty of Russian influence 'based on our deep conviction that such a tie [with the Soviets] must exist'. In the absence of evidence, 'deep convictions' are notoriously unreliable.

Dulles duly initiated a secret CIA operation to overthrow the government of Guatemala. It was known as Operation Success. Unvouched funds in the sum of $4.5 million were made available; a former Guatemalan army officer (Castillo Armas) was selected and groomed as a rebel leader; fighters were hired; aircraft requisitioned; and bases prepared. New York's fiercely anti-communist Catholic Cardinal Spellman was persuaded to provide support. Soon CIA agents 'were writing scripts or leaflets for the Guatemalan clergy'. On 9 April 1954, a pastoral letter was read in every Catholic church in Guatemala warning the faithful against a 'demonic force called communism that was trying to destroy their homeland'. Those who expressed reservations about the operation were sidelined, including *New York Times* foreign correspondent Sydney Gruson and the CIA station chief in Guatemala, both of whom were pulled out following pressure from the State Department.

In June 1954, US-trained rebel troops crossed into Guatemala with lists of left-wingers marked for elimination. US-piloted fighter-bombers strafed the capital. Air raids continued for several days, driving much of the country to near panic. A clandestine 'Voice of Liberation' radio station, operated by the CIA out of Florida, broadcast a stream of false reports about military rebellion and popular unrest. More fighter-bomber air support was called in and further strafing continued for another three days and nights, spreading alarm and causing hundreds of people to flee their homes. No one in Guatemala knew then that the CIA was behind the mayhem. The US State Department issued a statement saying that 'The department has no evidence that indicates this is anything other than a revolt of Guatemalans against the government'. It was dishonest.

Arbenz despatched his foreign minister (Toriello) to New York to seek assistance from Foster Dulles, unaware that he was the man behind the mayhem. Toriello's unknowing cable to Foster Dulles is poignant 'to the point of pathos':

> I regret to inform your Excellency that a savage attack
> with TNT bombs took place yesterday on the civilian
> population of Chiquimula, as well as strafing of that
> city and the cities of Gualan and Zacapa...Guatemala
> appeals urgently to your Excellency...and asks that your
> enlightened government, always respectful of the human
> rights of which it has been the standard bearer, be good
> enough to intercede with the Security Council.

The Guatemalan people had not discovered 'the great ruse of Operation Success'. Nor did they realise that the United States was not the standard bearer of human rights that Toriello thought it to be. When Arbenz gradually learned the truth, he began to lose his grip and was soon forced to step down. In his farewell radio speech, he told his countrymen: 'A cruel war against Guatemala has been unleashed. The United Fruit Company...together with US ruling circles, are responsible...' Arbenz sought and obtained political asylum in the Mexican embassy and the American ambassador arranged for Castillo Armas to proclaim himself as president. A succession of military juntas supported by the United States followed. They revoked most of Guatemala's democratic and social reforms.

Foster Dulles celebrated the overthrow as 'the biggest success in the last five years against Communism'. Churchill, who had tried in vain to encourage Eisenhower to 'extend a hand to the Soviets' after Stalin's death in 1953 – when Khrushchev initially adopted a conciliatory posture – was troubled. And his government objected. A spokesman observed: 'The Americans are making extremely heavy weather over all this and acting in a manner which is likely to alienate world sympathy'. Eisenhower's response was to dig in his heels. He told the State Department: 'Let's give them [the British] a lesson'.

Vietnam 1963

The United States encountered more 'heavy weather' in Southeast Asia, where it did everything possible for more than two decades to prevent a communist state in the former French colonial territory of Vietnam. Graham Greene's 1950s novel *The Quiet American* has a disquieting resonance. At the Geneva conference in 1954, which was intended to settle outstanding differences arising from both the Korean War and France's colonial war in Indochina, the United States opposed the unification of Vietnam. It actively sought to perpetuate the permanent division of both Vietnam and Korea in order to preserve a bulwark against communism. Secretary of State Foster Dulles attended the conference but he did not negotiate in good faith. When asked before the conference whether he would meet with the Chinese representative Zhou Enlai, he replied icily, 'Not unless our automobiles collide'. When Zhou approached him and held out his hand, he turned his back and walked away.

Foster Dulles was hoping to prevent an agreement on the unification of Vietnam. He failed. The final outcome of the Geneva conference provided for the temporary division of Vietnam at the 17th parallel, but only for a period of two years. The communist Vietminh and France reached agreement to hold elections in 1956 with a view to the formal unification of the country and the establishment of a national government. As a national government would almost certainly have been communist, Washington was opposed to the very idea of elections, whether agreed at the Geneva conference or not. It was the beginning of a long, doomed campaign that became a gradual slide into a catastrophic war.

Ngo Dinh Diem was the American choice for leader in South Vietnam. Although not well known in Washington, his anti-communist credentials were sufficiently clear: he had served as a junior minister in an earlier administration of Emperor Bao Dai, spent two years living in the United States at the Maryknoll seminary in Lakewood, New Jersey, and came recommended by New York's Catholic Cardinal Spellman. By 1954, he was residing in a Benedictine monastery in Belgium. When the French withdrew, Diem was parachuted – metaphorically speaking – into South Vietnam with the active support of Washington and the approval of the emperor. He took office as prime minister in July. The following year he became president. Encouraged by Washington, Diem duly ignored the Geneva agreement and refused to allow the intended elections to take place.

In Hanoi, Ho Chi Minh was the leader of the Vietminh and had the respect and support of the vast majority of the Vietnamese people. Communism was the dominant outlet for Vietnamese nationalism, for which the war against the colonial French had been waged from 1945 to 1954. At the beginning of the struggle against France, Ho declared the independence of Vietnam in a ringing declaration that would have sounded familiar to Americans. His words included: 'All men are created equal. They are endowed by their creator with certain inalienable rights. Among these are life, liberty and the pursuit of happiness'. President Eisenhower guessed that 'possibly eighty percent of the population' would vote for Ho Chi Minh at any election for a unified Vietnam. For that reason alone, as Odd Arne Westad has observed, the anti-communist minority in South Vietnam was 'bound to lose in any contest for national authenticity' and the 'US war in Vietnam was folly from the beginning'.

Diem refused to allow the intended elections and then attempted, with CIA support, to suppress communism in the south. The CIA propaganda included bizarre radio messages proclaiming that 'Christ has gone to the South' and that the 'Virgin Mary has departed from the North'. In response, the communists, who called themselves 'Vietcong' in the south, undertook a campaign of assassinations and bombings in support of a 'people's war', into which the United States increasingly allowed itself to be drawn. By 1963, there were over sixteen thousand American 'advisors' attached to all principal South Vietnamese military units. US military aircraft and helicopters transported Vietnamese troops, including into North Vietnam, and began to use herbicides such as Agent Orange for crop destruction.

When Vice President Lyndon Johnson visited Saigon in 1961, he came back convinced that if the communists were allowed to take South Vietnam, they would push their way to 'the beaches of Waikiki'. He even described Diem as 'the Churchill of Southeast Asia' (which was far-fetched) and that he was 'the only boy we got there' (which was true). In reality, Diem, who had been 'plucked from a religious group that represented only ten percent of the country's population', soon ceased to behave like the surrogate it was hoped he would be.

When Diem complained, with considerable justification, about 'all these soldiers I never asked to come here' and that the US advisors were making the situation worse – 'only intensifying the conflict by provoking strong responses from the North' – Washington began to have doubts about their man in Saigon. And when US Ambassador Nolting euphemistically informed Diem that the United States wished to 'share in the decision making process in the political, economic and military fields', Diem drew a line, telling the ambassador: 'Vietnam does not want to be a protectorate'.

Worse was to come, at least from Washington's perspective. Diem's brother and chief advisor, Ngo Dinh Nhu, suggested that the time had come to negotiate with the Vietcong. He told an interviewer, 'I am anti-communist from the point of view of doctrine, but I am not anti-communist from the point of view of politics or humanity'. As Buddhist monks engaged in self-immolation that was televised on American screens, and unrest about the war spread throughout South Vietnam, influential voices in the State Department began clamouring for Diem's overthrow. He was seen as a reluctant protégé and the view was that there was 'no possibility that the war can be won under a Diem administration'.

On a Saturday in late August 1963, the administration's chief East Asia specialist drafted a fateful cable. It directed the new ambassador in Saigon, Henry Cabot Lodge, to tell Diem that the United States 'cannot tolerate a situation' in which power lies in his brother's hands and that he should sever all political ties to him. It went on to say that if Diem 'remains obdurate and refuses, we must face the possibility that Diem himself *cannot be preserved*' and added that 'the Ambassador and country teams should urgently examine all possible replacement leadership and make *detailed plans as to how we might bring about Diem's replacement* if this becomes necessary' (emphasis added).

The cable needed presidential approval and Kennedy had not yet made up his mind, but Lodge was enthusiastic about the opportunity to effect regime change in Saigon. His cable to Washington on 29 August warned that unless the United States acted quickly, South Vietnam might fall into the hands of 'pro-communist or at least neutralist politicians'. Lodge adopted a melodramatic tone:

> We are launched on a course from which there is no respectable turning back: the overthrow of the Diem government. There is no turning back because *US prestige* is already publicly committed to this end in large measure, and will become more so as the facts leak out. [emphasis added]

It was morally vacuous but it seemed to convince Kennedy. In due course, he chose to endorse a coup to overthrow a government in Saigon that was losing the war against the communists in Vietnam. The conclusion of the officially titled 'Report of the Office of the Secretary of Defense Vietnam Task Force', better known as the Pentagon Papers, was damning:

> For the military coup d'etat against Ngo Dinh Diem, the US must accept its full share of responsibility...Beginning in August of 1963 we variously authorized, sanctioned and encouraged the coup efforts of the Vietnamese generals and offered full support for a successor government...We maintained clandestine contact with

them throughout the planning and execution of the coup and sought to review their operational plans and proposed new government.

There were a few voices of opposition in Washington but they were treated with disdain and incredulity. When the senior Vietnam expert, Paul Kattenburg, told a National Security Council meeting that the time had come 'for us to make the decision to get out honorably', he was slapped down by Secretary of State Dean Rusk, who fumed, 'We will not pull out until the war is won'. It never was. Kattenburg was rewarded with a diplomatic posting to Guyana. When the president's brother and US attorney-general, Robert Kennedy, mused whether an eventual communist victory in Vietnam 'could be resisted with any government' and if not, whether it was 'time to get out of Vietnam completely', the idea was considered so weird that one person at the meeting recalled it as 'a hopelessly alien thought in a field of unexamined assumptions and entrenched convictions'.

In Saigon, Lodge pressed ahead with the regime-change operation, which took on a life of its own. The ambassador, the CIA and a group of Vietnamese generals made sure of it. On 1 November, rebel troops moved on the capital. Diem called Ambassador Lodge, who feigned ignorance, telling Diem, 'If I can do anything for your physical safety, please call me'. Diem and his brother Nhu fled. The next day, Diem called General Don, the leader of the rebels, to say that he was ready to surrender at the Catholic church at Cholon in Saigon. Don despatched a squad to the church with an American M-113 armoured troop carrier. The two brothers were waiting to surrender. Instead, they were bundled into the troop carrier and their hands were tied behind their backs. When the troop carrier arrived back at general staff headquarters, the doors were opened to reveal their bodies riddled with bullets, lying in a pool of blood.

Photographs of the dead bodies of Diem and Nhu were despatched by the CIA to Washington and reviewed at a White House staff meeting on 4 November. Kennedy was disconsolate. His national security advisor, McGeorge Bundy, observed drily, 'This is not the preferred way to commit suicide'. But it was not suicide, and he knew it. Kennedy even reconsidered the commitment of the United States. On the eve of his fateful trip to Dallas a few weeks later, he told one of McGeorge Bundy's aides that he wanted to 'start a complete and very profound review of how we got into [Vietnam], and what we thought we were doing, and what we think we can do. I even want to think about whether or not we should be there'.

Kennedy was assassinated a few weeks later and nothing changed in Vietnam; it only got worse. The government of Diem was succeeded by a series of repressive dictatorships supported by the United States. Kennedy's successor President Lyndon Johnson increased troop numbers dramatically and US bombing extended to Laos and Cambodia. But the war was never capable of being won. The British prime minister, Harold Wilson, counselled against the escalation of war but Johnson, like Eisenhower before him, told the British to 'mind their own business'. In retrospect, as Sir Max Hastings tells it, the Vietnam War was 'an epic tragedy' in which, notwithstanding North Vietnamese atrocities, 'America's war leadership often flaunted its inhumanity' and devastated the society it purported to save.

Chile 1973

In 1973 – the year when the United States signed the Paris Peace Accords and announced to the world that it was withdrawing from Vietnam – the White House and the CIA were secretly plotting the overthrow of the democratically elected government of Chile. It was the culmination of a covert campaign by the CIA that had been waged since the early 1960s. The campaign, which took on new urgency when Salvador Allende won the presidential election in 1970, had the fullest support of President Nixon and national security advisor Henry Kissinger. Nixon later told an incredulous David Frost in one of his eponymous 'Nixon Interviews' that a military coup was necessary because the Soviets had a 'red sandwich between Havana and Santiago which could engulf all of Latin America'. Kissinger was 'if anything, even more alarmist'.

When Allende came to power, Chile was a country 'with a broad democratic tradition' and was 'well on its way to modernity, with a high literacy rate, a relatively large middle class and a strong civil society'. After the coup, Chile was ruled for seventeen years by General Augusto Pinochet under an American-supported dictatorship that was infamous for its longevity and brutality – 'more than three thousand people were killed without any semblance of law or process' and 'more than forty thousand were arrested...and many of them were tortured'. Pinochet was eventually indicted by the government of Spain for human rights crimes and arrested in the United Kingdom but died before trial.

Allende was a reformer whose policy goals included a peaceful transition to a democratic socialist state through 'the principle of legality, the development of institutions, political freedom, the prevention of violence and the socialization of the means of production'. He was also an establishment figure, a scholar and a freemason who was genuinely moved by injustice and outraged by the avarice of dominant American corporations in his country. He was not an advocate of violence or revolution. Nor was he a communist. But Nixon and Kissinger were convinced that if Allende came to power, he would establish 'some sort of communist government'. They decided that an Allende regime was 'unacceptable' to the United States – a phrase that continues to be used, especially by enthusiastic US ambassadors to the United Nations. They did their utmost to prevent Allende forming government and succeeded in stopping him in the 1964 election but not at the next election in 1970. When they failed to prevent Allende, they were determined to remove him. The CIA operation to prevent Allende coming to power was known as 'Track 1'. The operation to remove him was known as 'Track 2'.

Allende's 1970 electoral win caused near panic in the White House. In mid-September, Nixon ordered CIA Director Richard Helms to come up with a plan within forty-eight hours. Helms's famous scribbled note of Nixon's instructions includes remarks such as:

- worth spending
- not concerned risks involved
- no involvement of embassy
- $10,000,000 available, more if necessary
- *make economy scream* [emphasis added]
- 48 hours for plan of action

There was opposition to Nixon's 'madman' approach. The CIA chief of station in Santiago, who had worked on the operation to prevent Allende succeeding at the polls, reported that, given the election result, he did 'not consider any kind of intervention in the constitutional processes desirable'. Another CIA officer rejected the notion of a communist threat and wrote that Allende was not likely to take orders from Moscow or Havana. He cautioned that plotting against Allende would be 'repeating the errors we made in 1959–60 when we drove Fidel Castro into the Soviet camp'. Kissinger's chief advisor on Latin America, Viron Vaky, went further, warning that 'What we propose is patently a violation of our own principles and policy tenets'. These counsels of discretion had no effect. Nixon would not be deterred. In his language, Allende was a 'son of a bitch' and 'We're going to smash him'. There was 'constant, constant pressure' from the White House.

The CIA invoked a well-tried formula. An internal instruction stated:

> Sensitize feeling within and without Chile that election
> of Allende is a nefarious development for Chile, Latin
> America and the world...Surface ineluctable conclusion
> that military coup is the only answer...employ every
> stratagem, every ploy, however bizarre, to create this
> internal resistance...If we are successful...the pretext will,
> in all probability, present itself.

Another cable said that CIA agents in Santiago should use 'propaganda, black operations, surfacing of intelligence or disinformation, personal contacts, or anything else your imagination can conjure'. The response from the Santiago station was candid: 'You have asked us to provoke chaos in Chile...which is unlikely to be bloodless'.

A leading American scholar on Chile later wrote of the period between the September election and Allende's accession to power in November, that it:

> ...does not do credit to American ideals, since it includes an effort to prevent a freely elected president from taking office by fomenting a military coup; the assassination of a Chilean general, for which the United States was indirectly responsible; authorization, though not execution, of efforts to bribe the Chilean Congress; subsidization of a quasi-fascist extreme rightist group; and improperly close relationships between the US government and a major corporation.

Two days after Allende's inauguration in early November, Nixon convened a meeting of the National Security Council to discuss ways of deposing him. The robust language of the meeting emphasised that the United States should 'bring him down'. Within days, the United States ambassador warned the Chilean minister for defence, Sergio Ossa, in language that was as uncompromising as it was bullying, that 'We shall do all within our power to condemn Chile and the Chilean people to utmost deprivation and poverty'.

For two years, the subversion campaign cruelly disrupted the Chilean economy, but it failed to result in the collapse of the government. In December 1972 Allende came to New York to address the United Nations General Assembly. His acclaimed speech received enthusiastic applause and shouts of 'Viva Allende!' He denounced 'the economic aggression of which he said his country was a victim' and complained that 'We find ourselves opposed by forces that operate in the shadows, without a flag, with powerful weapons, from positions of great influence...' The speech had no effect on Nixon, who decided to overhaul his Chile team. He replaced Helms as CIA director and named him as ambassador to Iran. Helms then blithely denied at his confirmation hearing that the CIA had tried to block the election of Allende and was duly convicted of perjury. According to his code of morals, it was a 'badge of honor'.

After Nixon was sworn in for a second term as president in January 1973, the campaign against Allende stepped up. At every step, the CIA was there. The CIA headquarters in Langley, Virginia, directed the 'creation of a renewed atmosphere of political unrest and controlled crisis...to stimulate serious consideration for intervention on the part of the [Chilean] military'. In April, the Santiago station was directed to begin 'accelerated efforts against the military target'. Three weeks later, it was told to 'bring our influence to bear on key military commanders so that they might play a decisive role on the side of the coup forces'. When the army commander, General Prats, proved to be an obstacle to a coup – because he believed that the constitutional role of the military was to support the elected government – CIA agents in the Santiago station reported that 'Only way to remove Prats would appear to be by abduction or assassination'. Fortuitously, Prats resigned, to be replaced by Pinochet, who was a friend of the CIA.

It was the final act. In August 1973, the CIA approved another $1 million for the destabilisation campaign. Its agents in Santiago were fully informed, fully supportive and fully implicated. On 9 September, one agent cabled that 'A coup attempt will be initiated on September 11' along with other precise details of the operation. All went according to plan. It was the end of the road. A proclamation announcing the coup went to air; Allende refused to resign; the presidential palace was assaulted and bombed; and Allende died, allegedly by shooting himself at the palace. His tragic last words to the public included, 'I am sure that my sacrifice will not be in vain. I am sure it will be at least a moral lesson, and a rebuke to crime, cowardice and treason.'

Iraq 2003

The coups in Iran, Guatemala, Vietnam and Chile had a Cold War context but the reality was that in each of those cases the connection with Soviet Russia was tenuous or non-existent. Each of the American interventions was a repudiation of the principles and precepts that were central to the 'rules-based order' to which the United States professed allegiance. The deposed leaders Mossadegh, Arbenz, Diem and Allende were not communists; none of them acted at the direction of Moscow; all, except perhaps Diem, were genuinely committed to the legitimate social reform of their country. And inevitably, the violence of the military juntas and dictators that replaced them was 'much more deadly than that of the Left-wing groups who had challenged the existing order'. In pursuit of its objectives, the United States created and prolonged political instability, generated social unrest and caused the deaths of large numbers of innocent citizens.

The most significant of the post–Cold War interventions was the US-led invasion of Iraq in 2003. It heralded the twenty-first century – and marked the decline of the American Century. The military historian David Kilcullen suggested that the 'beginning of the end for the post-Cold War world' can be dated to that first US air strike – which failed – on the outskirts of Baghdad on 20 March 2003. The invasion of Iraq was never legally justified but nothing would stop it. The suggestion of compliance by the United States with the Charter of the United Nations was a pretence. According to a former Treasury secretary to George W Bush, the invasion was on the agenda from the first days of the administration – as early as January 2001. After the September 11 attack – an event with which Iraq and Saddam Hussein were not connected – senior figures in the administration were actively seeking to justify a regime change operation in Iraq. General Wesley Clark was told that the United States was 'going to war' with Iraq 'about ten days after 9/11'.

Secretary of Defense Donald Rumsfeld's disturbing note of 27 November 2001 contains the following entries:

- (building momentum for regime change)
- regime change
- How start?
  - Saddam moves against Kurds in north?
  - US discovers Saddam connection to September 11 attack or to anthrax attack?
  - Dispute over WMD inspections?
    - start now thinking about inspection demands
- Decapitation of government

Rumsfeld's focus on 'regime change' and 'decapitation of government' ignored the central tenet of the rules-based order – namely, that regime change could not, by itself, be a lawful objective of war by a state acting alone without the authorisation of the United Nations Security Council. Nor could it be a legitimate basis, on its own, for invading a sovereign country. It did not matter that a particular regime might be 'unacceptable to the United States'. And it was irrelevant that Saddam Hussein may have been a cruel and authoritarian leader. The Secretary-General of the United Nations, Kofi Annan, declared without qualification that the US-led invasion of Iraq was illegal: 'I have indicated that it was not in conformity with the UN Charter. From our point of view and the UN Charter point of view, it was illegal'. Richard Perle, senior advisor to Rumsfeld, later conceded as much, saying 'International law...would have required us to leave Saddam Hussein'.

Most countries also agreed. France, Germany, Russia, Belgium, Switzerland, Sweden, Norway, Greece, Austria, Finland and Lichtenstein opposed or condemned the war. All fifty-two member states of the African Union condemned the war. The leading countries of Central and South America condemned the war. The Arab League unanimously condemned the war. Pope John Paul II opposed the war and his representative warned that, without UN authorisation, the war would be a 'crime against peace and a crime against international law'. China issued a joint statement with France and Russia emphasising the requirement for a further United Nations Security Council resolution to justify war. India criticised the lack of United Nations approval. And Canada and New Zealand would not support the war.

Only four countries supplied combat forces directly participating in the war, in addition to the United States. They were the United Kingdom, Australia, Denmark and Poland. There have been recriminations in three of those countries. And Poland's participation appears to have been secured by an

American commitment to pay its costs. In the United Kingdom, the independent commission of enquiry headed by Sir John Chilcot produced a report that was highly critical of the British decision to invade Iraq at the request of the United States. It found that there was no formal record of the decision, that the precise grounds relied upon were unclear and that the decision to go to war without a resolution of the United Nations Security Council undermined the council's authority. In Australia there was no enquiry but Lieutenant General Peter Leahy, the Chief of Army at the time of the Iraq invasion, queried Australia's relationship with the United States when deciding to go to war:

> Let's have a discussion, not an enquiry, around our
> relationship with the United States, how we decide to go
> to war and very importantly how we decide every day
> when we are at war, to stay at war.

In Denmark, a judicial commission examining the basis for the war conducted hearings for two years before being controversially shut down – shortly before a former prime minister (Fogh Rasmussen) and a former foreign minister were due to give evidence. In the Netherlands, which did not supply combat forces, a judicial enquiry headed by former Dutch Supreme Court president Willibrord Davids concluded that the US-led invasion violated international law and that the notion of 'regime change' advanced by the invading powers had 'no basis in international law'.

The chorus of disapproval from the public and from lawyers and legal bodies was loud and long. The International Commission of Jurists, the US-based National Lawyers Guild, a group of thirty-one Canadian law professors and countless bar associations contended that the war was illegal. So did the most pre-eminent English lawyers. The acclaimed Lord Alexander of Weedon QC said the argument relied on by the United States was 'risible'; Professor Lowe said it was 'fatuous'; Professor Sands QC said it was 'a bad argument'; and Lord Bingham, the 'most eminent' of English judges, concluded that the invasion of Iraq by the United States, the United Kingdom, Australia and others was 'unauthorised by the Security Council' and constituted 'a serious violation of international law and the rule of law'.

Washington's implausible contention was that the invasion was already authorised by a prior resolution (No 1441) of the United Nations Security Council that required Iraq to provide 'immediate, unimpeded, unconditional and unrestricted access' to its facilities by Hans Blix's UN inspection team. When Blix reported ten days before the war commenced that Iraq was making 'significant progress' toward compliance but that its cooperation was still not 'immediate and unconditional', this was enough for Washington. Blix added that it would take 'but months' to resolve the key remaining disarmament tasks. But the war had been long-planned and the United States was not for waiting. It contended that Iraq was in material breach of the resolution and that the United States was itself entitled to enforce the resolution immediately 'to defend itself against the threat posed by Iraq...and protect world peace and security'.

There were two problems, as Lord Bingham explained. First, 'Hans Blix and his team of weapons inspectors had found no weapons of mass destruction, were making progress and expected to complete their task in a matter of months'. There was therefore no threat and no material breach. Second, it could not have been reasonably intended that a decision as to a breach by Iraq and enforcement against it could be made 'otherwise than collectively by the Security Council'. It was not up to the United States, or any other country, to take unilateral action.

The threadbare nature of the American argument is all the more evident when it is noted that the US Ambassador to the United Nations, John Negroponte, had assured the Security Council when Resolution 1441 was passed that, in the event of a further breach by Iraq, the resolution would require that 'the matter will return to the Council for discussions as required in paragraph 12'. The remarks of UK Permanent Representative Sir Jeremy Greenstock were even stronger. He emphasised that 'There is no automaticity in this resolution. If there is a further Iraqi breach of its disarmament obligations, the matter will return to the Council for discussion as required by [para 12]'. These inconvenient truths were ignored.

Like the legal reasons, the military reasons against the invasion were also compelling. There was no equivalence whatsoever between Al Qaeda and Iraq. Saddam Hussein was a secular nationalist who repressed fundamentalists, including supporters of Al Qaeda. Bush's chief counter-terrorism specialist, Richard Clarke, said that 'Having been attacked by Al Qaeda, for us to go bombing Iraq in response would be like our invading Mexico after the Japanese attacked Pearl Harbor'. Colin Powell, in an earlier moment of clarity, thought the Iraq project was 'lunacy'. Brent Scowcroft, who had been national security advisor to Bush senior, wrote in *The Wall Street Journal* that 'There is scant evidence to tie Saddam to terrorist organizations, and even less to the September 11 attacks... Worse, there is a virtual consensus in the world against an attack on Iraq at this time'. The British head of MI6 famously revealed after visiting Washington that 'the intelligence and

95

facts were being fixed around the policy'. And the senior State Department official Richard Haass observed, 'I just cannot explain the strategic obsession with Iraq, why it rose to the top of people's priority list'.

Hans Blix, the Swedish diplomat whose illustrious public record includes having been director general of the International Atomic Energy Agency for sixteen years before he accepted the United Nations monitoring role in Iraq, stated the obvious when he told the *Financial Times*: 'The US went in [to Iraq] to create democracy but they found no weapons of mass destruction and created anarchy'. For the United States, the result of the invasion was to make America less secure. Robert Hutchings, former chairman of the National Intelligence Council, commenting on the 2006 National Intelligence Estimate, said it was the consensus view of the directors of America's then sixteen intelligence services that the war in Iraq has made America less safe 'and frankly, it does not surprise me'. The report stated:

> We assess that the Iraq jihad is shaping a new generation of terrorist leaders and operatives…The Iraq conflict has become the 'cause celebre' for jihadists, breeding a deep resentment of US involvement in the Muslim world and cultivating supporters for the global jihadist movement.

CHAPTER 4

CRITICISM
Warnings from Within

Voices of Dissent

America's post-war exceptionalism and interventionism have troubled many critics, including distinguished members of the military and political establishment. But these voices of dissent have echoed only faintly in Washington and almost not at all among the flag-waving American public. Senator William Fulbright is one of those critics who is remembered but not heeded. So is George Kennan, the intellectual architect of the Cold War policy of containment. One category of critics – the old soldiers, the thoughtful philosopher-warriors who have endured the heat of battle and emerged to challenge the American military mindset – deserves special attention. Generals Eisenhower and Shoup railed, with varying degrees of condemnation, against the forces that they saw at play at the frontline of the defence, industrial and political establishment in the United States. In more recent times, Colonel Andrew Bacevich, Vietnam veteran and West Point graduate, has been an articulate spokesman for their views.

Eisenhower, Shoup and Bacevich were preceded by General Smedley Butler, who made his views known in his book titled *War Is a Racket* (1935). It was a trenchant condemnation of the profit motive behind war. Butler said that he spent most of his thirty-three years of active military service 'as a high class muscle man for Big Business, for Wall Street and the bankers'. Butler's thesis was remarkably similar to prevailing views about the relationship between fascism and big business – 'an informal and changing coalition of groups with vested psychological, moral and material interests in the continuous development and maintenance of high levels of weaponry...and in military-strategic conceptions of internal affairs', a concept articulated by Daniel Guérin in his 1936 book *Fascism and Big Business*.

Eisenhower

The same vested 'psychological, moral and material interests' of the defence industry and the military establishment troubled former army general President Eisenhower – even though, it must be said, the escalation of the arms race and the multiplication of nuclear warheads dramatically increased during his presidency. Three months after his inauguration in January 1953, Eisenhower told the American Society of Newspaper Editors:

> Every gun that is made, every warship launched, every
> rocket fired, signifies in the final sense, a theft from those
> who hunger and are not fed, those who are cold and are

not clothed. This world in arms is not spending money alone. It is spending the sweat of its laborers, the genius of its scientists, the hopes of its children.

By the end of his two terms in office, Eisenhower worried even more about American militarism. It was, as he saw it, driven by a powerful interlocking web of commercial and defence interests, promoted by an ever-expanding arms industry and propelled by the lure of profit. For his Farewell Address the departing president wanted to leave to the American people and the world something of substance, not a mere litany of achievements. The speech was under consideration for months. In the early stages, one of his speechwriters referred in a memo to the danger of a 'permanent war-based economy':

> ...for the first time in history, the United States has a permanent war-based economy...Not only that, but flag and general officers retiring at an early age take positions in [a] war-based industrial complex shaping its decisions and guiding the direction of its tremendous thrust. This creates a danger that what the Communists have always said about us is true. We must be careful to ensure that the 'merchants of death' do not come to dictate policy.

Eisenhower liked the theme, developed it and coined the expression 'military-industrial complex'. This state of affairs, he said, in the final version of the speech in January 1961, created the 'potential for the disastrous rise of misplaced power' whose grave implications 'we must not fail to comprehend'. The speech went on:

Our military organization today bears little resemblance to that known by any of my predecessors in peace time...Until the latest of our world conflicts, the United States had no armaments industry...But now...we have been compelled to create a permanent armaments industry of vast proportions...We annually spend on military security more than the net income of all United States corporations. The conjunction of an immense military establishment and a large arms industry is new in the American experience. The total influence – economic, political, even spiritual – is felt in every city, every state house, every office of the Federal government.

Eisenhower's Farewell Address should have been powerful and memorable but the response from the American public and the media, let alone from Washington and the Pentagon, was at best tepid. They did not seem to appreciate the dangers, and did not want to know, then or now.

Shoup

Almost a decade later, at the height of the Vietnam War, the illustrious General David Monroe Shoup thought that Eisenhower's self-described 'potential for the disastrous rise of misplaced power' had become a reality. His verdict was that the United States had become a 'militaristic and aggressive nation'. Shoup, a recipient of the Medal of Honor, was Eisenhower's choice for Commandant of the Marine Corps and became Kennedy's favourite general. In an article published in *The Atlantic* in 1969 after he retired, he described a phenomenon that he labelled as the 'New American Militarism' and posed the question:

> We have an immense and expensive military
> establishment, fuelled by a gigantic defense industry,
> and millions of proud, patriotic, and frequently bellicose
> and militaristic citizens. How did this militarist culture
> evolve?

This American 'militarist culture', he said, had been 'born of the necessities of World War II, nurtured by the Korean War, and became an accepted aspect of American life during the years of cold war emergencies and real or imagined threats from the Communist bloc'. A consequence of it was America's 'belief in military solutions to world problems' and its readiness 'to seek military solutions to problems of political disorder'. And, like Eisenhower and Butler, he warned that the 'relationship between the defense industry and the military establishment is closer than many citizens realize', singling out among others 'the multibillion dollar aerospace industry, which thrives upon the boundless desires of the Air Force'. Shoup pointed the blame at the 'influential nucleus of aggressive, ambitious professional military leaders who are the root of America's evolving militarism' and 'the rich and powerful defense industries' that were 'standing closely behind' them.

Shoup was just as unstinting in his criticism of America's war in Vietnam. He lamented its pointlessness and prophesied its shameful end. He said that the Johnson administration had sold the war on a false pretence – on the basis that 'we must stop some kind of unwanted ideology from creeping up on this nation'. He ridiculed the idea that events in Vietnam '8,000 miles away with water in between' posed a national security threat to the United States. And he described as ludicrous the fear 'that just because we lose in South Vietnam that very soon somebody is going to be crawling and knocking at the doors of Pearl Harbor'. The people of Vietnam deserved, he said, the chance to determine their own fate – 'if we leave them alone to solve their own problems in the manner that they want to solve them, they would be proud of their solution'. He added, referring to Third World nations in general, that if the United States:

> ...would keep our dirty, bloody, dollar-crooked fingers
> out of the business of these nations...they will arrive at
> a solution of their own...at least what they will get will
> be their own, and not the American style, which they do
> not want and above all, do not want crammed down their
> throats by Americans.

On the reality of the threat of communism, Shoup was again refreshingly pragmatic. And he blamed President Truman's confrontational Cold War policy for inflaming the Soviet threat. After 1945, he pointed out, Russia had no nuclear weapons but 'We encircled her with nuclear bombs and missiles...From here it was easy to get these people to forego butter for guns. To sacrifice and toil cheerfully so they could have some weapons to protect their homeland from the threat of [American] destruction'. Others have referred to this 'encirclement' and the Russian national paranoia bred from centuries of foreign aggression:

> The present actuality of nuclear bases around [Russia's]
> borders feeds back into, and reinforces, the historical

memory of the Tatars, of Napoleon, of World War I,
of the [American] intervention against the [Russian]
revolution itself, and of Japan and Germany from the
1930s on through World War II.

Shoup was right about the Soviet threat, as time and Soviet archives have demonstrated. In his view, it was mostly hype and propaganda. He told a student audience: 'Do not let yourself get too shook-up by the over-advertised encroachment of communism'. Writer Stephen Glain explained it:

In the 1950s, Americans were told the Soviets had not
only the means to destroy the United States but the
desire to do so. In reality, Moscow lacked the former
and so gave little thought to the latter, while Washington
squandered billions of dollars on needless weaponry.

Shoup regarded the solution to communism as straightforward. He put it in simple language: 'Help people get things and the idea of communism will strangle by its own umbilical cord'. And his response to the proponents of the domino theory, to which Washington fixedly adhered, was caustic: 'They just keep trying to keep the people worried about the communists crawling up the banks of Pearl Harbor, crawling up the Palisades, or crawling up the beaches of Los Angeles, which of course is a bunch of pure unadulterated poppycock'.

While others sought to 'educate and influence', Shoup set out to 'chastise and denounce'. Even when Shoup predicted the final, ignominious end to America's war in Vietnam in testimony before Fulbright's Senate Foreign Relations Committee in 1968, he was not taken seriously. He told Senator Albert Gore:

'Some place up the line' the United States is going to say, 'it is too much for us' and that we cannot help. He was right. Not long afterwards, the war did become 'too much' and President Nixon sought 'peace with honour', but not before he authorised the worst of the bombing campaign of North Vietnam from B-52 formations flying out of Guam. The last of the American troops did not withdraw until 1973.

Bacevich

The third of the old soldiers is the only one still living. Retired United States Army colonel Andrew Bacevich is an emeritus professor at Boston University. He served in Vietnam, and his son, also an army officer, served and died in Iraq. The theme of Bacevich's writings is that Americans have become seduced by the culture of war and the pursuit of military dominance, and that this illusion has reached dangerous levels. Bacevich counsels restraint but there is no sign that Washington is listening. Like the warnings of other luminaries, Bacevich has been ignored.

The heart of the problem for Bacevich is the American expectation, based on outsized military pretensions, 'that through the determined exercise of its unquestioned military dominance, the United States can perpetuate American global primacy and impress its values on the world at large'. If it persists in this expectation, he warns, America:

> will surely share the fate of all those who in ages past
> have looked to war and military power to fulfil their
> destiny. We will rob future generations of their rightful
> inheritance. We will wreak havoc abroad. We will

CRITICISM

endanger security at home. We will risk the forfeiture of all that we prize.

Bacevich rues the steady progression of extreme conservative views belonging to a new generation of exceptionalists in the defence, national security and foreign policy establishment. Ideas that once might have seemed 'reckless or preposterous [have now come] to seem perfectly reasonable'. Neoconservatives have transformed themselves into establishment figures and their views have 'entered the mainstream of public discourse and became less controversial'. For these true believers, he suggests, America is, and always has been, 'the one true universal church', the Reagan era 'a golden moment' and military power an instrument for transforming the international system and cementing American primacy. For them, the outcome of the Cold War was a vindication of the values of the United States and an opportunity 'to achieve the final triumph of American ideals'.

Underlying this stance, says Bacevich, are a series of convictions, including the 'certainty that American global dominion is benign' and that others welcome it; the presumption that if the United States does not maintain its imperium, the inevitable result will be 'global disorder, bloody, bitter and protracted'; and the insistence that 'nothing could be allowed to inhibit the United States in the use of that power'. The doctrines of preventative war and permanent military supremacy, now officially enshrined in the national security and defence strategies of the United States, give effect to these convictions. But in truth, they are misconceptions, characterised by an 'hostility toward realism'.

For those with such an outlook, says Bacevich, Roosevelt's vision for a post-war world was a chimera and 'collective

105

security is a mirage'; any proposal for organising the world around anything other than American power is 'woolly-headed and fatuous'; the United Nations 'is a guarantor of nothing [and] except in a formal sense, it can hardly be said to exist'; a decline in American power necessarily means 'a rise in world chaos and a dangerous twenty-first century'; and the only 'alternative to [American] unipolarity is chaos'.

The natural corollary to views such as these is the belief that the United States needs 'more military power than ever before'; that its military supremacy must be sustained and enhanced; and that its military power must be not merely dominant, but it should 'overmatch'. This is where we are today. Thus, it is 'incumbent on the Pentagon to maintain the capability to intervene decisively in every critical region of the world', whether or not a proximate threat exists. This means, as one proponent put it, that 'America must be able to fight Iraq and North Korea...and contemplate war with China or Russia...' And that the United States military should be a force 'that can win any conflict, anywhere'.

Bacevich regards such views as not merely dangerous but delusional. The truth, 'however unwelcome', he points out, 'is that since 1945 US forces have not achieved a conclusive success in any contest on a scale larger than policing actions...' Nor, says Bacevich, is there evidence to suggest that America's interventions in other states have advanced the cause of global peace, while there is much evidence to suggest that its pursuit of dominance is a self-defeating project. Bacevich urges a policy of restraint, adding that 'The proper aim of American statecraft, therefore, is not to redeem humankind or to prescribe some specific world order, nor to police the planet by force of arms'. He adds that America should lead by example not by military force. Its mission should be to 'model freedom rather than impose it'. By 'demonstrating the feasibility of creating a way of life based on humane, liberal values, the United States might help illuminate the path ahead for others who seek freedom'. It should, he says, tackle at home Martin Luther King's 'giant triplets of racism, extreme materialism and militarism'.

The views of the military men, Eisenhower, Shoup and Bacevich, are echoed in those of the former political insiders Senator William Fulbright and George Kennan.

Fulbright

Senator William Fulbright was the longest-serving chairman in the history of the United States Senate Foreign Relations Committee. In his political role he had more insight into the nature of American leadership in the world than almost anyone else. His classic book *The Arrogance of Power* (1966) is an expression of genuine concern for the American future. Fifty years before President Trump, Fulbright warned of the trend toward 'a more strident and aggressive American policy'; despaired of modern 'super patriots'; and counselled restraint, moderation and the wise use of power. He adopted the phrase 'arrogance of power' to describe the tendency to equate power with virtue and responsibility with a universal mission. In his view, the American people were beset by the assumption that 'force is the ultimate proof of superiority' and that 'when a nation shows that it has the stronger army, it is also proving that it has better people, better institutions, better principles and, in general, a better civilization'. For Fulbright, the perceived need to prove that the United States is 'bigger, better, or stronger than other nations' was a national affliction.

Fulbright was wary of the influence of ideology and faith on foreign policy and had no time for the 'crusades of high-minded men', whom he described as these 'self-appointed emissaries of God who have wrought so much violence in the world', setting out 'upon self-appointed missions to police the world, to defeat all tyrannies'. Such enthusiasts, like former secretary of state John Foster Dulles:

> ...are men with doctrines...who believe in some cause
> without doubt and practice their beliefs without scruple,
> men who cease to be human beings...and become
> instead living, breathing, embodiments of some faith or
> ideology.

Fulbright made fun of the American instinct for universal mission, recounting the story of the three boy scouts who reported to their scoutmaster that their good deed for the day was helping an old lady to cross the street. When the scoutmaster commented, 'That is fine but why did it take three of you?' The boys replied, 'She did not want to go'. In Fulbright's view, the analogy was apt. For 'the good deed above all others that Americans feel qualified to perform is the teaching of democracy'. His verdict is salutary:

> Maybe we are not really cut out for the job of spreading
> the gospel of democracy...And maybe – just maybe – if
> we left our neighbours to make their own judgments
> and their own mistakes, and confined our assistance
> to matters of economics and technology instead of
> philosophy, maybe then they would begin to find the
> democracy and dignity that have largely eluded them...

As far as Fulbright was concerned, the idea of an 'American empire' was romantic nonsense, which called to mind 'the slogans of the past' about 'manifest destiny' and 'making the world safe for democracy' and the 'demand for unconditional surrender in World War II'. As he put it, 'the idea of being responsible for the whole world seems to be flattering to Americans [but] I am afraid it is turning our heads'. And he invoked the wisdom of George Bernard Shaw: 'All this struggling and striving to make the world better is a great mistake, not because it is not a good thing to improve the world if you know how to do it, but because striving and struggling is the worst way you could set about doing anything'.

Fulbright's answer to those Americans who subscribed to the theory of exceptionalism was blunt and obvious:

...we are not God's chosen saviour of mankind but only one of mankind's more successful and fortunate branches, endowed by our creator with about the same capacity for good and evil, no more or less, than the rest of humanity.

And his assessment of communism exhibited the same robust common sense and humanity. What was obvious to Fulbright then – and what is obvious to most thinking people today – ran counter to the contemporary wisdom of the defence and foreign policy establishment in Washington, let alone the crusaders at the CIA. Fulbright correctly saw Stalinism as 'a passing phase of Soviet communism'. Communism was 'not monolithic', he said, and showed itself to be 'more open-ended than we had supposed, capable of varying degrees of humanization if not democratization'. It was undoubtedly a 'harsh system of organising society' but its 'doctrine has redeeming tenets of humanitarianism...[and] some countries are probably better off under communist rule than they were under preceding regimes... some people may even want to live under communism'. Most importantly, he reiterated: 'it is neither the duty nor the right of the United States to sort out all these problems for the... societies of Asia, Africa and Latin America'.

Adherence by the United States to international law was yet another issue of enduring importance to Fulbright. It was, he made clear, a question of national self-interest. His principled belief was in marked contrast to that of past and present administrations, for whom compliance with international law has often been treated as optional. The particular event that stimulated Fulbright's concern at the time was the 1965 intervention by the United States in the Dominican Republic on the grounds of 'a communist danger'. The intervention was in violation of America's treaty obligations to respect the sovereignty and territory of other states. Fulbright remarked:

> These clauses are not ambiguous. They mean that,
> with one exception, all forms of forcible intervention
> are absolutely prohibited...we are committed to it,
> not partially or temporarily or insofar as we find it
> compatible with our vital interests but almost absolutely.
> It represents our word and our bond...

Like others before and since, Fulbright completely failed to see why it was not 'a matter of vital interest [to the United States] to honour a clear and explicit treaty obligation'. Ignoring basic obligations in international law was a failure of leadership that did far more damage than good. Fulbright's reasoning was compelling and his logic self-evident:

When we violate the law ourselves, whatever short-term advantage may be gained, we are obviously encouraging others to violate the law; we thus encourage disorder and instability and thereby do incalculable damage to our own long-term interests.

Decades before the Iraq invasion, and Washington's invocation of the doctrine of preventative war, he explained in language that has since been pointedly ignored in Washington, that:

a pre-emptive war in defense of freedom would surely destroy freedom, because one simply cannot engage in barbarous action without becoming a barbarian, because one cannot defend human values by calculated and unprovoked violence without doing mortal damage to the values one is trying to defend.

Ultimately, Fulbright urged the United States to choose between 'the humanism of Lincoln or the arrogance of those who would make America the world's policeman'. He observed that 'Only at an advanced level of civilization, it seems, do men acquire the wisdom and humility to acknowledge that they are not really cut out to play God'. Fulbright left open his verdict on whether the United States had reached this 'advanced level of civilization' but his adverse opinion of the grandiose claims by American statesmen about 'putting the world right' was clear. He favoured a more modest approach 'that accepts the world as it is, with all its existing nations and ideologies, with all its existing qualities and shortcomings'. In his view, the most one should hope to achieve is not democracy or freedom, not liberation or regime change – but 'to make life a little more civilized, a little more satisfying, and a little more serene'.

Kennan

The final distinguished critic is George Kennan, the architect of the policy of containment and a former United States ambassador to the Soviet Union. Like Fulbright, his concerns have gone unheeded. Writing during the Reagan era, two decades after publication of Fulbright's *Arrogance of Power*, Kennan reproached past American statesmen who had been 'unduly legalistic and moralistic' in their judgment of the actions of other governments. He said they might impress a domestic audience but the result was 'to lose effectiveness in the international arena'. And he emphasised that the primary obligation of government is to the interests of the national society not to 'the moral impulses that individual elements of that society may experience'. He insisted that the interests of society that government is charged with protecting have 'no moral quality'. They consist only of the nation's 'military security, the integrity of its political life and the well-being of its people'.

Kennan emphasised the practical difficulties of a judgmental and moralistic foreign policy, stressing that when others fail to conform to America's own principles of justice and propriety, 'what we cannot do is to assume that our moral standards are theirs as well, and to appeal to those standards as the source of our grievances'. He reserved particular criticism for American interventions in foreign countries in the name of 'democracy'. Such interventions were, he said, often based on behaviour that is 'not seriously injurious to our interests' but merely offensive to our 'sensibilities'. Frequently, they are undertaken by 'men with doctrines' intent on demonstrating 'not only...the moral deficiencies of others but...the positive morality of ourselves'. Such men are motivated, Kennan explained, by a supposed 'moral duty to detect these lapses on the part of others, to denounce them before the world and to assure...that they were corrected'.

And too often the denunciation – liberally sprinkled with pejorative, often facile, epithets like 'rogue', 'despot' or 'communist' – merely reflected 'pressures generated by politically influential minority elements that have some special interest'. The result is an evident lack of consistency:

> Practices or policies that arouse our official displeasure
> in one country are cheerfully condoned or ignored in
> another. What is bad in the behaviour of our opponents
> is good, or at least acceptable, in the case of our friends.
> What is unobjectionable to us at one period of history is
> seen as offensive in another.

As for the benefits of 'spreading democracy', Kennan regarded as wrong-headed the longstanding argument from Washington that the 'encouragement and promotion of democracy elsewhere is always in the interests of the security, political integrity and prosperity of the United States'. It is debatable, he thought. Indeed:

> ...it is not invariably the case. Democracy is a loose
> term. Many varieties of folly and injustice contrive to
> masquerade under this designation. There are forms
> of plebiscitary 'democracy' that may well prove less

favourable to American interests than a wise and
benevolent authoritarianism.

Notably, Kennan asserted that 'Democracy, as Americans understand it, is not necessarily the future of all mankind, nor is it the duty of the US government to assure that it becomes that'. And in a rebuff to those who assert a missionary responsibility to spread the benefits of American-style democracy and freedoms, Kennan added that 'not everyone in this world is responsible, after all, for the actions of everyone else, everywhere'.

And then there is the considerable problem of the consequences of intervention. As Kennan pointed out, while the United States is often 'quick to allege that this or that practice in a foreign country is bad and deserves correction', the reality is that the alternative 'might be worse'. Washington, he thought, 'seldom if ever' seems to concern itself 'seriously or realistically with the conceivable alternatives', even though history, including recent events in Iraq, provides no shortage of examples of this phenomenon. The practical result, said Kennan, is that the United States effectively demands 'a species of veto power' over the practices of foreign states of which it disapproves, 'while denying responsibility for whatever may flow from the [forced] acceptance of our demands'.

Kennan – like Fulbright before him – suggested that America's moral commitment would be best demonstrated by the exercise of restraint, the practice of example and the recognition that the 'avoidance of the worst should often be a more practical undertaking than the achievement of the best'. He added that 'some of the strongest imperatives of moral conduct should be ones of a negative rather than a positive nature', citing the strictures of the Ten Commandments as the best illustration of this proposition. And he emphasised the importance of understanding that 'in world affairs, as in personal life, example exerts a greater power than precept'.

Kennan concluded by addressing three aspects of contemporary American society that, in his view, raised profound moral questions. On these matters, he was remarkably prescient but his warnings have had no effect. In each case, in the thirty-five years since he wrote, the circumstances have worsened considerably or the relevant behaviour has increased exponentially. The first matter was the burgeoning of the covert paramilitary operations of the United States government; the second was the 'national addiction' to the annual spending of hundreds of billions of dollars on defence; and the third was 'the devastating effect of modern industrialization and overpopulation on the world's natural environment'.

Kennan's verdict on covert paramilitary operations was firm. He regretted, in the light of the experience of the intervening years, the decision taken in the aftermath of World War II – in which he was complicit – to set up a facility for such clandestine operations on behalf of the government. He warned that this branch of governmental activity – 'not to be confused with secret intelligence' – should not be allowed to become, as it has done, 'a regular and routine feature of the governmental process, cast in the concrete of unquestioned habit and institutionalized bureaucracy'. As he said:

Operations of this nature are not in character for this country. They do not accord with its traditions or with its established procedures of government. The effort to conduct them involves dilemmas and situations of moral ambiguity in which the American statesman is deprived

of principled guidance and loses a sense of what is
fitting and what is not. Excessive secrecy, duplicity and
clandestine skulduggery are simply not our dish...such
operations conflict with our own traditional standards
and compromise our diplomacy in other areas.

On the national addiction to defence spending, Kennan saw then
what has become a profound dilemma today. It was caused, he
thought, by America's 'exorbitant dreams of world influence, if
not world hegemony – the feeling that we must have the solution
to everyone's problems and a finger in every pie – that continue
to figure in the assumptions underlying so many American
reactions in matters of foreign policy'. More than three decades
before the ever-worsening statistics of the twenty-first century,
Kennan pointed to 'a budgetary deficit and an adverse trade
balance both so fantastically high that [the nation] is rapidly
changing from a major creditor to a major debtor'; an 'enormous
internal indebtedness [that] has been permitted to double in less
than six years'; and military expenditures that have been allowed
to grow 'so badly out of relationship to the other needs of its
economy and so extensively out of reach of political control'.

The result, Kennan concluded, was that the United States 'is
so obviously living beyond its means, and confesses itself unable
to live otherwise' that it 'is simply not in a position to make
the most effective use of its own resources on the international
scene'. In his view, the issue raised moral considerations. It
was an aspect of 'the duty of bringing one's commitments and
undertakings into a reasonable relationship with one's real
possibilities for acting upon the international environment'.

Kennan's final point was about the destruction of the natural
environment and the threat of nuclear war. Of both threats, he

said, with a confidence that might not be justified today: 'there are few thoughtful people – except perhaps in some sectors of American government and opinion – who would not agree that our world is at present faced with two unprecedented and supreme dangers':

> The one threatens the destruction of civilization through
> the recklessness and selfishness of its military rivalries,
> the other through the massive abuse of its natural habitat.
> Both are relatively new problems, for the solution of
> which past experience affords little guidance. Both are
> urgent.

Kennan emphasised that 'the environmental and nuclear crises will brook no delay' and that the 'need for giving priority to these two overriding dangers has a purely rational basis – a basis in the national interest – quite aside from morality'. This was because the worst that could happen as a result of other calamities 'would be a far smaller tragedy than that which would assuredly confront us (and if not us, then our children) if we failed to face up to these two apocalyptic dangers in good time'.

And, he added, there was a moral element to the problem of environmental destruction:

> Is there not, whatever the nature of one's particular God,
> an element of sacrilege involved in the placing of all this
> at stake for the sake of the comforts, the fears and the
> national rivalries of a single generation? Is there not a
> moral obligation to recognize in this very uniqueness of
> the habitat and nature of man the greatest of our moral

responsibilities, and to make of ourselves, in our national
personification, its guardians and protectors rather than
its destroyers?

Kennan concluded by urging a foreign policy founded on
restraint, and a conception of the American national interest
that was reasonably, not extravagantly, conceived. Instead, it
should be one that 'would seek the possibilities of service to
morality primarily in our own behaviour, not in our judgment
of others'; it would restrict our undertakings 'to the limits
established by our own traditions and resources'; and it 'would
see virtue in our minding our own business...' Kennan lived
contentedly in Princeton until his death in 2005 at the age of
101 but his voice has been lost in Washington.

PART 3
CONSEQUENCES

CHAPTER 5

MILITARISM
Dominance & Overmatch

War Culture

Despite the warnings, despite the criticism, the United States has continued on the same path for more than seventy years. The consequence is that it can now be said confidently that 'To a degree without precedent in US history, Americans have come to define the nation's strength and well-being in terms of military preparedness, military action, and the fostering of military ideals'. This belief and attitude have become 'deeply entrenched'. Military strength and power have come to be seen as 'the truest measure of national greatness' and as indispensable, mandatory requirements for a successful society.

Militarism is, so it is argued, an 'ideology and a set of practices that have invaded America in every sector of its economic, political and cultural life'. It has been referred to as a cultural disease – like insatiable consumerism or excessive gun violence. Some have referred to America's expanded military projection since the end of the Cold War, and its ballooning military expenditure since 2001, as 'hyper-militarisation' – with a faint nod to 1930s Germany. Andrew Bacevich wrote that since the end of the Cold War, 'the tempo of US military intervention has become nothing short of frenetic'. And Stephen Glain noted that 'Since the collapse of the Soviet Union, US presidents have ordered troops into battle twenty-two times, compared with fourteen times during the Cold War'.

But as President Eisenhower lamented, the burden of arms results in a 'wasting of strength'. Eisenhower had been an outstanding army general at the centre of the American war machine during World War II. As president, he presided over a nuclear arms race, but paradoxically, his underlying ethical belief was that spending on arms and armies is inherently undesirable; that it constitutes a misappropriation of resources; and that 'by diverting social capital from productive to destructive purposes, war and the preparation for war, deplete rather than enhance a nation's strength'. This is what he was adverting to when he said at the beginning of his first term that 'every warship launched, every rocket fired, signifies, in the final sense, a theft from those who hunger and are not fed, those who are cold and are not clothed'.

Eisenhower reflected again in his post-presidential memoir, *Waging Peace* (1965). He confessed that, as his administration progressed, he felt 'more and more uneasiness about the effect on the nation of tremendous peacetime military expenditure' and 'the almost overpowering influence' of the nation's defence contractors. No subsequent civilian president appears to have quite perceived the dangers or shared the same degree of concern. A consequence of the influence and expenditure that so troubled Eisenhower was a military way of thinking: a 'cast of mind that defines international reality as basically military' and tends to 'discount the likelihood of finding a solution except through military means'. It was famously dubbed 'military metaphysics' by C Wright Mills, a professor of sociology at Columbia.

The current national security and defence strategies of the United States are redolent of this military way of thinking. Their premise is 'US leadership in the world' coupled with more military, more weapons, more security, more alarm, more invective about real or imagined enemies and more anxious desperation to maintain leadership. The 'enemy' – for which greater spending is now said to be required – is less the radical Islamic terrorism of the last two decades and more the so-called 'revisionist powers of China and Russia'. But the key is military strength. It always has been. What was previously referred to as full spectrum military dominance is now described in the national security strategy as 'military overmatch'. The official language states:

> The United States must retain *overmatch* – the
> combination of capabilities in sufficient scale to prevent
> enemy success and to ensure that America's sons and
> daughters will never be in a fair fight. *Overmatch*
> strengthens our diplomacy and permits us to shape the
> international environment...To retain military *overmatch*,
> the United States must restore ability...restore readiness...
> and grow the size of the force. [emphasis added]

New weapons systems are required 'that clearly overmatch [adversaries] in lethality [killing power]'. The task is 'to ensure that American military superiority endures'. The military must be rebuilt 'so that it remains pre-eminent, deters our adversaries, and if necessary, is able to fight and win'. Adversaries must be convinced that 'we can and will defeat them – not just punish them'. The United States must 'build a more lethal force'. Preparedness for war must be 'prioritized' and key military capabilities must be 'modernized'. More and more resources must be devoted to 'solidify our military advantage'.

The core requirements are preparedness for war all over the world, global military presence, more weapons and a bigger military force. It is not enough that the United States has 'unmatched military advantages', it must, urges the national security strategy, with a degree of repetition bordering on paranoia, 'build upon our strengths' by 're-building our military so that it remains pre-eminent'. This includes prioritising investments in space and cyberspace. They, like terrestrial combat zones, have become 'warfighting domains' being integrated into 'the full spectrum of military operations'. The undersea is another warfighting domain. The American military ambition is to 'own the undersea domain', which it increasingly targets as Arctic ice diminishes.

The reality is that these warlike declarations in the national security and defence strategies of the United States do not represent a fundamentally new direction. They are merely the latest steps in a seventy-year continuum that has moved to a new level since 2001. As some commentators have noted, the current administration has opted 'to fetishize the military at the expense of everything else...But although [it] has made matters worse, the underlying problem is much older'.

The first 'manifesto of American militarism' was the top-secret report of the National Security Council in April 1950

(NSC-68). It envisioned permanent mobilisation for a clash of civilisations and a quadrupling of the defence budget. Replete with startling overstatement, it was a work of advocacy and according to one respected commentator, 'a first-rate specimen of gratuitous, alarmist cant'. Like the current national security and defence strategies, NSC-68's prose was designed to encourage support for greater defence spending. Exaggeration, hyperbole and threat elevation were deployed to stir fear. And rhetoric was adopted to galvanise the undecided.

One of the primary architects of NSC-68 was Truman's Secretary of State, Dean Acheson, the son of an Episcopal bishop. He confessed that 'dramatization and magnification were necessary to push the people where they should go'. Loyal to their task, Acheson and the authors of NSC-68 described Soviet Russia as a 'slave state' and insisted that the 'implacable purpose' of Soviet Russia was 'to eliminate the challenge of freedom'. Americans were assured that they faced 'the ever-present possibility of annihilation'; that the nation and its citizens 'stand in their deepest peril'; and that what was at stake was 'the fulfilment or destruction not only of this Republic but of civilization itself'. This dire situation, concluded the authors with disconcerting certitude, 'imposes on us, in our own interests, the responsibility of world leadership'.

NSC-68 was a pivotal moment. It coincided with the Korean War and marked the true beginning of the American Century. When the report was approved by President Truman in September, it changed the world. The trend toward a militarist culture, defence-first thinking and ever-larger military spending commenced its long post-war upward movement. But the Soviet threat was never what it was made out to be. According to a 1984 study, 'Washington's war-making capability in 1955 was some forty times greater than Moscow's. Nearly a decade later, the United States was still nine times more powerful militarily'. In the 1950s, air force general Curtis LeMay boasted that he could destroy the Russian war-making capacity 'without losing a man to their defenses'.

The reality in those early Cold War days was that the Soviet Union lacked both the means to destroy the United States and the desire to do so. Stalin 'trembled with fear' at the prospect of war with the United States. As did his successor Nikita Khrushchev, despite his sabre-rattling. Khrushchev once referred to the Soviet Union as 'a great big target range for American bombers operating from airfields in Norway, Germany, Italy, South Korea and Japan'. He would look across the Black Sea from Crimea and tell visitors, 'I see US missiles in Turkey aimed at my dacha'. This disequilibrium did not prevent the hardliners and militarists in Washington loudly and publicly attributing to the Kremlin a destructive capacity 'that leaders in both hemispheres knew existed only in the minds of Soviet propagandists'. As the Indian-American political scientist Fareed Zakaria has observed:

> The consequences of exaggerating the Soviet threat
> were vast: gross domestic abuses during the McCarthy
> era; a dangerous nuclear arms race; a long futile and
> unsuccessful war in Vietnam; and countless military
> interventions in various so-called Third world countries.

Then as now, the militarists advocated a 'pre-emptive strike' – before Moscow had a chance to undertake its 'diabolical plan for world domination'. It was like the Stanley Kubrick film *Dr Strangelove*. The Joint Chiefs called for bigger defence budgets to sustain this capability. Later, they would assert that there was a 'bomber gap' and a 'missile gap'. But there never was. The bomber and missile gaps of the Cold War were dissembling – even 'fraudulent' – just like the Gulf of Tonkin incident that stepped up the US military deployment in Vietnam or the notion that Saddam Hussein possessed weapons of mass destruction in Iraq that he intended to use pre-emptively. They were part of 'the Pentagon's lucrative tradition of threat elevation'. There has always been a reason to justify greater defence expenditure. The practice of 'hyping threats and exaggerating the capabilities and resources of adversaries' has been longstanding. In memos written after September 11, Defense Secretary Donald Rumsfeld unashamedly urged his staff to 'keep elevating the threat' to 'make the American people realize they are surrounded in the world by violent extremists'.

By 1991, when the Cold War ended and the Soviet Union disintegrated, the next generation of militarists, led by Defense Secretary Dick Cheney and the Pentagon's Under Secretary for Policy Paul Wolfowitz, advanced a new case to justify increased militarism and greater defence spending. They contended that America's future global mission should be to ensure that no rival superpower be allowed to emerge; that the United States should have sufficient military might to deter any nation from challenging its primacy; that other nations should be discouraged 'from challenging our leadership or seeking to overturn the established political and economic order'; and that potential competitors should be deterred 'from even aspiring to a larger regional or global role'. 'What is most important', their policy document reiterated, is 'the sense that the world order is ultimately backed by the US' and that 'the United States should be postured to act independently when collective action cannot be orchestrated'. It was a clear rejection of the strategy of collective internationalism through the United Nations and a call for even greater military capacity to maintain American supremacy.

The oft-repeated catch-cry – global military supremacy, pre-eminence, primacy, dominance or overmatch – coupled with a resolve to act unilaterally whenever considered necessary remains the bedrock of American policy. The cast of mind that defines international reality as basically military has not changed in Washington. It has endured from the era of Truman to the era of Trump. And it has become institutionalised. An aura of never-ending threat necessitating increased vigilance, greater military expenditure, ever-higher debt and continuing global military power projection continues to be promoted. It is why Professor Rosa Brooks from Georgetown University adopted the graphic title *How Everything Became War and the Military Became Everything* for her penetrating recent book.

Global Projection

The concept of global military projection is part of the American credo. It is little understood and rarely questioned. Army strategist Major Danny Sjursen explained: 'Today, not a single square inch of this ever-warming planet of ours escapes the reach of US militarization' and 'every square inch of [the planet] not already occupied by a rival state has been deemed a militarized space to be contested'. Integral to this reach is the uniquely American division of the entire planet into military command structures. The result is that the whole of the earth is the subject of exacting military surveillance directed from the Pentagon and its combatant commands. No country, ocean, island, coral reef or rocky outcrop on the surface of the planet is outside the area of responsibility of one or other of the combatant commands.

The terrestrial combatant commands of the United States are the Indo-Pacific Command, Africa Command, European Command, Central Command, Northern Command and Southern Command. The area covered by the Indo-Pacific Command stretches from the eastern Pacific to halfway across the Indian Ocean, and from the Arctic to the Antarctic. It includes 52 per cent of the earth's surface and more than half its population. Central Command is responsible for the Middle East and Central Asia; Northern Command for North America and Mexico; Southern Command for Latin America; Africa Command for Africa; and European Command for Europe.

In 2019, a further combatant command known as Space Command was established. Its precise reach is uncertain and its jurisdiction effectively uncontrolled. There is no international law defining the edge of space and the United States is resisting regulatory control that would constrain it. NASA and the United States Air Force define the edge of space to be fifty miles (eighty kilometres) above sea level for the purpose of awarding their personnel with 'outer space badges'. The conventional starting point for space is the Kármán line, at an altitude of one hundred kilometres, approximately at the intersection of the thermosphere and the mesosphere. This is about the point where the atmosphere becomes too thin to support aeronautical flight.

There are other commands. A Special Operations Command, unrestricted by any geographic limitations, is responsible for 'unconventional warfare' wherever and whenever directed by the president or defence secretary. Its forces include Rangers,

Green Berets and SEALS. A Strategic Command takes care of the euphemistically described 'strategic deterrence and global strike' capabilities anywhere in the world – in other words, the nuclear capabilities. It is headquartered at the Nebraska air force base where the *Enola Gay*, the B-29 aircraft which dropped the first atomic bomb over Hiroshima, was built. Associated with all of the combatant commands is a global Transportation Command. In addition, in 2018 Cyber Command was elevated to the status of a combatant command.

The earth's surface, the undersea and space above are enmeshed in a tightly fitting American military and communications grid. The oceans and lands are divided within carefully calibrated coordinates of longitude and latitude. And the limits of Space Command, if any, are yet to become clear. For each combatant command's area of responsibility, there is a war plan. And each combatant commander wields more practical authority than an ambassador. These senior officers are said to be 'the most powerful men on Earth', invested with power reminiscent – so it is said – of the Roman proconsuls and 'commonly referred to as such'. It is conventional to describe ambassadors as 'serving under' the military combatant commander in their geographic region and combatant commanders as 'supervising the affairs' of the countries within their jurisdiction. Chalmers Johnson gives the example of General Zinni, formerly commander of Central Command, who 'had twenty ambassadors serving under him and a personal political adviser with ambassadorial rank'.

Within their regions, the combatant commanders oversee United States naval, military and air force bases, arms sales, intelligence, special operations, space assets and nuclear forces, as well as more and more civilian work. They report directly to the president and defence secretary, while ambassadors report to the secretary of state. They enjoy near total control 'over the human, financial and material resources under their authority'. And they exercise considerable leverage over the host governments in their regions. This capability and influence are a function of the resources at their disposal. It also represents a paradigm shift in the way the power of the United States is exercised. The combatant commanders are the muscular uniformed face of modern American 'kinetic diplomacy'.

The corollary of this military muscularity is that conventional American diplomacy has become a poor relation to its military equivalent. In 2008, Defense Secretary Robert Gates warned of the 'creeping militarization of America's profile abroad'. And Senator Joe Biden lamented the 'migration of functions and authorities from the civilian agencies to the Department of Defense'. In much of the developing world, the face of America is overwhelmingly military – represented 'not by civilian medics or agrarians or educators but by armed men and women in military fatigues and body armor'. The hallmark of the American overseas presence is now fewer diplomats and more armed forces. As at March 2018, US special forces were present in more than twice as many countries as US ambassadors; marines were stationed at 181 embassies and consulates; and CIA officers were, and always are, ubiquitous. At the same time, 70 out of 188 US ambassadorships had not been filled. By March 2019, fifty-two US ambassadorships to countries and international organisations remained vacant. By November 2019, more than 25 per cent of key US State Department positions still remained unfilled.

In contrast, China now boasts the world's largest network of diplomatic posts. For the first time, the number of Chinese embassies and consulates surpasses that of the United States. In 2019, William Burns in *Foreign Affairs* magazine called this trend 'The Demolition of US Diplomacy' and remarked:

> The White House regularly pushes historic cuts to diplomacy and development spending, which is already 19 times smaller than the defense budget. Career diplomats are sidelined, with only one of 28 assistant secretary-rank positions filled by a Foreign Service officer, and more ambassadorships are going to political appointees in this administration than any in recent history. One-fifth of ambassadorships remain unfulfilled, including critical posts.

While the State Department is being hollowed out and its budget is anaemic, that of the defence department has reached scarcely fathomable levels of profligacy. A consequence is that the Pentagon, which is said to have more lawyers than the State Department has diplomats, and more members of military bands than there are Foreign Service officers, has 'all but eclipsed' the latter at the centre of American foreign policy. The dominance of the Pentagon reflects a preference for a way of thinking that values military strength above all else in international relations, discourages compromise and fears weakness, while downplaying the role of the softer arts of negotiation and conciliation. The preferred negotiating stance of the militarists is firmness, underpinned by military strength. Any concession is derided as appeasement. Ted Strickler, a former political advisor to US Strategic Command, explained this tendency in a paper entitled '10 Things the Foreign Service Needs to Know'. His view, albeit with some simplification and generalisation, was that US military doctrine is a 'combination of the Bible and the Boy Scout Handbook' and that 'Military characterizations frequently are in absolute terms...while the Foreign Service is more sensitive to shades of grey'.

Foreign Bases

A key feature of the Pentagon's global power projection is its amorphous empire of foreign military bases. The sheer number of bases and the lack of transparency make any analysis challenging. A defence department 'base structure report' in 2005 stated that the US military maintained more than 700 bases in 120 countries but the report failed to include bases in Iraq, Afghanistan, Kosovo, Israel, Kyrgyzstan, Qatar and Uzbekistan. Stephen Glain said that the Pentagon acknowledged '909 military facilities in forty-six countries and territories' in 2007. A more reliable assessment at 2015 is approximately 800 foreign bases. Such extra-territorial deployment of military force was unknown in the history of the United States before World War II. The twenty-first century Pentagon, one can be confident, directs and controls 'more bases in other people's lands than any other people, nation or empire in world history'.

The bases are almost everywhere. They stretch from far northern Australia to Denmark's Greenland; from the middle of the Indian Ocean to the islands of the western Pacific; and from the Horn of Africa to the Persian Gulf. There are hundreds of large bases which are highly visible air-conditioned islands of American culture. And there is a vast number of smaller facilities, not always officially acknowledged, that operate as listening posts, tracking stations and intelligence-gathering missions operated by the Pentagon, the National Security

Agency, the National Reconnaissance Office or one or other of the seventeen separate American intelligence bodies that jostle with each other. Almost twenty years ago, an NBC News journalist remarked, with only some exaggeration, that 'Today, one could throw a dart at a map of the world and it would likely land within a few hundred miles of a quietly established US intelligence-gathering operation.' Since then, the security network has expanded and been made considerably more complex by the US's self-fulfilling fear of China and Russia and advances in encryption and fibre optic technology.

Once established, America's foreign military facilities frequently take on a life of their own, resisting attempts to remove or reduce them. Seventy-five years have passed since World War II but there are still 113 bases in Japan, 83 in South Korea and hundreds in Germany and Italy. The United States military rarely lets go. A congressional investigation concluded that 'Original missions may become outdated, but new missions are developed, not only with the intent of keeping the facility going, but often to actually enlarge it'. And with every military intervention since the end of the Cold War, the Pentagon has left behind clusters of new bases in areas where it never before had a foothold – from Kosovo and the Balkan states, to Iraq and the Persian Gulf states, and into Afghanistan and some Central Asian states. The massive fortified military bases left behind in Seoul and Baghdad are not going anywhere.

The usual justification for this boundless military presence is that it keeps the peace and makes the world, and the United States, safer and more secure. But such a proposition is not self-evident and frequently wrong. More often than not, the presence of America's foreign military bases heightens military tensions and discourages diplomatic solutions. In unstable regions, their stabilising effect, if any, is short-term while their long-term destabilising consequences 'can actually make war more likely and America less secure'. And frequently they act as a self-fulfilling prophecy by increasing threats to the security of nearby countries and provoking a military response. Research has shown – indeed it seems unarguable – that United States military bases and troops in the Middle East have been a 'major catalyst for anti-Americanism and radicalization', leading to Al Qaeda recruitment. The American military presence in Saudi Arabia, for example, was part of Osama bin Laden's professed motivation for the September 11 attacks. And the creation of new military bases and intelligence installations near the borders of countries like China, Russia, Iran and North Korea helps create the very threat against which they are supposedly designed to protect.

A case in point is the Korean Peninsula. The troops, bases and missile systems in South Korea contribute to a state of increased tension and make Pyongyang and Beijing bristle – just as Soviet missiles on Cuba made Washington apoplectic in 1962. The effect is to make peace, let alone denuclearisation by North Korea, more difficult to achieve. And although the state of war on the Korean peninsula has continued since 1950, Washington has never been interested in a peace treaty. It set its face against a peace treaty from the outset, ignoring the terms of the armistice to which it agreed in 1953, which expressly required that steps be taken toward a political resolution.

The likelihood that 'it's been in the interest (conscious or unconscious) of some US officials to maintain a state of war, to have a justification for maintaining troops and bases in Korea and thus on the Asian mainland' is not just 'a reasonable argument', as scholar David Vine has politely suggested, it is a near certainty. This state of affairs, and the numerous American bases, no doubt explain why South Korea is the only place in the world where Google Maps is not permitted to operate. Sam Roggeveen, director of the international security program at the Lowy Institute, is one of an increasing number of voices who have suggested that 'the United States should get out of South Korea'.

Another example of conduct that helps create the very threat against which it is designed to protect is the American-led expansion of NATO into the countries of Eastern Europe, right up to the borders of Russia. Combat-ready NATO troops are now deployed '1,000 miles closer to Moscow than before 1989'. The expansion explains, in part, Russia's annexation of the Crimean Peninsula in 2014. George Kennan thought such expansion was a fateful error that would 'inflame the nationalistic, anti-Western and militaristic tendencies in Russian opinion' and 'restore the atmosphere of the cold war to East-West relations'. It has done just that.

When the United States Senate approved the expansion of NATO in 1998, Kennan lamented that the decision 'shows so little understanding of Russian history and Soviet history. Of course, there is going to be a bad reaction from Russia, and then [the NATO expanders] will say that we always told you that is how the Russians are – but this is just wrong'. He added, correctly in hindsight:

> I think it is the beginning of a new cold war. I think
> the Russians will gradually react quite adversely and it
> will affect their policies. I think it is a tragic mistake.
> There was no reason for this whatsoever. No one was
> threatening anybody else. The expansion would make the

Founding Fathers of this country turn in their graves...
What bothers me is how superficial and ill-informed the
whole Senate debate was.

Kennan was not the only voice of opposition at the time. In
1995, a group of almost two dozen retired senior officials
from the state and defence departments penned an open
letter opposing NATO expansion, contending that it risked
exacerbating instability and 'convincing most Russians that the
United States and the West are attempting to *isolate, encircle
and subordinate* them' (emphasis added). They clearly are. Tom
Switzer, the experienced Australian journalist and presenter, has
repeatedly labelled the expansion of NATO as the single worst
foreign policy decision by the United States in modern times,
with the sole exception of the invasion of Iraq. But the rhetoric of
contemporary anti-Russian feeling in Washington is sometimes
off the scale. When Senator Rand Paul recently opposed the
inclusion of Montenegro in the NATO alliance on perfectly
sensible grounds, the late Senator John McCain accused him of
acting treasonously and 'working for Vladimir Putin'. Thomas
Friedman's more recent assessment in *The New York Times* is
sobering: 'I opposed expanding NATO toward Russia after the
Cold War, when Russia was at its most democratic and least
threatening. It remains one of the dumbest things we've ever
done and, of course, laid the groundwork for Putin's rise'.

Exorbitance

The global military power projection of the United States is
sustained by a fountain of money – between $700 billion and
$1 trillion every year. No other country is remotely comparable.

No country spends more on its military; no country exports more weapons and lethal armaments; and no country has more foreign military bases. America spends as much on its supposed 'defence' as the next eight or nine highest-spending countries combined. Despite having a population that represents less than 5 per cent of the world total, the United States is responsible for more than a third of all global military expenditure and more than a third of all global arms exports. Consistent military spending of this scale brings to mind the chilling warning of a *New York Times* reporter in 1938 who wrote that 'When and if fascism comes to America, it will not be labelled "made in Germany"; it will not be marked with a swastika; it will not even be called fascism; it will be called, of course, "Americanism"'.

The Pentagon's official defence budget for 2019 was $693 billion. The budget for 2020 is $738 billion. The proposed 2021 budget is higher still. This level of military expenditure is two to three times as much as China's current level of spending and more than ten times as much as Russia's. The figures are similarly high as a percentage of GDP. The Stockholm International Peace Research Institute recorded that the military expenditure of the United States in 2018 was 3.2 per cent of GDP, while China's was 1.9 per cent, the United Kingdom's was 1.8 per cent and Germany's was 1.2 per cent. The three unlikely nations with the closest similar percentage levels to the United States were Sudan, Morocco and Colombia, although some countries have even higher levels.

An annual figure of approximately $700 billion for defence is only part of the picture. There is much more. The Pentagon's budget does not include other defence and national security expenditure that is separately budgeted in other departments. Nor does it take account of the interest on the funds borrowed by Washington to pay for its war spending and national security. The amounts spent on defence and national security by other departments and agencies such as Energy, Veterans Affairs, Homeland Security, State and Treasury add several hundred billion dollars and more to the overall defence budget.

The nuclear budget, for example, supports a production network for nuclear warheads and nuclear reactors across the United States. It is the responsibility of the Department of Energy, not Defense. And President Trump has vowed to give it more money. The Veterans Affairs budget has tripled since 2001 as a result of the ballooning claims and entitlements of the new generation of veterans spawned by America's twenty-first century wars. There have been 2.7 million veterans since 2001, with a Pentagon projection of 4.3 million by 2039. The cost of their care, rehabilitation and support is not the responsibility of Defense but of Veterans Affairs. The budget of the Department of Homeland Security (DHS) has expanded massively. The DHS is responsible for almost a quarter of a million employees and the protection of the United States against threats, particularly terrorism 'within, at or outside its borders'. The budgets of the State Department and the US Agency for International Development contribute billions of dollars to a 'Foreign Military Financing' program. And Treasury spends billions of dollars underwriting veterans' retirement plans. When these costs are added to the Defense budget, the total expenditure by the United States on defence and national security is more than $1 trillion every year.

To put it in context, the official defence figure of approximately $700 billion is more than half of the total annual discretionary spending of the United States government. And it is many, many times greater than the amounts given each year to the State Department, or to education, health, housing or infrastructure. The amount proposed for the State Department and USAID in the 2020 budget was a mere $40 billion; for education $62 billion; for health and human services $87 billion; and for housing and urban development $44 billion. The proposed 2021 budget contemplates further cuts in non-defence areas. As Ben Freeman of the Centre for International Policy pointed out:

> ...just the approximately $80 billion annual increase in the [Pentagon's] top line between 2017 and 2019 will be double the current budget of the State Department; higher than the gross domestic products of more than 100 countries; and larger than the entire military budget of any country in the world, except China's.

Another perspective comes from America's export of munitions and armaments. Munitions and armaments serve only one purpose – to kill human beings and destroy structures. Yet the United States stands head and shoulders above all other countries in the world in the arms trade. And President Trump described his 2019 arms deal with Saudi Arabia as involving the sale of 'beautiful military equipment'. In the five years from 2013 to 2018, arms exports by the United States grew by 29 per cent, its share of total global arms exports rose from 30 to 36 per cent and the gap between the United States and the next largest arms exporter increased from 12 to 75 per cent. The major beneficiaries of American weapons exports are Saudi Arabia, Israel, Egypt and Qatar. In fact, Saudi Arabia, which is not necessarily as closely allied to the United States as it once was, has become the world's largest arms importer.

Statistics such as these are part of the reason why the 2019 Global Peace Index recorded the United States as languishing near the bottom of its militarisation domain, alongside North Korea, Russia and Israel. The index ranked America 161 out of 163 countries for 'militarisation' and 128 out of 163 countries for 'peace'. The militarisation score is one of the three key ingredients of the Global Peace Index and is based on indicators such as military expenditure, numbers of armed personnel, exports of arms and weapons, nuclear and heavy weapons capabilities and ease of access to small arms and light weapons.

A notable feature of this militarist culture is that the massive amounts for defence voted every year by the United States Congress generate 'no visible public outrage'. Modern American patriotism presupposes unquestioning, hand-on-heart support for military spending that must, it seems, exceed that of any other country. Instead of opposition, there is, with only a few exceptions, an 'enduring consensus' on both sides of Congress. It is an unstated pact. Neta Crawford from the Costs of War Project at Brown University said that the attitude of Congress 'seems to be that the Pentagon deserves whatever funding they ask for, no matter the cost, and regardless of whether or not this spending is efficient or wise'. It is treated as part of the natural order.

There is a moral and ethical dimension to such exorbitant spending on the military and defence. But it is difficult to imagine a modern president saying what President Eisenhower dared to say almost seventy years ago:

The cost of one modern heavy bomber is this: a modern brick school in more than 30 cities. It is two electric power plants, each serving a town of 60,000 population. It is two fine, fully equipped hospitals. It is some fifty miles of concrete pavement.

We pay for a single fighter plane with a half million bushels of wheat. We pay for a single destroyer with new homes that could have housed more than 80,000 people...

This is not a way of life at all, in any true sense.

It is even more difficult to imagine that Eisenhower's cry from the heart would carry any weight in today's more militarised, more singular, America, where the list of beneficiaries who derive profit, power and privilege from defence spending grows longer all the time. Defence spending in the United States lubricates and sustains politics, businesses, intellectual opinion and careers. It has generated a lucrative 'industry' on a scale that has been unknown in any other democratic country in history. At the centre of this Hydra is the Pentagon.

The Pentagon

The actual size of the Pentagon 'enterprise' is beyond ready comprehension. A few years ago a defence department publication revelled in these facts: the 'Defense enterprise is the largest and most complex organization in the world' with 'roughly three million employees'... 'almost 5,000 locations'... and '2.2 billion square feet in building space, with the Army alone utilizing the equivalent of more than twice the total office space in New York City'. The enterprise is larger than any American corporation, including Exxon Mobil, Walmart or any other corporate behemoth. It is the world's largest employer and the world's biggest single user of oil and petroleum products – twenty-four hours a day all over the globe. Its landholdings in the United States consist of 'over 29 million acres'. It has over 1.4 million active duty personnel, 1.1 million reservists and guard members and 861,000 civilian employees. Approximately 450,000 of its employees are stationed overseas in 163 countries. The Pentagon building itself is the world's largest office building – with, it is suggested, 'More office space than Manhattan'.

Associated with this Pentagon 'enterprise' is a hidden and vastly expensive top-secret intelligence world. America's wars since 2001 and its new determination to treat China and Russia as strategic enemies have not just amplified the defence enterprise, they have added an Orwellian dimension to intelligence spending. It first emerged in its full-blown complexity after the September 11 attacks:

> With a quick infusion of money, military and intelligence
> agencies multiplied. Twenty-four organizations were
> created by the end of 2001, including the Office of
> Homeland Security and the Foreign Terrorist Asset
> Tracking Task Force. In 2002, 37 more were created to
> track weapons of mass destruction, collect threat tips and
> coordinate the new focus on counterterrorism. That was
> followed the next year by 36 new organizations; and 26
> after that; and 31 more; and 32 more; and 20 more each
> in 2007, 2008 and 2009.

In 2010, *The Washington Post* concluded, following a two-year investigation, that more than 1200 government organisations and almost 2000 private companies were working on programs relating to counter-terrorism, intelligence and homeland security in approximately 10,000 locations across the United States; that an estimated 854,000 people (more than the population of Washington DC) held top-secret security clearances; and that thirty-three building complexes for top-secret intelligence work, amounting to approximately 17 million square feet of space – equivalent in size to three Pentagons or twenty-two Capitol buildings – were under construction or had been built since 2001.

In 2020, every day across the United States, many hundreds of thousands of military and civilian personnel with top-secret security clearances are scanned into offices protected by electromagnetic locks, retinal cameras and fortified walls impenetrable to eavesdropping equipment. Their movements are watched by surveillance cameras and their baggage is checked by X-ray machines. Inside most buildings is a room known as an SCIF – an enclosed internal area that is used to process classified information derived from sensitive intelligence sources, methods or analytical processes. According to *The Washington Post* investigation team, such facilities have 'become a measure of status in Top Secret America'. Some SCIFs are small. Others are 'four times the size of a football field'. Almost all establishments have armed security details. Some have their own police force, armoured vehicles and canine units. Some clandestine programs operate in concrete structures fitted with false windows designed to look like office buildings. The script could have been written by HG Wells.

Whistleblower Edward Snowden was not wrong about the scale of American intelligence gathering. When *The Washington Post* conducted its investigation ten years ago, the National Security Agency – one of seventeen current intelligence agencies – intercepted and stored 1.7 billion emails, phone calls and other communications every day. So much intelligence information was collected that insiders told *The Washington Post* investigation team that the 'overload of hourly, daily, weekly, monthly and annual reports is actually counterproductive'. The sheer bulk of information results in message dissonance, reduced effectiveness and duplication. Access to many hundreds of ultra-secret programs known as 'Special Access Programs' or SAPs is so severely limited that few, if any, people have a complete understanding. James Clapper, a former Director of National Intelligence, told the investigation team that 'There's only one entity in the entire universe that has visibility on all SAPs – that's God'.

Meanwhile, as antagonism toward China and Russia reaches new heights, Congress funds more facilities, more personnel and equipment, more satellites, more security, more weaponry and more fleets of armoured vehicles for the intelligence community. To an extent previously unknown in the history of the United States, the defence and foreign policy establishment has been replaced by a more militarised, more expensive and more dangerous defence and intelligence establishment.

Hidden Costs

The hidden costs and long-term economic consequences of America's militarism are quietly insidious. Unlike previous conflicts in Vietnam, Korea and World War II, the wars undertaken by the United States since 2001 in Iraq, Afghanistan and adjoining Pakistan, not to forget Libya or its intervention in Syria since 2014, have been funded entirely by borrowings.

The costs of these twenty-first century wars have been, and continue to be, simply added to the national debt, on which interest accumulates. The final reckoning is then left to other administrations and a new generation of taxpayers:

> The consequence of this war funding policy has been to transfer the financial cost – including not only trillions of dollars of current spending, but also the long-term liabilities such as veterans care – to future generations.

In an earlier time, waging war abroad meant austerity at home. It was usual to fund wars by increasing taxes, cutting domestic spending and encouraging the purchase of war bonds. President Truman set a top marginal tax rate of 92 per cent to fund the Korean War. During the Eisenhower administration the top marginal rate was 90 per cent. And President Johnson, although more reluctant, imposed a Vietnam War surcharge that increased top tax rates to 77 per cent. There is a new attitude in twenty-first century America. Presidents Bush and Trump have waged wars in multiple conflict zones and presided over historic increases in military spending – at the same time as introducing tax cuts.

This attitude may be contrasted with an earlier era. The patriotic message displayed on an American government poster during World War II exhorted thrift and financial prudence. It was headed 'For Victory – And My Personal Post War World'. The poster promoted the '7-key plan to hold prices down'. The seven points were as follows:

1. Buy and hold War Bonds.
2. Pay willingly our share of taxes.

3. Provide adequate life insurance and savings for our future.
4. Reduce our debts as much as possible.
5. Buy only what we need and make what we have last longer.
6. Follow ration rules and price ceilings.
7. Cooperate with our Government's wage stabilization program.

Nothing could be further from Washington's current prevailing attitude. Thrift and prudence are out of favour. The cost of firing one rocket-propelled shell on the newly built, super-sophisticated but trouble-prone, USS *Zumwalt* is said to be 'a cool $915,000 per round'. And a Chinese study quoted by David Kilcullen, refers to America's 'unlimited extravagance in war' and makes the point that a US aircraft bomber is 'like a flying mountain of gold, more costly than many of its targets'. While almost no military expense is too much for Washington, the administration no longer countenances the necessity of encouraging American citizens to pay more taxes and buy government bonds to support the nation's warfare. The American people are shielded from the financial reality. The Institute for Economics and Peace noted that the wars in Iraq and Afghanistan represent 'the first time in American history that the Government cut taxes as it went to war'. The actual costs of the wars, including trillions of dollars in accrued long-term liabilities, are simply being deferred. One scholar has referred to America's modern military conflicts as 'the credit card wars'.

The cost of these modern 'credit card wars' is massive. Brown University's Costs of War Project estimates that the true cost to the United States of war-related government spending from 2001 to 2019 is $4.9 trillion – to which must be added a further $1 trillion to reflect the cost of future care of existing veterans of the 'post 9/11 wars'. At a rally in Ohio in April 2018, President Trump estimated the costs at $7 trillion over seventeen years and concluded that there was nothing to show for it 'except death and destruction'. The Brown University researchers concluded that in total, the United States 'has spent or is obligated to spend $5.9 trillion in current dollars through FY2019'. And they warned that it will only get worse:

> ...the costs of war will likely be greater than this because,
> unless the US immediately ends its deployments, the
> number of veterans associated with the post-9/11 wars
> will also grow. Veterans' benefits and disability spending,
> and the cost of interest on borrowing to pay for the wars,
> will comprise an increasingly large share of the costs of
> the US post-9/11 wars.

The unseen interest burden has a particular significance given Washington's preference for debt and deficit funding. A few years ago, the Project on Government Oversight, a non-partisan, non-profit organisation based in Washington, calculated 'the share of the interest on [the national debt] generated by defense-related programs at more than $100 billion annually'. Last year, researchers concluded that 'of the more than $500 billion in interest taxpayers fork over to service the government's debt each year, about $156 billion can be attributed to Pentagon spending'. This is part of the reason why, as one commentator colourfully described it, 'the Pentagon devours the budget'. It is also a part of the reason why Alastair Walton, the Australian Consul-General in New York, wrote recently that the 'fundamental fiscal, debt and related social challenges which will confront the United States over the next three decades are...unprecedented in American history and may profoundly shake the very core of its financial, political and social compact'. The COVID-19 crisis has brought forward the challenge to America's compact.

Naturally, the major weapons contractors do not complain about the ever-higher defence budgets or the state of permanent war. The characterisation of the Pentagon budget as 'corporate welfare for weapons makers' is readily understandable. Lockheed Martin, for example, is the largest vendor to the biggest client on earth. It is the United States government's single biggest contractor. It is also the manufacturer of the controversial F-35 joint strike fighter aircraft, which is priced at approximately $100 million each. The United States defense department wants 2456 of these aircraft. Lockheed Martin's pipeline of government orders and work in progress guarantees its taxpayer-funded cash flow for years ahead. Its inventory includes fighter jets, transport planes, ballistic missiles, missile defence systems, computers, radar, Apache helicopters, space systems, satellites and infra-red systems. Other billion-dollar weapons suppliers who gorge on the Pentagon budget include Boeing (F-18 Super Hornet jets), Northrop Grumman (B-21 nuclear bombers), General Dynamics (Ohio-class ballistic missile submarines) and Raytheon (guided missiles).

The list is beyond extensive. But there is more to this defence expenditure than just the exorbitant amounts outlaid to achieve greater killing power. It is a question of priorities. As President Eisenhower said: 'It is spending the sweat of its laborers, the genius of its scientists, the hopes of its children'.

The issue is ethical, but it is also practical. A militarist culture and excessive military spending not only reduce the quality of life by detracting from expenditure on public services such as transport, infrastructure, clean energy, housing, education and roads. But it has been argued convincingly that such spending has a long-term negative effect on the economy. This is because the 'relentlessly predatory effects of the military economy erode industrial productivity, the foundation of every nation's economic growth'. Some commentators refer to the 'vampiristic effect' of the defence sector on the whole economy and link America's military spending with its growing de-industrialisation and the decay of its manufacturing cities.

This negative effect arises because there is a basic functional difference between military spending and civilian spending. From an economic standpoint, the former is non-productive. It involves an 'absence of economic functional usefulness'. Advocates for the stimulus effect of military spending disagree, of course. And no one can deny that many major inventions and technological advances owe a lot to warfare. But numerous studies have demonstrated that after an initial stimulus, military spending destroys jobs and prosperity. The gains are short-lived and the stimulus benefits affect only certain industries. In fact, 'most economic models show that military spending diverts resources from productive uses, such as consumption and investment, and ultimately slows economic growth and reduces employment'.

George Washington's warning more than two centuries ago seems remarkably apt. Like Eisenhower, he was a general before he was president. And like Eisenhower, he told his countrymen to 'avoid those overgrown military establishments which, under any form of government, are inauspicious to liberty, and which are to be regarded as particularly hostile to republican liberty'. Founding Father and fourth US president James Madison was even more direct about the price of militarism and the costs and consequences of war:

> Of all the enemies of true liberty, war is, perhaps, the
> most to be dreaded, because it comprises and develops the
> germ of every other...
> War is the parent of armies; from these proceed debts and
> taxes...
> No nation can preserve its freedom in the midst of
> continual warfare.
> War is in fact the true nurse of executive
> aggrandizement...

More directly visible is the human effect of America's twenty-first century wars. As always, the civilian non-combatants of other countries suffer far more than the American servicemen and women deployed to bring them 'freedom'. It was the same in Vietnam and Korea. Washington's transparency over civilian casualties is questionable but the best independent estimates indicate that by late 2018, the United States' wars in Iraq, Afghanistan and adjoining Pakistan had resulted in direct deaths numbering between 480,000 and 507,000. The majority of those deaths – nearly a quarter of a million – have consisted of civilian non-combatants, being Iraqi, Afghani and Pakistani men, women and children. They were followed by national military, police and opposition fighters. In addition to the deaths, many more lives have been ruined and families dislocated. Over 8 million civilians in Iraq, Afghanistan and

Pakistan – at least 21 million if you include Syria – have become refugees or asylum seekers or been internally displaced. Iran and Turkey now host millions of disaffected refugees whose resentment adds to American security concerns.

The human cost to the United States is also considerable but hardly comparable. Up to 2019, almost seven thousand American military combatants have been killed. Many other American servicemen and women have become amputees – 1645 by 2015. More than 300,000 have suffered traumatic brain injuries. And there is an unquantifiable number of veterans who experience lasting difficulties in adjusting to civilian life, resulting in unemployment, crime, depression, domestic violence, divorce and suicide. These facts and figures only scratch the surface of the human consequences of war.

The years of war initiated by the United States in Afghanistan and Pakistan since 2001, and in Iraq since 2003, have transformed the region for the worse. Not only have the wars resulted in the killing and maiming of hundreds of thousands of innocent people but they have created a greater security risk than existed before. The United States National Intelligence Estimate in 2006 concluded that the wars were 'breeding a deep resentment of US involvement in the Muslim world and cultivating supporters for the global Jihadist movement'.

The consequences are nearly always the same – whether in Iraq or Vietnam, Korea or Afghanistan, or in dozens of other war zones where the United States has intervened during the last seventy years. Nobel Peace Prize recipient Martin Luther King highlighted these negative effects in his famous speech at the Riverside Church in New York in 1967, when he quoted a Vietnamese Buddhist leader:

It is curious that the Americans, who calculate so
carefully on the possibilities of military victory, do
not realize that in the process they are incurring deep
psychological and political defeat. The image of America
will never again be the image of revolution, freedom and
democracy, but the image of violence and militarism...

CHAPTER 6

UNILATERALISM
America First

Treaties & Conventions

Militarism fuels confidence, encourages unilateralism and leads to hubris. It explains, at least in part, why seventy-five years after the United Nations Charter, the United States has become increasingly disruptive, and dangerous to the economic and political stability of the modern world that it helped to create. It also explains morally tenuous conduct – out of step with other leading civilised nations – such as the controversial use of torture and targeted assassinations. Some Americans refer to 'a new orthodoxy' that contends that 'the US should aggressively pursue its own interests regardless of what others think'. Writers, even some with impeccably conservative credentials, have adopted pointed titles and descriptions, often using the word 'rogue'. They include *Rogue Nation – America's Unilateralism and the Failure of Good Intentions* and 'From

Diplomatic Leader to Rogue Nation' and *Rogue State: A Guide to the World's Only Super Power*. The last was apparently a favourite of Osama bin Laden. But rather than being a new orthodoxy, such singular unilateralism has a long post-war history. It is not a new phenomenon. It has simply become extravagantly overt under President Trump.

Niall Ferguson, the acclaimed economic historian, observed that President Truman made his intentions clear at the outset of the Cold War when he said that the only way to 'save the world from totalitarianism' was for 'the whole world [to] adopt the American system', for 'the American system' could survive only if it becomes 'a world system'. The response from James Warburg, the influential banker and financial advisor to Franklin Roosevelt, was straight to the point. He called this notion 'isolationism turned inside out' and that it meant 'We are willing to become citizens of the world but only if the world becomes an extension of the United States'. Nowhere is this inconsistency more evident than in Washington's attitude to the United Nations and international treaties and conventions. But it goes much further than that.

Despite being the founder and major sponsor of the United Nations, and currently contributing approximately $10 billion annually, the United States is by far the largest debtor to the organisation – owing approximately $1 billion out of $1.3 billion in outstanding funding obligations. It has become an outlier. Its recalcitrance is reflected in its refusal to ratify, or even sign, treaties, conventions and protocols that most major nations in the world support. In fact, since 1994 the United States Senate has not ratified a single UN convention or treaty that has come before it. Some of the important topics on which the United States has placed itself outside the pale include: the rights of the child, discrimination against women, human rights, climate and the environment, the law of the sea, missile reduction and the arms trade. Hundreds of nations have ratified the UN treaties and conventions on these subjects but Washington will not participate or only does so with heavy qualifications. The nations that have nearly always ratified include the leading countries of Europe (France, Germany and the United Kingdom) and those of the former British Commonwealth (Australia, Canada and New Zealand). In many cases, but not always, they also include China and Russia.

The Convention on the Rights of the Child aims to protect and promote the rights of children around the world but the United States is the only country that has not ratified it. Opposition comes from American religious groups, conservatives, supporters of parental rights and home-schooling and those who favour the juvenile death penalty. No other country either has these concerns or has allowed them to influence government policy. The protection of women from discrimination is another example. The UN convention was adopted in 1979 and requires all countries to eliminate discrimination against women and girls in all areas of life. Almost every country in the world (189 states) has ratified the convention but the United States is conspicuously absent, along with a handful of countries such as Palau, Iran, Somalia, Sudan and Tonga. Social and religious conservatives claim that the convention seeks to impose a liberal, progressive, feminist standard which is detrimental to traditional values.

The position on human rights is the same. The United States was once the world leader, the champion and the pioneer of human rights. In the eighteenth century, its founding fathers invoked 'natural rights' and 'inalienable rights' in support of the new republic. And after World War II, Eleanor Roosevelt chaired the committee that drafted the ground-breaking Universal Declaration of Human Rights, the precursor to all subsequent human rights treaties. But modern America has developed an aversion to international human rights treaties and demonstrated a unique reluctance to ratify them. It stands 'alone among other industrialized Western countries in its reluctance'.

This reluctance to ratify also includes the International Covenant on Economic, Social and Cultural Rights, which was adopted by the United Nations General Assembly in 1966. It is one of the two treaties that give legal force to the Universal Declaration of Human Rights. Among other things, it recognises the right of all peoples to self-determination, including the right to 'freely determine their political status'. The covenant has 169 parties but the United States is one of only four countries, along with the tiny states of Palau, Cuba and Comoros, who have signed but not ratified it. One of the goals of the covenant is international accountability but this is precisely what makes it objectionable to the United States, which tends to frame concerns about international scrutiny as an infringement of its sovereignty.

The same dislike of international accountability underlies the recent peremptory withdrawal of the United States from the UN Human Rights Council. The decision was a clear reaction to, and came the day after, the Human Rights Commissioner 'slammed' the Trump administration's policy of separating migrant parents from their children at the Mexican border. The then United States Ambassador Nikki Haley used the most undiplomatic language to complain about the membership of the council. But the real complaint seems to have been that the United States was just one of the forty-seven member states on the council and that most of them did not share its views on Israel or the treatment of Palestinians.

Ms Haley also complained that not all member states upheld the highest standards of human rights in their own countries. This is true but the council has performed a useful international function and a collective organisation is certainly better than nothing. Kenneth Roth, the executive director of Human Rights Watch, observed that 'the UN Human Rights Council has played an important role in such countries as North Korea, Syria, Myanmar and South Sudan, but all Trump seems to care about is defending Israel'. As is well known, Israel is a constant preoccupation in Washington. It is a given today that 'questioning the United States' virtually unconditional support for Israel can imperil a policymaker's hope of ever serving in government again'.

International Scrutiny

In twenty-first century America, international scrutiny of its conduct or of that of its armed forces and citizens has become unacceptable. The modern United States has drawn an emphatic red line against almost any form of international accountability. This includes adjudication by the International Court of Justice and the International Criminal Court. This aversion does not sit easily with the fact that the United States was a founding proponent of both the International Court of Justice and the Nuremberg War Crimes Tribunal. The former is one of the components of the scheme created by the United Nations Charter. And the International Criminal Court is a proud successor to the tradition of prosecuting war crimes and crimes against humanity established at Nuremberg. In that earlier, less unilateralist era, the push for both was led by the United States.

Any resort to an international forum or tribunal as a platform for criticising or sanctioning the United States now generates wholesale suspicion and disdain, even outrage, in Washington. The United States 2005 National Defense Strategy remarkably exclaimed that the use of international tribunals and judicial processes constituted the 'strategy of the weak'. It stated that 'Our strength as a nation state will continue to be challenged by those who employ a strategy of the weak, *using international fora, judicial processes* and terrorism' (emphasis added). Terrorism is understandable, but 'international fora' and 'judicial processes' – a strategy of the weak?

The US aversion to scrutiny by the International Court of Justice appears to have crystallised in 1986 with an adverse decision against the United States in a case brought by Nicaragua. In the court's words, the government of Nicaragua had taken 'significant steps towards establishing a totalitarian Communist dictatorship' as part of an internal struggle largely being played out between the Sandinistas and the Contra rebels. President Reagan and the United States Congress seemed to think that these circumstances justified the intervention by the United States in Nicaragua, contrary to the principles established by the United Nations Charter.

The court was puzzled by the logic of the American argument, saying that 'However the regime in Nicaragua be defined, adherence by a State to any particular doctrine does not constitute a violation of customary international law; to hold otherwise would make a nonsense of the fundamental principle of State sovereignty'. It added that it was beyond contemplation that one state could intervene against another simply 'on the ground that the latter has opted for some particular ideology or political system'. A state cannot intervene simply because another state's system does not conform to its 'values'. It matters not whether the state has adopted an authoritarian, communist, socialist or any other political system. This straightforward and obvious proposition appeared to be inexplicable to the United States. Its reaction to the decision of the International Court of Justice was indignant and dismissive. It withdrew its consent to the court's general jurisdiction, which had been in place for forty years; refused to recognise the judgment; and moved strenuously to block enforcement of the judgment in the United Nations Security Council.

Thus began a 'decades-long trend toward US disengagement from the ICJ'. It has gathered pace in the twenty-first century as America walks away from an institution of its own creation. The International Court of Justice no longer fits into a belief system that puts patriotism before globalism; nationalism before global responsibility; and individual sovereignty before collective decision-making. Values and attitudes in Washington have changed so much since 1945 that the United States is now undertaking a conscious process of decoupling. In Jeffrey Sachs's dark words, 'the United States is completing the move from post-war leader to twenty-first century rogue state'.

After it withdrew from the court's general jurisdiction in 1986, the United States subsequently withdrew from the court's jurisdiction under specific treaties. In 2005, it responded to several unfavourable decisions of the court by withdrawing from a protocol to the Vienna Convention on Consular Relations. The United States was the first country to successfully invoke the protocol when it sued Iran over the taking of fifty-two American diplomats and citizens as hostages in 1979. But when the court later ruled in favour of a group of Mexican foreign nationals on death row and directed that they be given meaningful review of their convictions and sentences, the Bush administration reacted by withdrawing from the protocol. A law professor quoted by *The New York Times* said 'it is a sore loser kind of move. If we cannot win, we are not going to play'.

More recently, Iran challenged in the International Court of Justice the re-imposition of sanctions by the United States following its decision to unilaterally withdraw from the Iran nuclear deal known as the Joint Comprehensive Plan of Action (JCPOA). And Palestine brought a claim in the court contending that the United States' decision to relocate its embassy in Israel to Jerusalem violated the Vienna Convention on Diplomatic Relations. The convention requires that a state's capital must be on its own territory and the longstanding position of the United Nations Security Council has been that Jerusalem is not the sovereign territory of the state of Israel. In each case, Washington reacted by withdrawing from the respective treaty or convention by which it had previously consented to the jurisdiction of the court in such disputes. President Trump's national security advisor conceded that the two withdrawals had 'less to do with Iran and the Palestinians than with the continued consistent policy of the United States to reject the jurisdiction' of the International Court of Justice.

While the United States once supported the International Court of Justice, then changed its mind, its attitude to the International Criminal Court has been largely hostile from inception. The Rome Statute, which established the court, was adopted by a vote of 120 to 7 at a diplomatic conference in Rome in 1998. The seven countries that voted against the treaty were Iraq, Israel, Libya, China, Qatar, Yemen and the United States.

Although the United States subsequently signed the treaty, it did not ratify it and later curiously purported to 'unsign' it. In contrast, 123 states have signed and ratified the Rome Statute. The last to do so was Malaysia. All of the leading countries of Europe and the former British Commonwealth have ratified the treaty.

No one can reasonably deny that the object of the International Criminal Court is laudable: to bring to justice the perpetrators – from any country – of the worst crimes known to humankind such as war crimes, crimes against humanity, genocide and crimes of aggression. The court does not have a roving commission. Its jurisdiction applies only where a state is itself unable or unwilling to prosecute its own nationals. Yet the opposition of the United States to the International Criminal Court has become virulent to the point of hysteria. The official American position, announced by the National Security Advisor John Bolton in September 2018, was laden with threats:

> If the court comes after us, Israel or other US allies, we will not sit quietly. We will take the following steps, among others:
> – We will negotiate even more binding, bilateral agreements to prohibit nations from surrendering US personnel to the ICC...
> – We will respond against the ICC and its personnel...We will ban its judges and prosecutors from entering the United States. We will sanction their funds in the US financial system, and we will prosecute them in the US criminal system. We will do the same for any company or state that assists an ICC investigation of Americans.

- We will take note if any countries cooperate with ICC investigations of the United States and its allies, and we will remember that cooperation when setting US foreign assistance, military assistance, and intelligence sharing levels.
- We will consider taking steps in the UN Security Council to constrain the court's sweeping powers, including that the ICC does not exercise jurisdiction over Americans...

This bullying diatribe against individual judges, the court, companies and countries who dared to cooperate with the International Criminal Court was, in the words of a British observer, the 'unacceptable face of American exceptionalism'. A more reasoned, but equally caustic, response came from the American diplomat David Scheffer, who was his country's first ambassador-at-large for war crimes issues. Scheffer led the American negotiating team in the United Nations talks on the International Criminal Court and signed the Rome Statute on behalf of the United States. His words were telling but they appear to have had little effect:

The Bolton speech today isolates the United States from international criminal justice and severely undermines our leadership in bringing perpetrators of atrocity crimes to justice elsewhere in the world.

The double standard set forth in his speech will likely play well with authoritarian regimes, which will resist accountability for atrocity crimes and ignore international efforts to advance the rule of law.

> This was a speech soaked in fear and Bolton
> sounded the message, once again, that the United States
> is intimidated by international law and multilateral
> organizations. I saw not strength but weakness conveyed
> today by the Trump administration.

Even before the position announced in September 2018, the United States had gone to extraordinary lengths to prevent the prosecution of Americans by the International Criminal Court. In any given case, it could easily do so by launching its own investigation of the suspect, thereby removing the jurisdiction of the court, which applies only when a state is unable or unwilling to prosecute its own citizens. Instead, the Bush administration passed the American Service-Members' Protection Act, which allows the United States to take all means necessary and appropriate, including force, to 'free US or allied personnel detained by or on behalf of the International Criminal Court'. It amounts to authorisation of the use of military force to liberate any American or allied citizen being held by the court in The Hague. International diplomats wryly refer to this legislative exceptionalism, with its imagery of US Navy SEALS being parachuted into the Netherlands, as 'The Hague Invasion Act'.

Trade, Tariffs & WTO

The same idea that the United States is 'intimidated by international law' – to use the words of Ambassador Scheffer – emerges from its stance toward the World Trade Organisation (WTO). The world economy has never been as closely integrated as it is today. The international trade in goods and services alone has doubled as a share of world GDP since the mid-1980s. The WTO, which has 164 member states representing 98 per cent of global GDP and 95 per cent of all global trade, serves an important function in ensuring that trade relations are conducted fairly. It represents the 'rules-based order' for international trade, which it enforces by agreed trade rules and an agreed process for the binding resolution of trade disputes between nations.

In earlier times, trade relations were determined by relative power, which ensured that smaller and less powerful nations had little protection against protectionism, economic nationalism and bullying. This system was widely criticised as 'economically wrong-headed and arbitrary, subjecting trade policy to the vagaries of domestic lobbying and international power relations rather than the rule of law'. The United States was a founding proponent of the WTO and 'one of the main drivers of the multilateral approach'. At the outset, it pressed for a binding dispute resolution system with three-member panels of independent arbiters and an appellate body consisting of judges drawn from member countries. And in due course, it became 'the most prolific user of the WTO's dispute settlement system'. Many hundreds of trade disputes have been resolved. The trend has been that the complaining government usually wins. As at 2017, 'The US has won 91% of the cases it has filed in the WTO and lost 84% of those filed against it. Its overall batting average is .500.'

But attitudes have changed and the United States has grown weary. Washington bridles more than ever against adverse WTO decisions, complains about WTO judges and publicly denigrates the WTO. It wants a return to the old days of negotiated solutions and diplomatic coercion – on the basis that 'the US may be able to get more by throwing its weight around in small negotiations than it can in broader deals or in open litigation' in the WTO. Former Australian ambassador in Asia Trevor Wilson put it bluntly when he explained the current crisis in international trade:

> The main reason is the US decision that it will no longer accept any external judgment on US policies: for example, that its domestic subsidies are wrong, that its labour policies should conform with international norms, that it should recognise widely-accepted intellectual property protections, that it should contribute to international climate change programs...

Washington is seeking to undermine the WTO, as it has done with the International Criminal Court. In pursuit of its objective, it has adopted a deliberately destructive policy of 'strangling the WTO dispute settlement system by refusing to appoint new judges to its appellate body'. Since 2017, American officials have blocked all appointments of any new WTO judge as the terms of existing judges expire. It says it is doing so because 'the systemic concerns that we have identified remain unaddressed'. The so-called 'systemic concerns' have an air of contrivance about them. They are procedural rather than substantive. The consequence is a slow death. Three judges are required for each appeal. If there are not three judges, the appeal system will grind to a halt. And without the appeal system, the process for the resolution of international trade disputes by the WTO will become inoperable because panel decisions cannot be adopted until an appeal has been resolved. As a report from the Centre for Strategic and International Studies explained:

Accordingly, once the Appellate Body no longer has
a quorum, any member could block the enforcement
of a panel report simply by filing an appeal. With the
WTO's formal appeals process and its ability to issue
binding rulings paralyzed, countries might abandon the
multilateral system altogether and resort to unilateral
retaliatory measures to settle trade disputes.

This is what the Trump administration wants. Its trade war against China, in particular its dramatic tariff increases, is an example of such 'resort to unilateral retaliatory measures'. And unless Washington agrees to the appointment of new judges, China's complaints against the United States in the WTO in response to the unilateral tariff increases will be unable to be finally resolved. The cause of this behaviour is Washington's all-consuming fear of China. Trump's presidential assistant, close advisor and director of trade and manufacturing policy is Peter Navarro. Navarro's books include *Death by China*, *Crouching Tiger* and *The Coming China Wars*. Their content is as alarmist as their titles. The institutional fear of China in Washington is part of the reason why the United States no longer wishes to play by the WTO rules. It is a reaction to China's competitive economic ascendancy.

As is well known, China's rise since joining the WTO in 2001 has been phenomenal. It has developed the world's largest banking sector, second largest stock market and third largest bond market. It has become the major buyer of resources in the world, the world's largest exporter of goods, the world's largest trading nation, the world's largest manufacturer and the world's largest holder of foreign currency reserves. There may well be a legitimate argument that China and other countries like India, despite their lower per capita GDP, no longer deserve the favourable treatment to which their classification as a 'developing country' under the WTO rules entitles them. The resolution of that debate is still to come.

But Washington's tactic of singling out China for massive unilateral tariff increases is 'trashing the global economic system and the rules and norms the US has championed in the post-war era'. The most important principle of the WTO is that 'countries cannot normally discriminate between their trading partners'. It means that if tariffs are low, as they generally are in the United States, the same low rate must apply to all countries – not all but one. Until recently, the average American tariff rate on industrial imports was 2 per cent. But by late 2019, many tariffs on Chinese goods were in excess of 20 per cent.

The only possible justification under the WTO rules for such discriminatory tariff increases against China lies in the 'national security' exception of the General Agreement on Tariffs and Trade. But it could hardly apply and it is not entirely clear that the Trump administration cares. Its invocation of national security to justify increased steel tariffs against Canada was fanciful. The national security exception allows a country to take 'any action which it considers necessary for the protection of its essential security interests' but only insofar as they relate to 'fissionable nuclear materials' or 'the traffic in arms, ammunition and implements of war' or which are necessary because of 'war or other emergency in international relations'. Even if Washington invokes the last item, it is far from obvious that there is an 'emergency' with China; and there is no war. In any event, whether there is an emergency or not is a matter for the WTO to determine, not the United States.

There will never be a determination, however, unless Washington is prepared to release its deadlock on the WTO's dispute resolution process. In the meantime, the European Union and Canada are attempting to work around Washington's obduracy by setting up their own 'multilateral investment court' presided over by retired WTO judges. This is what the *Financial Times* chief economics writer, Martin Wolf, recommended: 'If the US succeeds in rendering the dispute system inquorate, the other members could agree to abide by an informal mechanism instead'.

But Washington is not interested. In the words of the former United States labour secretary Robert Reich: 'Trump wants to abandon the rules of the World Trade Organisation – giving him authority to raise tariffs without congressional consent, isolating America, and playing into Putin's and Xi's vision of ultra-nativist nationalism'. And in the opinion of Shiro Armstrong, the director of the East Asian Bureau of Economic Research at the Australian National University: 'The era of a rules-based trade is ending. The US has gone from underwriting the rules for the past 70 years to becoming their biggest threat'. It appears that Washington may not have entirely abandoned the WTO, at least when it suits its political interests not to do so. In January 2020, it cooperated with Japan and Europe to put forward proposals to the WTO – clearly directed at China – to curb excessive state subsidies that are said to be distorting the worldwide economy.

Economic Sanctions

Another aspect of American unilateralism is its increasing resort to unilateral economic sanctions – without multilateral support, regardless of the position of the United Nations and sometimes in defiance of its resolutions. Massive unilateral tariff increases such as those directed at China are just a form of economic sanction. Sanctions in general have become a 'policy tool of choice for the United States in the post–Cold War world'. They are a form of intervention but their legitimacy can sometimes be doubtful and their propensity to cause abuse is obvious.

Secondary sanctions raise even more acute problems. They are extra-territorial measures directed from Washington that threaten to cut off foreign individuals or companies from the United States financial system if they trade with a sanctioned entity or country – even if none of that conduct touches the United States directly. A recent policy brief issued by the European Council on Foreign Relations expresses the view that 'Many European officials worry that secondary sanctions are increasingly addictive for both the White House and the US Congress'. There is no doubt that China and Russia share the same view.

The effect of broadly based economic sanctions is to impose indiscriminate suffering and deprivation on the innocent citizens of foreign countries. In war, civilians cannot be targeted but in the case of broad economic sanctions, civilians are the target – despite the protestations of Washington officials that they have no quarrel with, for example, the people of Iran or Cuba or North Korea or even Russia. The United Nations Human Rights Council – from which the United States has chosen to withdraw – has repeatedly resolved, by majority, to condemn such unilateral coercive measures on the ground that broadly based 'economic sanctions demonstrably cause death, aggravate economic crises, disrupt the production and distribution of food and medicine, constitute a push factor generating emigration, and lead to violations of human rights'. It might be thought that these consequences are hardly open to doubt.

Apart from their practical effect, the real point of principle about unilateral economic sanctions is that they are inconsistent with the collective approach established by the Charter of the United Nations. They violate its basic principles. The Charter gives the United Nations Security Council the power to impose sanctions in cases of an actual or threatened breach of peace and security. It does not authorise individual states to do so in accordance with their own varied prejudices, political objectives and cultural obsessions. The conduct of war is constrained by the Charter. So also is, or should be, the unilateral imposition of broadly based economic sanctions by individual states. Such sanctions are, after all, a form of economic warfare. Often they are little more than an attempt at economic asphyxiation. Washington has used them in an attempt to achieve regime collapse and regime change. The attempt to strangle Chile in 1973 is a past example of such extremism directed from Washington. North Korea, Cuba and Iran are current and continuing examples. In the latter two cases, the United States is out of line with most of the rest of the world. And the sanctions have not had the desired effect.

Cubans call the American embargo on their country 'El Bloqueo' – the blockade. It has its origins in the Cold War but can no longer be supported on a rational basis, whatever personal views Americans may have about the Cuban government or the legacy of Fidel Castro. The United Nations General Assembly has been robust in its criticism of the American sanctions against Cuba. Year after year, for more than a quarter of a century now, the General Assembly has voted to call on the United States to end its harmful and idiosyncratic embargo on

Cuba. It is the only country that imposes sanctions on Cuba. Nearly every other country in the world has supported the repeated resolutions of the General Assembly. Washington does not care. The November 2018 resolution was passed by 189 countries in favour and 2 against. The only two opponents were the United States and Israel.

The legislation passed by the United States Congress authorising sanctions against Cuba is masked in titles such as the 'Cuban Democracy Act' and the 'Cuban Liberty and Democracy Solidarity Act'. Their objective is to maintain sanctions on Cuba as long as its government refuses to move toward 'democratization and greater respect for human rights'. They are an attempt to change the political system of a sovereign country. One piece of legislation passed by Congress purports to penalise foreign companies that do business in Cuba by preventing them from doing business in the United States. This has only caused friction, resulting in Canada and the European Union passing their own legislation making it unlawful for companies to comply with US sanctions boycotting Cuba. Old-fashioned ideological extremism is part of the problem. John Bolton justified the sanctions against Cuba as a way of ending 'the glamorisation of socialism and communism'.

Washington will not accept the lesson of the International Court of Justice – that it is beyond contemplation that one state could intervene in the affairs of another simply because the other state 'has opted for a particular ideology or political system'. Fifteen years ago, George Shultz, who served as secretary of state under President Reagan, called the continuing embargo on Cuba 'insane'. And Pulitzer Prize-winning journalist Nicholas Kristof wrote in *The New York Times* that 'It has been 60 years since Fidel Castro marched into Havana, so it is time for both Cuba and the United States to grow up. Let's let Cuba be a normal country again'. Reason has not prevailed. The United States is not interested in what other nations think or the United Nations General Assembly resolves.

Iran is another extreme example. President Trump's sanctions are driven by a politically motivated aversion to the Iran nuclear deal – to which the Obama administration agreed – and fuelled by an almost obsessive determination to confront Iran. The United States has ignored the conclusions of the International Atomic Energy Agency (IAEA) and its own intelligence assessments, isolated itself and antagonised its European allies, let alone China and Russia. The IAEA is actually an American idea. It was established in 1957 on the urging of President Eisenhower. Its first director general was a former US congressman. It now has 171 member states, including all major countries in the world. It is independent, autonomous, highly reputable and has been responsible for verifying and monitoring Iran's nuclear-related commitments. Its verification processes are said to constitute 'the most robust verification system in existence anywhere in the world'.

In December 2015, the IAEA concluded that Iran had long ago abandoned any pretensions to a nuclear weapons program and that the case against it was closed. The report stated that the last time Iran conducted activities relevant to the development of a nuclear device was before the end of 2003 and that, even then, 'these activities did not advance beyond feasibility and scientific studies, and the acquisition of certain relevant technical competences and capabilities'. The report added that since 2009 there had been no credible indications of such activities by Iran whatsoever. Washington received the same intelligence from its own agencies. A key judgment of the United States 2007 National Intelligence Estimate was to similar effect: 'We judge with high confidence that in Fall 2003, Tehran halted its nuclear weapons program'.

The Iran nuclear deal is a binding agreement between Iran and the world's major powers – China, Russia, the United Kingdom, the United States, France, Germany and the European Union. It was entered into following clearance from the IAEA. It is not a treaty and no party has a legal right to withdraw. Yet in May 2018, in breach of its terms, the United States announced its unilateral withdrawal and the imposition of a 'maximum pressure' campaign against Iran. The maximum pressure includes the re-instatement of economy-wide sanctions designed to 'crash' the Iranian economy. Until the withdrawal by the United States, the deal was working. And Iran's compliance had been verified by both the IAEA and American intelligence. By late 2018, the IAEA had 'verified 12 times that Iran has abided by the terms' of the nuclear deal. And as late as January 2019, the Worldwide Threat Assessment by the United States Director of National Intelligence confirmed that 'We continue to assess that Iran is not currently undertaking the key nuclear weapons-development activities we judge necessary to produce a nuclear device'.

Despite these assurances, the United States withdrew from the deal and re-imposed economic sanctions on Iran, increasing them further in March 2020 as Iran reeled from the COVID-19 pandemic. The sanctions are causing hardship, social disruption and currency devaluation, as they are intended to do. They are also fuelling further distrust and enmity toward the United States and making it more, not less, likely that Iran will develop nuclear weapons. The United States does not appear to care, or to recognise the consequences. When Iran successfully sued the United States in the International

Court of Justice and obtained orders requiring Washington to lift the sanctions that affect the importation of medicine, food and civil aviation products, the Trump administration refused to comply. Instead, it withdrew from the treaty that formed the basis of the ruling. Meanwhile, Iran has been carrying out a staged reduction in its commitment to the nuclear deal, under the supervision of the IAEA, in the hope of at least forcing Europe and the other parties to the agreement to comply with their obligations. So far, the reductions are reversible. Iran and the other parties want the deal to work but the United States clearly does not.

Of broader effect are Washington's secondary sanctions against foreign companies and individuals doing business with Iran. The secondary sanctions – all in the name of United States foreign policy – have led to criticism, resentment and huge financial losses by innocent non-Iranian third parties. The negative reaction from affected companies and countries presages the beginnings of a fragmentation of the dominant US financial system. According to Bloomberg and the European Council on Foreign Relations, the estimated fallout to European businesses resulting from sanctions by the United States on Iran amounts to multibillion-dollar losses. They include $1.5 billion for Siemens on a railway contract with Iran; $2 billion for Total on its investment in the South Pars gas field; and $19 billion for Airbus on its contract with Iran Air. They are not the only businesses that have suffered losses. Even the popular Italian coach of the much-loved Tehran football team, Esteghlal, was forced to resign because the American sanctions 'led to his Italian bank freezing his account'.

Washington's immense power to cause such damage arises because of its broad control over international banking transactions, primarily through the SWIFT system, which relies on a network of correspondent banks. SWIFT stands for Society for Worldwide Interbank Financial Telecommunications. It links more than 11,000 financial institutions in more than 200 countries. The apex of the worldwide correspondent system is the New York Federal Reserve Bank, which is controlled and regulated by American banking authorities. The flow of global financial platforms through the United States enables it to 'weaponize' sanctions. European businesses have a special vulnerability because of the substantial integration of Europe's financial markets with the larger American market. Even small- and medium-sized enterprises that may have no direct exposure to the US market still need to use banks that want to retain access to the US dollar, US financial markets and their US clients.

The financial journalist Stephen Bartholomeusz explained how 'the US uses the dominance of its currency as a weapon':

> The US might account for only 10 percent of the world's trade and 15 percent of the global economy but about a third of countries peg their currency to the dollar to some degree, 50 percent of global trade is invoiced in US dollars, more than 60 percent of the world's foreign exchange reserves are denominated in US dollars and two-thirds of global security issuance is in US dollars...
>
> It's been a key element of America's post-war geopolitical dominance. Its reserve currency status has enabled the US to use the dollar to impose punishing sanctions on countries and individuals.

There is resistance to this extra-territorial overreach, which is administered by the Orwellian-named Office of Foreign Asset Control in Washington. Its eager staff are able to dedicate unparalleled resources to a brew of sanctions, designations, implementation and enforcement in every conceivable corner of the world. A few have urged restraint. United States Treasury Secretary Jack Lew warned four years ago that America's unilateral sanctions risked creating a larger problem:

> The risk that sanctions overreach will ultimately drive
> business activity from the US financial system could
> become more acute if alternatives to the United States as
> a center of financial activity, and to the US dollar as the
> world's preeminent reserve currency, assume a larger role
> in the global financial system...the more we condition use
> of the dollar and our financial system on adherence to
> US foreign policy, the more the risk of migration to other
> currencies and other financial systems in the medium-
> term grows.

This is what is happening. Alternatives to the United States as a centre of financial activity and to the US dollar as the world's pre-eminent reserve currency are now being actively considered in Europe, and gradually implemented in China and Russia. The pushback first emerged in the mid-1990s when the United States Congress imposed extra-territorial sanctions on Cuba, Libya and Iran. European governments lodged a complaint in the WTO and the European Union adopted a 'Blocking Statute', which prohibited compliance by European companies with American sanctions purporting to have extra-territorial effect. Europe has not been alone in objecting to the pressure of such secondary sanctions. For some time, 'China, India, Russia and Turkey have attempted to bypass the impact of such US unilateral measures'.

In response to the latest sanctions on Iran, China set up a financial payments system which runs parallel to US dollar-denominated channels and allows its banks to deal with countries subject to US secondary sanctions. It has established an alternative to SWIFT known as the Cross-Border Inter-Bank Payments System (CIPS) and is also looking closely at possible collaboration with a European special purpose vehicle for trade with Iran known as the Instrument for Supporting Trade Exchanges (INSTEX). INSTEX is not yet effective but it is designed to facilitate non-US dollar transactions and circumvent the traditional global financial platforms that the United States relies upon to enforce its secondary sanctions. The mechanism is the brainchild of Germany, France and the United Kingdom. But in November 2019, six other European countries – Belgium, Denmark, Finland, Sweden, the Netherlands and Norway – announced that they were also joining INSTEX and that, unlike the United States, they 'attach the utmost importance' to the preservation and implementation of the nuclear deal with Iran. Russia, India, Turkey, South Korea and Japan have all expressed interest in participating in INSTEX.

The European Council on Foreign Relations has put forward other wide-ranging recommendations for consideration, which are designed to avoid the effect of secondary sanctions imposed by Washington and reduce dependence on the US dollar and US financial platforms. The suggestions include the creation of an independent replica of SWIFT or the taking of steps to ensure its independence and political neutrality so that it is not restricted by the unilateral measures of the United States.

Another involves the drafting of a new iteration of the European Blocking Statute, to 'pre-empt Washington's introduction of further restrictions on SWIFT', for example in relation to Russian or Chinese banks. Yet another involves pressing for the nationalisation of SWIFT or threatening to do so. A fourth suggestion includes the possibility of connecting European central banks directly to Iranian entities. Other suggestions include the creation of extra-territorial countermeasures that can be imposed defensively against American interests; leading a global dialogue on the use and regulation of sanctions; and significantly strengthening the global role of the euro to facilitate a more multi-polar monetary system.

The last matter is also close to the heart of China and Russia. The European Union is not the only major power that aims to bolster its currency in order to reduce the financial power of the United States and counter its unilateralism. Since 2014, Russia has been busy 'de-dollarising' parts of its financial system and developing its own methods for financial transfers and payments that protect it from harsher US sanctions and the risks of dependency on the US-dominated global financial system. In July 2019, Russia and China agreed that all future settlements between them will be conducted in their respective currencies, taking billions of dollars off the SWIFT network. Russia, like China, has also launched its own domestic alternative to SWIFT known as the System for Transfer of Financial Messages (SPFS). And the Russian central bank is said to be working on a new digital currency, although details are sparse at this stage. China meanwhile not only has its own alternative to the SWIFT system but has sought to elevate the yuan more generally by setting up foreign exchange agreements with other nations and by encouraging the use of the yuan in infrastructure projects under its Belt and Road Initiative.

Dissatisfaction with the United States dollar has reached an inflection point. In January 2020, an article in *The Economist* was headlined 'Dethroning the dollar – America's Aggressive Use of Sanctions Endangers the Dollar's Reign'. The European Council on Foreign Relations has confirmed that 'European countries are now beginning to realise how much they would benefit from reduced dependence on the dollar'. And Mark Carney, former governor of the Bank of England, has said that 'the dollar-centric system won't hold', even floating 'the idea of a network of central-bank digital monies that could serve as a global invoicing currency' – to which America may not be invited. Elvira Nabiullina, the head of Russia's central bank, echoed her British compatriot when she remarked recently, 'I see a global shift in mood. We are gradually moving towards a more multi-currency international monetary system'.

John Maynard Keynes was probably right to resist the American dollar all those years ago at Bretton Woods. And the United States Treasury secretary was probably wise to warn more recently that 'the more we condition use of the dollar and our financial system on adherence to US foreign policy, the more the risk of migration to other currencies and other financial systems in the medium-term grows'. As one commentator observed:

> This strong-arming may have lasting consequences for
> American stewardship of the global economy, which
> has long been based in part on the assumption that
> Washington would not weaponize the dollar's dominance
> in pursuit of purely unilateral aims.

Summits, Arms & Climate

Some other illustrations of modern American unilateralism include the international summits that are no longer collaborative, the arms treaties from which the United States is progressively withdrawing, the climate agreements which it has disavowed and, of course, the United Nations Convention on the Law of the Sea (UNCLOS), to which it has never agreed. The most recent arms treaty withdrawal – from the United Nations Arms Trade Treaty – was announced by President Trump in April 2019 at a meeting of the National Rifle Association. The announcement was greeted with delirious chants of 'USA, USA' from the foot-stomping crowd. The sound effects were eerily similar to those of fascist rallies of a bygone era. This particular cohort of Americans mistakenly thought that withdrawal from the treaty was an endorsement of the principle of universal gun ownership and an assertion of American sovereignty. They had no idea, it would seem, that the treaty had nothing to do with gun ownership by citizens of the United States, and everything to do with the international regulation of the illicit trade in conventional weapons.

The United Nations Arms Trade Treaty neither regulates internal transactions nor interferes with the acquisition of arms by civilians. When the resolution was adopted by an overwhelming majority in the United Nations General Assembly in 2013, only three states opposed it: North Korea, Iran and Syria, although some countries abstained. It was signed by 137 states and ratified by 105 states. The United States signed but never ratified the treaty, and has now, in any event, 'withdrawn' its signature.

Another arms treaty from which the United States has recently withdrawn is the Intermediate-Range Nuclear Forces (INF) Treaty.

This landmark 1987 arms control agreement with Soviet Russia prohibited cruise and ballistic missiles with range capabilities between 500 and 5500 kilometres. It had been substantially effective over a long time although a dispute had arisen in recent years about the range of a particular Russian missile known as the SSC-8. Russia contended, probably cynically, that its range was only 480 kilometres. Washington disagreed, but its complete withdrawal from the treaty was hardly an appropriate response. China was the real reason for the withdrawal; and further United States militarisation of the Asia-Pacific was the real objective.

The Carnegie Endowment for International Peace cited US officials as saying:

> ...the major reason for withdrawing is to contest China's growing military power and assertiveness...the United States needs to deploy conventional ground-based intermediate-range missile systems against China – systems that the INF Treaty prohibits the United States from fielding. And because Beijing is not a party to the treaty, the People's Liberation Army (PLA) has a tremendous advantage.

The movement of the United States away from arms treaties is not just a recent phenomenon. In 2001, President George W Bush announced America's unilateral withdrawal from the Anti-Ballistic Missile (ABM) Treaty. The other parties were Russia and several successor states of the former Soviet Union. The treaty had been proposed originally by the United States and had operated successfully for almost thirty years. Soviet leader Leonid Brezhnev agreed to it in 1972. It limited anti-nuclear missile strategic defensive systems, discouraged the build-up of offensive systems and effectively constrained nuclear proliferation. But President Bush called the treaty a hindrance. The unsurprising consequence of United States withdrawal has been a correlative build-up of Russia's nuclear capabilities.

Then there is the 1996 Comprehensive Nuclear Test Ban Treaty (CTBT). It has been signed by 184 countries and ratified by 168. The United States was never prepared to allow it to come into force and withheld ratification. Only seven other states have refused to sign or ratify the treaty: Iran, Israel, Egypt, India, Pakistan, China and North Korea. The treaty, which was adopted by the United Nations General Assembly, bans all nuclear explosive testing for both civilian and military purposes. Within a few years of the treaty's adoption in the United Nations, the Bush administration stepped even further away from it by announcing a 'nuclear posture review' that included the possibility of resuming nuclear testing and using nuclear weapons in a first-strike attack. Successive United States nuclear posture reviews have continued to move in the opposite direction to nuclear non-proliferation. President Trump even announced that the United States 'must greatly strengthen and expand its nuclear capability' and that it would 'outmatch' and 'outlast' other potential competitors in a nuclear arms race. His 2021 budget request, if accepted by Congress, would cause the US nuclear budget to 'skyrocket'. In contrast, for twenty-six consecutive years, Japan – the only country to experience the explosion of nuclear bombs on its cities – has sponsored a resolution in the United Nations General Assembly calling for the abolition of nuclear weapons. The 2018 version was endorsed by 160 countries and the 2019 version by 148 countries. The United States has never supported the Japanese initiative.

An earlier glaring example of the unwillingness of the United States to follow most of the rest of the world on arms limitation is the first additional protocol to the 1949 Geneva Conventions, which was agreed in 1977. One of the objects of the protocol is the prevention of repetition of the 'area' bombing of German and Japanese cities that was a chilling feature of World War II. Article 51 prohibits indiscriminate and disproportionate bombing, including attacks not limited to specific military targets; attacks that do not distinguish between civilians and military objectives; bombardments that treat cities, towns and villages as a single military objective; and attacks that are 'excessive in relation to the concrete and direct military advantage anticipated'. Despite 174 nations ratifying the protocol, the United States will not agree. The other outliers include Israel, Iran, Pakistan, India and Turkey.

It is a similar story with international attempts to address the effects of climate change. One of the most significant and inspirational international climate treaties was the 1997 Kyoto Protocol. Its premise was that the industrially developed countries (thirty-seven states plus the European Union) had been historically responsible for the rise in global greenhouse emissions and should submit to binding targets to reduce emissions. Developing countries such as China and India were not subject to binding targets in the first five-year commitment period but were required to do their best. This was satisfactory to almost every country in the world, including the collective European Union. A total of 192 parties signed and ratified the Kyoto Protocol. It was almost as close to a working global agreement on climate change that one could hope for – with the exception of the United States.

Only a handful of other countries did not sign and ratify the Kyoto Protocol – minnows such as Andorra, Palestine, Afghanistan and South Sudan. The United States initially signed the protocol, but was never prepared to ratify, and President George W Bush renounced it anyway. Canada withdrew in 2012 at the end of the first commitment period, citing, among other things, the fact that the treaty did not bind the United States. By that stage, even without American participation, the Kyoto Protocol had been a qualified success and laid the foundation for the Paris Climate Agreement.

The Paris Climate Agreement reflects a similar story of American unilateralism. The agreement was made in 2016 and commits all parties to the progressive reduction of greenhouse gas emissions and the maintenance of long-term temperature increases to below 2 degrees Celsius above pre-industrial levels. Each country is required to report on its contribution to the mitigation of global warming but no mechanism compels a party to set a specific target by a particular date. The Paris agreement is effectively a collective statement of international will. On the day it was opened for signature, 174 countries and the European Union signed up. And on 1 April 2016, in what would be considered an unlikely collaboration today, China and the United States issued a joint statement confirming that both countries would sign the agreement.

By 2019, at least 195 parties had signed the Paris agreement and 187 parties had ratified it – representing almost 97 per cent of global greenhouse emissions. However, the support of the United States was brief and temporary – notwithstanding that it represents approximately 15 per cent of global greenhouse emissions and has the world's highest per capita CO_2 emissions. Within seven months of the Paris agreement coming into force,

President Trump announced that the United States would withdraw from it. Washington commenced the formal process of withdrawal precisely on 4 November 2019, the first date on which it was legally entitled to do so. No other country has withdrawn. The destructive consequences of this failure of leadership are multiple. The world-leading climate scientist, physicist and founder of Climate Analytics Dr Bill Hare explained why:

> The US withdrawal is having wide-ranging adverse impacts on the will of countries in both subtle and unsubtle ways. Those countries that never wanted to do anything are now using the opportunity to walk backwards. Many countries that were moving forward are finding that their constituencies, particularly in industry, are now saying the US is out of the game so why should we move forward...Others are simply hiding behind the US and saying we have to wait until the US comes back in before we can do anything. So I am seeing now, for the first time in this process, really extensive damage being caused by the US withdrawal.

International summits reveal another picture of damaging unilateralism by the United States. The G7 summits in particular have lately become 'a bit of a nightmare for all concerned' and the G20 summits not much better. Historically, both the G7 and G20 summits have been critical forums for the world's leading powers to confront crises. Their coordinated message and shared action have helped calm markets during the global financial crisis, spur global recovery and confront the worst of the European debt crisis. And every year since 1975, the G7 participants have issued a joint communiqué following the meeting. That is no longer possible and Washington is to blame.

In 2019, the G7 host, President Macron of France, concluded that an attempt to issue a joint communiqué was pointless given the disagreements with the United States. At the G7 summit in Canada in 2018 hosted by President Trudeau, President Trump's withdrawal from the joint communiqué left that summit in chaos. After the 2019 summit, the American writer Peter Nicholas wrote in *The Atlantic* magazine that 'with Trump at odds with much of the free world, the free world seems to be moving on without him'. A few years earlier, the respected Australian journalist Chris Uhlmann famously described President Trump at the G20 summit in Hamburg in 2017 as an 'uneasy, awkward and lonely figure', who was 'isolated and friendless', whose disastrous foreign policy had 'pressed fast forward on the decline of the United States' and who was himself 'the biggest threat to the values of the west'.

This growing isolation of the United States – on a wide range of issues on which other civilised countries have a broad consensus – has been happening for a considerable time. But it is accelerating in the twenty-first century and it is being hastened by an 'America First' approach to the rest of the world. This approach, perhaps it is a doctrine, was reputedly characterised by one senior White House official in the Trump administration as 'We're America, Bitch'. President Trump's announcement – at the height of the COVID-19 pandemic – of the suspension of US funding to the World Health Organisation is, perhaps, an illustration. Even more troubling – also at the height of the pandemic – was the news that the Trump administration intended to withdraw from the 1992 international treaty known as 'Open Skies', might abandon the nuclear arms reduction treaty known as 'New START' and would spend China and Russia 'into oblivion' on nuclear arms.

Fareed Zakaria was not entirely joking when he wrote:

> Only three countries in the world do not use the metric
> system – Liberia, Myanmar and the United States. For
> America to continue to lead the world, we will have to
> first join it.

PART 4
THE FUTURE

CHAPTER 7

ASIA FIRST
A Changing World

Waging War

A contemporary contrast between America and China is revealing. Former president Jimmy Carter, at the age of ninety-four, understands it. He warned recently that the United States was the 'most warlike nation in the history of the world' and that 'while America waged war all over the world, China was investing its resources into infrastructure projects such as high-speed rail'. In fact, China owns two-thirds of the world's high-speed rail infrastructure and is ahead of schedule to build 30,000 kilometres of high-speed railway line by 2020. Carter then posed the question: 'Do you know how many times China has been at war with anybody since 1979? None. And we have stayed at war', adding that China's 'peace dividend' has allowed and enhanced its economic growth.

The former Singaporean diplomat Kishore Mahbubani, author of the important books *Has the West Lost It?* and *Has China Won?*, made the same point:

> China is the only major power in the world which has
> not gone to war in 40 years, and has not fired a single
> bullet in 30 years. In contrast, in the last year of former
> US president Barack Obama's presidency, the US dropped
> 26,000 bombs on seven countries.

Fareed Zakaria wrote to similar effect:

> [China] has not gone to war since 1979. It has not
> used lethal military force abroad since 1988. Nor has
> it funded or supported proxies or armed insurgents
> anywhere in the world since the early 1980s. That record
> of non-intervention is unique among the world's great
> powers. All the other permanent members of the UN
> Security Council have used force many times in many
> places over the last few decades – a list led, of course, by
> the United States.

The effects of America's constant war-making are still playing out but the diminution in its authority was palpable even before President Trump accelerated the process. While the United States has spent trillions of dollars 'flailing about' in the twenty-first century, invading Iraq, bombing Afghanistan, baiting Russia, sanctioning Iran, raising tariffs on China and assassinating foreign military leaders, most of Asia has moved forward – rapidly and increasingly independently. And despite Washington's preoccupation with China, Asia is much more than China. China represents only one-third of Asia's population; its GDP is only half the GDP of the region; and it represents less than half of the inbound investment into the region. India is actually growing faster than China and the nations of ASEAN – the Association of Southeast Asian Nations – are attracting more foreign investment than China. A World Economic Forum paper in 2019 stated that 'Next year, in purchasing power parity (PPP) terms, Asian economies will become larger than the rest of the world combined for the first time since the 19th century'. PPP terms 'provide a better measure of the *volume* of goods and services produced by an economy as compared to GDP at current market exchange rates, which is a measure of *value*'.

Asian Wave

There is a new wave of Asian growth taking place. Some refer to it as the 'fourth wave' after Japan (the first wave), the 'tiger' economies of South Korea, Taiwan and Singapore (the second wave) and China (the third wave). According to Parag Khanna, author of *The Future is Asian*, the fourth wave Asian countries represent 2.5 billion people; many of their economies are growing faster than the Chinese economy; and every one of them has a younger population than China by median age. China, however, is one of the largest investors in these countries. And their growth is mutually reinforcing.

There should be nothing surprising about the rise of Asia. Asian countries and China in particular have been the dominant economic force in the world for most of the last two millennia, including up to the early modern period from 1400 to 1800. Lord Patten was not the first to recognise that 'for eighteen of the last twenty centuries, China's economy has been the biggest in the world'. The proposition is amply demonstrated in a frequently cited chart by the international consultants McKinsey & Company. It shows the enormous length of time during the last two millennia in which China and India were the world's largest economies, until a decline around 1800 followed by a precipitous drop coinciding with the European industrial revolution.

Western economic superiority is actually only a recent occurrence. And it is not to be conflated with Western-centric beliefs about the significance of ancient Athens and Rome, the benefits of democracy or the supposed superiority of Christianity. A millennium before Athens' Golden Age under Pericles (495–429 BC), the Chinese were casting in bronze and weaving silk. Their inventions and discoveries in the centuries before Christ are a catalogue of wonder. They include, among other remarkable things: acupuncture, ball bearings, the theory of the circulation of blood, cast iron, crop rotation, the crossbow, deep drilling, extendable ladders, the use of natural gas as fuel, the theory of equilibrium, fertilisers, fumigation, geological prospecting, lacquer, malt sugar, topographical maps, paper, polar-equatorial coordinates, porcelain, refraction, the spindle wheel, stringed instruments and vinegar. And when it came to ship-building and maritime exploration, the colossal nine-masted Chinese treasure ships of the early fifteenth century were not to be compared – in size or range of voyaging – with their European counterparts.

Then there were the cities. At the beginning of the sixteenth century, the largest and most important cities in the world were almost all in Asia and the greatest number was in China: Beijing, Hangzhou, Guangzhou and Nanjing among them. Other major global cities in Asia at that time included the Ottoman capital of Constantinople, the Persian city of Tabriz, the Egyptian metropolis of Cairo and the Indian cities of Vijayanagara and Gaur. Paris was smaller than almost all of them and London was insignificant, with a population of only about 50,000 people mostly living within its medieval walls. By that stage, all of 'the principal civilisations of Asia had attained a level of technical and economic development superior to that of Europe'. Before 1800, the Chinese Ming and Qing empires, and the empires of the Mughals, Persians and Ottomans all 'carried much greater political and even military weight than any or all of Europe'. And until that turning point, the major economies of Asia were more advanced than any of sixteenth-century Portugal, seventeenth-century Netherlands or eighteenth-century Britain.

Observations about the wealth of China used to be a common theme in centuries past. Ibn Battuta, the fourteenth-century Moroccan scholar, geographer and traveller, recorded that 'nowhere in the world are there to be found people richer than the Chinese'. While Adam Smith, the Scottish economist and philosopher, acknowledged the economic superiority of China in his seminal work *The Wealth of Nations* (1776), noting that Europe was a late arrival in the development of the wealth of nations and that 'China is much richer than any European country'. A similar observation was made by the French Jesuit historian and China specialist Father Du Halde – to whom Voltaire attributed 'the widest and the best description the empire of China has had worldwide'. Writing at a similar time to Adam Smith, Du Halde remarked:

> ...the particular riches of every province [of China], and the ability of transporting merchandise by means of

rivers and canals, have rendered the empire always very flourishing...The trade carried on within China is so great, that all of Europe is not to be compared therewith.

Decline & Fall

But as the eighteenth century came to a close, the long period of Asian, especially Chinese, economic pre-eminence began to falter. The European industrial revolution and the expansion of European colonialism dramatically shifted the balance of power in favour of the Western world, profoundly altering European perceptions and promoting its cultural and racial superiority. The change began to take effect during the late Enlightenment, after the reshaping of the world at the end of the Seven Years War in 1763. In the long sweep of history, however, Western dominance has been an aberration of short duration. The tide is now turning again. It is obvious, at least to those who usually know best, such as investors, if not always to Western politicians, that 'The Asian Century has arrived'. The same ingredients of 'industrial capitalism, internal stability, and search for global markets that propelled Europe's imperial ascendancy and the United States' imperial status are converging in Asia'. The re-emergence of Asia is a fundamental structural shift.

This sobering fact is the defining truth of our times. The cycle of Western domination of the world is in decline. It is coming to a natural end. The Western share of the global economy is shrinking and will continue to do so. This is 'inevitable and unstoppable'. Few major Western leaders have yet displayed the courage to acknowledge it. But as Kishore Mahbubani has observed, 'Their populations, on the other hand, can feel these large changes in their bones, and in the job markets. This, in part, explains supposedly aberrant – at least to elites – events like Trump and Brexit'. President Trump's rust belt base understands well the statement by the economist Branko Milanovic that the great winners of the redistribution of global wealth 'have been the Asian poor and middle classes; the great losers, the lower middle classes of the rich world'.

Consider this – since the end of World War II, the ordinary working-class person in America has never had it so bad. RW Johnson, emeritus fellow of Magdalen College, Oxford, explained why:

> At the heart of the problem is the stagnation of real wages...Between 1948 and 1973, productivity rose by 96.7 percent and real wages by 91.3 percent, almost exactly in step...But from 1973 to 2015 – the era of globalization, when many of those jobs vanished abroad – productivity rose 73.4 percent while wages rose by only 11.1 percent...On average in 1965 an American CEO earned 20 times what a worker did. By 2013, on average, the number was 296 times.

And alarmingly, at least until the COVID-19 pandemic blew it up, the capitalisation of the United States stock market was massively out of alignment with GDP. In the ten years after the global financial crisis, US stock market capitalisation rose 307 per cent while GDP grew only 50 per cent. The disparity was never sustainable.

Niccoló Machiavelli famously warned that 'there is nothing more difficult...more perilous to conduct...than to take the lead in the introduction of a new order of things'. A 'new order of things' is happening before our eyes. Among many indicators, since 2015 the economies of the E7 emerging states (China, India, Brazil, Mexico, Russia, Indonesia and Turkey) have overtaken those of the powerful G7 states (Canada, France, Germany, Italy, Japan, United Kingdom and United States). And with some exceptions in countries like Iraq, Afghanistan, Syria and Libya where the United States has sought to impose military solutions through invasion, bombing, sanctions and assassinations, the world's underprivileged are getting better, healthier, more literate and more prosperous. No one would have predicted in 1990 that in the next twenty-five years, 'world hunger would decline by 40 percent, child mortality would halve and extreme poverty would fall by three quarters'.

China Inc.

China is the tip of the Asian spear. In recent years, its GDP has accounted for almost a third of global growth. Everyone knows the famous quip by Napoleon Bonaparte 'Let China sleep, for when she wakes she will shake the world'. Jonathan Spence, the prolific English-born China historian at Yale, put it aptly fifty years ago: 'China, which once surpassed the West, then almost succumbed to it, now offers to the world her own solutions'. China's return to global economic dominance is, in large measure, an inevitable consequence of the weight of numbers and markets. Its population of 1.4 billion is more than four times that of the United States and close to double that of the West – North America, the United Kingdom, Western Europe, Australia and New Zealand; and its authoritarian government has a less expansive sense of its global responsibilities. No one seriously disputes the fact that China will be the richest and most powerful country in the world in the twenty-first century. It will surpass the United States as the future global economic hegemon.

An authoritative recent prediction was that, barring unforeseen wars and economic crises – or black swan events such as game-changing pandemics – China's economy could be worth $42.4 trillion by 2030 compared with $24 trillion for the United States – in other words 77 per cent larger. A pre-COVID-19 chart adopted by the *Financial Times'* Martin Wolf, which predicts world GDP output based on the International Monetary Fund's forecasts in purchasing power parity terms, shows China returning to the global dominance of past centuries by 2022, surpassing the United States and Europe, both of which will progressively decline in relative terms. The pandemic will result in global economic contraction but China, as well as most of east Asia, is likely to recover faster and fare better. For those hopeful of China's economic decline, Westad cautioned in 2019:

> Today, China's economic power relative to the United
> States exceeds what the Soviet Union's relative power
> was by a factor of two or three. Although that growth
> has now slowed, those who believe that China will soon
> go the way of Japan and fall into economic stagnation
> are almost certainly wrong…China has enough of an
> untapped domestic market to fuel the country's economic
> rise for years to come.

Washington's reaction is, of course, to do everything within its power to blunt China's rise. A significant number of policymakers is investing time, resources and money into plotting and planning how to undermine China's economic progress. It is an article of faith – almost a creed – inspired by a belief that what is good for China cannot be good for the United States; fuelled by a national defence strategy that insists that China is an 'adversary' and a strategic enemy; and rooted in an America First idea that trade deficits are detrimental. And as the COVID-19 pandemic hits the United States harder than any other country, many in Washington are stoking the fires of conflict, and base populism, with renewed vigour.

China's economy does face significant challenges and uncertainties in the short and medium term as it deals with an adverse demographic trend, high debt levels, the transition from high speed to high quality production and from manufacturing to service industries. Changes of fortune such as the 2020 pandemic add an extra layer of uncertainty and complication. But President Trump's advisors are like King Canute's courtiers, who loyally believed that their monarch could reverse the tide. Mahbubani was blunt: 'The biggest act of strategic folly that America could commit would be to make a futile attempt to derail China's successful development'. China's pace may well be constrained but its long-term trajectory is unlikely to deviate.

Some critics of China adopt a moral stance, often a dangerously simplistic one. China's high level of state control over individual freedoms may be inimical to Westerners but to those who condemn China as 'nasty, authoritarian and communist' or even more remarkably as 'fundamentally evil', there is another side. In fact, some would say, perhaps with reasonable justification, that the United States is 'nasty, capitalist and unequal'. As Parag Khanna put it: 'American millennials have grown up with a war on terror, declining median income, mounting racial tension, arbitrary gun violence and political demagoguery'. He might have added poor health care and rampant inequality. To this, Khanna contrasted the experience of billions of young Asians, Chinese included, growing up in the past two decades, who have 'experienced geopolitical stability, rapidly expanding prosperity, and surging national pride'.

Lord Patten's approach is preferable. His conclusion was that 'China's economic progress is good, not bad, for America, Europe and the rest of the world' – to which he added a note of pragmatism, adopting a Chinese aphorism: 'What you cannot avoid, welcome'.

The Singaporean Prime Minister, Lee Hsien Loong, also tried to explain that China's economic progress 'is good, not bad' for the world:

China's development and success have benefited the world too. China has become a massive production and manufacturing base, lowering costs for the world's producers, first for labour-intensive goods, and now increasingly for high value and technology-intensive production. It is also a huge market, importing everything from commodities and electronic equipment to aircraft and fine wines...China's growth has shifted the strategic balance and the economic centre of gravity of the world, and the shift continues.

Whatever side one takes, it must be conceded that in a single generation, China's government has lifted many hundreds of millions of people out of poverty and transformed their lives for the better. It is 'the largest increase in human material welfare in history...better food, better housing, better education and health care – all things that we recognise as having real moral weight'. A December 2019 Lowy Institute report reiterated the same message:

> ...life expectancy and literacy rates [in China] have
> increased sharply, the number of people living in abject
> poverty has fallen by more than 800 million, and
> millions of households have moved into relative affluence.
> China's impact on the world economy has also been
> substantial, with China now the largest trading partner
> for almost 60 countries...

It is, of course, beyond argument that an essential feature of any sovereign society is the security and integrity of its institutions, defence systems and communications networks. We are entitled to expect nothing less. China sometimes brazenly overreaches against perceived unfriendly states but there is nothing new in such behaviour among the great powers. The recent caution by Linda Jakobson, founding director of the independent policy institute China Matters, to all concerned Western citizens, and especially to those in defence and security establishments, is salient:

> China is going to be a trendsetter, a standard-setter in a
> whole host of areas we have not even thought about. This
> is a country we need to engage with deeply *whether we
> like them or not.* Many in the security establishment who
> have been quite active in the public arena, simply do not
> want to acknowledge this. [emphasis added]

The reality is that the rise of China is the biggest shift in international settings in modern times – more significant than the collapse of the British Empire, the decolonisation of Asia or the dissolution of the Soviet Union. But according to future specialists like McKinsey & Company, the future of Asia is 'no longer just a story about China'. Their 2019 report concludes that 'This is not a China-only story'. The report added: 'It is not about if and when Asia will rise, but how Asia is going to lead'. In the decades ahead, the authors write, 'Asian economies will go from participating in global trade and innovation flows to *determining their shape and direction*' (emphasis added).

Belt & Road Initiative

The new Asian narrative represents a broader, deeper story. China is a central pillar but not the sum of Asian economic growth. Intra-Asian trade now exceeds Asian trade with the rest of the world. And trade between Europe and Asia 'now far exceeds either of their trade with the United States'. And Asia is becoming more interconnected – a phenomenon that is being facilitated by China's Belt and Road Initiative (BRI), which has so far – at least until 2020 – led to major improvements in the construction, coordination and harmonisation of infrastructure across Asia including the Central Asian states, as well as Africa, Latin America and parts of Europe. The US Council on Foreign Relations called the BRI 'one of the most ambitious infrastructure investment projects ever conceived'. And President Xi Jinping called it 'the project of the century'. Many agree with him – although the economic contraction resulting from the COVID-19 pandemic is having a dampening effect as the recovery of China's huge manufacturing capacity takes priority.

Given the ambition and ubiquity of the BRI, it is difficult to be precise, but on one account, its visionary economic corridors have captured the imagination of 'more than 160 countries and international organisations' with whom 'more than 190 cooperation agreements' have been signed. This includes recent additions New Zealand and the Australian state of Victoria. British historian Peter Frankopan concluded that more than eighty countries representing over 63 per cent of the world's population were part of the initiative. And the Council on Foreign Relations counted 'more than sixty countries...and two-thirds of the world's population'.

The BRI's actual and prospective economic corridors across Asia cover a large energy and resource-rich part of the world. They are impressive in their scope but their geographic obviousness is breathtaking. A World Bank document described them as 'six corridors of integration'. When completed, they will spread like superhighways from Chinese industrial centres and ports in the east across Asia to Europe, Indochina and the Indian Ocean. Just as all roads once led to Rome, there is a sense in which all roads may one day lead to Beijing. A combined population of 4.4 billion people live along these 'new Silk Roads' between China and the Eastern Mediterranean. The more the BRI becomes a multilateral exercise, the more it connects not just Asian countries to China but also all Asians to each other.

One economic corridor, sometimes referred to as the 'Silk Road Economic Belt', traverses Central Asia and links China with the Turkish port of Istanbul through Kazakhstan, Kyrgyzstan, Tajikistan, Uzbekistan, Turkmenistan and Iran. A northern corridor connects with Russia through Mongolia and Siberia. Another, known as the 'China–Pakistan Economic Corridor', connects the free economic zone of Kashgar in Xinjiang province with the Pakistan deep-water port of Gwadar on the Arabian Sea. Another is proposed to link the Indochina Peninsula through Vietnam, Thailand, Laos, Cambodia, Myanmar, Malaysia and Singapore. And another is proposed to link China, Bangladesh, India and Myanmar.

The BRI is not without its difficulties. The current worldwide economic contraction is just the latest. But the concept has the potential – it has probably already done so – to elevate entire economies into the twenty-first century. There is no shortage of naysayers, especially American ones. The US State Department has been conducting a worldwide diplomatic campaign against the BRI. But the opposition of the United States is politically motivated – part of its undeclared war against China. India is traditionally wary of China and has so far resisted joining, but it was a founding member of the China-led Asian Infrastructure Investment Bank (AIIB), which funds many BRI projects. India is also the bank's second largest shareholder and biggest borrower. Other countries more conventionally aligned with the United States, such as Japan and Australia, currently adhere to the Washington line that the BRI will enhance Chinese hegemony and diminish American influence, although there are signs of Japanese ambivalence.

There is no doubt that China will eventually benefit economically, and probably also strategically from the BRI. On one respected view, the BRI is fundamentally 'market-based, not driven by ideology': though some of its projects may be loss-leading, 'it is a commercial initiative, not a charitable one'. In President Xi's words, the BRI will 'boost mutual understanding, mutual respect and mutual trust among different countries'. It is hard to disagree if the investments produce a beneficial outcome at a reasonable price. But not all the results have been uniform. And the global economic downturn will further expose more vulnerable economies.

In response to legitimate concerns about excessive debt burdens assumed by some participating countries, China reacted in 2019 by formulating a 'Debt Sustainability Framework', which it largely borrowed from the World Bank and the International Monetary Fund. It has also demonstrated a willingness to renegotiate some deals and has accepted 'numerous unilateral debt write-downs and contract terminations...[for] it fears the backlash that would ensue if it does not show generosity'. And it has pledged to address shortcomings evident in some projects. This is part of the recalibration that Xi Jinping announced at the second Belt and Road Forum. Further recalibration and more constraints will inevitably follow from the global economic contraction. China will 'no longer be in a position to shower BRI partners with loans'. And instead of 'building anything that is buildable, new BRI projects will probably be more strategically chosen'. For the time being, according to the American business magazine *Forbes*:

> Work has stopped along the China-Pakistan Economic Corridor, Cambodia's Sihanoukville Special Economic Zone has come to a standstill, the Payra coal power plant in Bangladesh has been delayed and projects across Indonesia, Malaysia and Myanmar have been stuck in holding patterns.

As projects sit idle, loan repayment schedules are being adjusted. But the idea that most BRI projects have created a debt trap for vulnerable countries is more propaganda than fact. The case most often cited is the Sri Lankan port at Hambantota, which was leased to China Merchant Port Holdings Limited for ninety-nine years in 2017 for a price of $1.2 billion. As at 2019, Sri Lanka's debt repayments to China EXIM Bank relating to Hambantota port amounted to only around 5 per cent of the country's total annual foreign debt repayments. The reality is that Sri Lanka leased out Hambantota port largely due to a persistent balance of payments crisis that 'went well beyond China'. The money obtained 'through leasing Hambantota port was used to strengthen Sri Lanka's dollar reserves in 2017–18, particularly in light of the huge external debt servicing due to the maturity of international sovereign bonds...' For the same reason, the Sri Lankan government has been considering leasing the Rajapaksa Airport to India.

The size and ambitious nature of the BRI, and the financial inexperience and enthusiasm of some poorer participant countries, have inevitably contributed to problems of execution and implementation. Many projects have prospered. Others have been stalled, cancelled or deferred. Others have had their terms revised. That is business. The looming economic crisis will cause 'project failures, insolvency and bankruptcies... along BRI routes in the months, if not years, to come'. China will be forced to divert attention and resources away from the BRI. And the next year will be a period of difficulty and hibernation, especially perhaps in Africa. But the show will go on. The BRI is enshrined in the constitution of the Chinese Communist Party; it has Xi Jinping's personal imprimatur; and is a symbol of China's emergence as a leading global power. There will be a slowing but there is no going back.

As one sceptical Indian commentator noted, 'the BRI has been incrementally making progress'. And at the end of

2019, the Council on Foreign Relations concluded that 'BRI contracts again saw a significant uptick'. In 2020, China's international infrastructure trail will slow, and in some cases stall, but substantial changes have already occurred, alliances are shifting and more countries are looking east – to China in particular and Asia in general.

CHAPTER 8

SHIFTING ALLIANCES
Looking East

China & Russia

Russian elites once saw themselves as European but Moscow has adopted an explicit Asia strategy and is positioning itself as a pillar of the Asian system. Among BRI member countries, Russia ranks first in its 'trade, financial and policy coordination ties with China'. The Kremlin is more committed to engagement with Asia than it has ever been, and it is strategically closer to China than at any time since the brief alliance that was made between Mao and Stalin in 1950. Russia's border with China is over 4200 kilometres long, more than 80 per cent of its territory is Asian and most of the country's enormous oil and gas reserves are located in Siberia and serve Asian markets. Well before President Obama announced America's 'pivot to Asia', Russia had launched its 'pivot to the East'. Russian oligarchs may have a fondness for London real estate and a preference for English public schools, but their country is reorienting to the East.

The cornerstone of Moscow's engagement with Asia is the China–Russia partnership. And the ties that bind are growing stronger. Former diplomat and Russia expert Bobo Lo explained, 'No relationship matters more to the Kremlin. China is much more than a bilateral partner; it is crucial to Russia's modern vision'. Ironically, the hostility of the United States is accelerating the closeness of China and Russia. At the end of 2019, the *South China Morning Post* described their relationship as one of 'unparalleled friendly ties and cooperation'. Personal connections exist at the highest level. Presidents Putin and Xi Jinping have met each other more frequently than any other two international leaders – 'almost 30 times in the last six years'. And Jack Ma, the founder of Chinese technology conglomerate Alibaba, 'meets regularly with Vladimir Putin'. When Donald Trump called for Russia to be readmitted to the G7 at the group's summit in Canada in 2018, Putin was 'busy receiving China's highest award while attending the Shanghai Cooperation Organisation summit'.

It is not just personal, it is commercial. By 2019, bilateral trade between China and Russia had reached record levels; China had become Russia's largest trade partner, surpassing Germany; and Russia had overtaken Saudi Arabia to be the number one source of Chinese oil imports. In recent times, Russia has been earning more from grain exports than from arms exports. As temperatures have risen in the Arctic, Russian wheat exports have doubled, overtaking the United States and creating a new world record in the 2018 season. Sales to China reached their highest-ever levels. Russia has become Asia's twenty-first century breadbasket. China and Russia have 'agreed to boost two-way trade to $200 billion by 2024'. And it is not just wheat. Soybeans from the Russian Far East are now competing with soybeans from Iowa and Illinois. The Russian economic ministry has said that it expects to double its global food exports, 'ready to replace US agricultural products in China'.

Not surprisingly, Russia has embraced China's BRI and its facilitation of trade and commerce across Central Asia and the former Soviet republics. China is participating in the upgrade of Russian railway links 'such as that from Moscow to Kazan and the fabled Trans-Siberian Railway'. And Chinese banks and investment funds are investing in port and rail facilities from Murmansk to Arkhangelsk along the northern sea route from the Barents Sea to the Bering Strait, which the Chinese like to call the 'Polar Silk Road' or sometimes the 'Ice Silk Road'. A vessel heading to Europe from Shanghai could cut several thousand kilometres from its journey. In Ukraine, 'China is investing $7 billion in upgrading Ukrainian infrastructure...as a logistics hub for BRI'. Ukraine even declared 2019 the 'Year of China'.

Russia's energy ties with China are also deepening. Gazprom's 'Power of Siberia' pipeline exports natural gas directly to China. Transneft's 'Eastern Siberia-Pacific Ocean' pipeline has delivered 300,000 barrels of Russian crude oil to China on a daily basis. On the Yamal Peninsula in north-western Siberia, Chinese state banks are the major financiers and the Chinese Silk Road Fund is a major shareholder in a Russian Arctic energy project that is the largest liquefied natural gas extraction in the world. And technological cooperation between China and Russia has expanded significantly – especially in 5G, artificial intelligence, robotics, biotechnology, new media and the digital economy. The two countries now hold an annual 'High-Tech Forum' and an 'Innovation Dialogue'; have established a dizzying number of joint technology parks; and are increasing their joint investment in special funds for advanced technology development. Russian–Chinese academic cooperation is also proliferating. Huawei has opened centres in Moscow, St Petersburg, Kazan, Novosibirsk and Nizhny Novgorod and Western computers are disappearing from Russian offices and being replaced by Chinese ones.

The military relationship between China and Russia is also growing, like never before. The two countries have moved to an informal alliance which they call an 'all-embracing strategic partnership of co-ordination'. President Putin declared it to be 'a trusting relationship', and President Xi chimed in, 'promising to push the China–Russia relationship to new heights'. Two-thirds of Chinese military hardware imports come from Russia, including the formidable S-400 missile defence system and Sukhoi Su-35 fighter jets. Washington's instinctive response to their acquisition was to impose sanctions on the procurement department of China's Ministry of Defence. But other Asian countries have agreed, or are contemplating, the acquisition of the same Russian military hardware.

At sea, China and Russia have been conducting joint naval manoeuvres since 2012 – not only in Chinese home waters such as the Yellow Sea, but in Russian operational areas such as the Baltic and the Mediterranean, and also in politically sensitive areas such as the South China Sea and the Sea of Japan. The exercises have helped China develop its naval capabilities to the point where, according to a German Institute report entitled 'Partnership on the High Seas', China has not only surpassed Russia as a maritime power but its PLA Navy now has 'more warships than the US Navy' and 'the biggest naval fleet in the world'. Some commentators refer to Russia 'feeding the dragon'.

On land, joint military drills between China and Russia scaled new heights with China's participation in Vostok-2018, Russia's largest strategic military exercise in its history. The *Japan Times* called it 'unprecedented' and the 'first time' that China had participated in Russia's annual strategic exercise. The pattern was repeated with Russia's next annual strategic exercise staged in Western Russia known as Tsentr-2019. And it is the same story in the air. In July 2019, Chinese and Russian air forces conducted 'their first ever joint long-range aerial patrol in the East China Sea and Sea of Japan' and more can be expected.

It is not altogether surprising that Admiral Davidson, the newly appointed commander of US Indo-Pacific Command, conceded that 'China is now capable of controlling the South China Sea in all scenarios', to which he added the sole qualification 'short of war with the United States'. The implication that 'war with the United States' would alter the current state of affairs may be false optimism.

The Middle East

Not only Russia is marching east toward China. Key Middle East states such as Turkey, Iran, Saudi Arabia and Egypt are looking to the East. Cultural and political differences with the West, including broad anti-American sentiment arising from decades of US-led interference in the region, are part of the reason. But the economic opportunities so far offered by China's BRI, and arms and energy deals offered by Russia, are significant factors. Turkey is a prime example. Once a cornerstone of NATO's Cold

War strategy located at the intersection of Europe and Asia, it may be 'spinning out of NATO's orbit' – although President Erdogan is nothing if not mercurial. Turkey's people are almost entirely Muslim; most of its territory and population lies squarely in Asia; and its ethnic, linguistic and cultural affinities stretch 6000 kilometres across the Caucasus and Central Asia as far as Mongolia. Under Erdogan, Turkey's 'overtures to its Turkic brethren' have intensified.

Modern Turkey regards China, Russia, Iran and the Central Asian states as its more natural strategic partners and cultural affiliates. It is poised to join the China-led Shanghai Cooperation Organisation and its accession negotiations for membership of the European Union have stalled. Along with China and the Central Asian states, Turkey is working to consolidate the region from the oil-rich Caspian Sea to China's western Xinjiang region. This is the geographic heart of the world through which the old and new silk roads traverse. It is being knitted together through increased connectivity and infrastructure.

The Silk Road Economic Belt through the Central Asian states and Iran complements Turkey's own 'Middle Corridor' project, which links Turkey to Georgia and Azerbaijan by rail, crosses the Caspian Sea and extends to China through Turkmenistan and Kazakhstan. China and Turkey share the same vision for the region and have signed a memorandum of understanding aligning their two projects. Turkey was one of the first countries to endorse the BRI. It is already the passageway for Caspian energy to Europe and 'soon it will be the conduit for natural gas from Turkmenistan' – as well as from Iran and Russia. The Turkey–Russia–Iran energy triangle is playing an increasingly important geopolitical role.

China's involvement with Turkey is not limited to the BRI. Their economic relationship is growing and trade volumes have risen more than twenty-fold since 2000. China is Turkey's largest import partner and has pledged to open its markets to Turkish products. Its central bank has provided a $1 billion cash infusion for the Turkish economy. The Industrial and Commercial Bank of China (ICBC), the world's largest bank, has bought the Turkish Tekstilbank, recapitalised it, changed its name to 'ICBC Turkey' and made available a $3.6 billion package for Turkey's energy sector. ZTE Corp, a Chinese telecom giant similar to Huawei, has taken over Turkish Netas Telekom with the aim of making Netas and Turkey its technology hub in the Europe, Middle East and African region. And Chinese construction companies are building thousands of kilometres of new high-speed and conventional rail lines for Turkish State Railways.

Russia is reinforcing Turkey's orientation to the East. It has sold its S-400 missile defence system to Turkey and the two countries collaborated to support and stabilise the Assad regime in Syria – although they are at odds over the north-western Syrian province of Idlib, where the Erdogan government wishes to prevent an autonomous Kurdish area on its frontier. In January 2020 in Istanbul, presidents Putin and Erdogan launched the long-awaited TurkStream natural gas pipeline, which runs directly from southern Russia to Turkey. Washington's reflexive threat to impose sanctions on Turkey because of its purchase of the Russian missile defence system – and because the TurkStream pipeline would supposedly strengthen Europe's energy dependence on Russia – only hastened the deterioration of US–Turkey relations. President Erdogan retaliated by promising to close, if necessary, the

Incirlik Airbase, which houses US nuclear missiles, and Kurecik base, which is the site of a NATO radar station. The harder Washington blows, the more Turkey tips toward Asia.

A recent official statement by President Erdogan calls for a new world order – a 'multipolar balance' – not one led by the United States:

> Turkey and China have major responsibilities as a new
> world order emerges...Turkey shares China's vision...
> The world seeks a new, multipolar balance today. The
> need for a new international order, which will serve
> the interests of humanity, is crystal clear. Turkey and
> China, the world's most ancient civilizations, have a
> responsibility to contribute to building this new system.

*

Iran, like Turkey, is also part of the changing order in the Middle East. And despite – or perhaps because of – Washington's hostility, it has powerful allies. Russia and China have fundamentally common strategic interests with Iran. And for Turkey's President Erdogan, Iran is 'one of the most important strategic partners for us'. The Turkish Minister of Economy went further: 'The stronger Iran gets in this region, the stronger Turkey becomes as well, and the stronger Turkey becomes, the stronger Iran gets as well'. In Beijing on New Year's Day 2020, in a clear reference to the United States, the Chinese Foreign Minister entertained his Iranian counterpart, Javad Zarif, and stated that the two countries should stand together against 'unilateralism and bullying'. President Trump's decision a few days later to order the assassination of the revered Iranian military leader Major General Qasem Soleimani seemed to prove the point.

Significantly, China and Russia have begun, very publicly, to demonstrate their military support for Iran. In 2018, spy chiefs from China, Russia and Iran came together in Pakistan to coordinate their counter-ISIS strategies. And in late December 2019, as Western Christmas festivities wound down, the navies of China, Russia and Iran conducted joint exercises in the Indian Ocean and Gulf of Oman. The unprecedented war games were dubbed 'Marine Security Belt'. It was the first time since the Islamic revolution in 1979 that 'Iran has held a joint manoeuvre with two major world naval powers of this scale'. A few weeks after the joint exercises, an article in *Foreign Affairs* magazine noted 'not only is the US pressure campaign against Iran failing to achieve its stated aims but it is also benefitting the two great powers that the National Security Strategy is designed to confront'.

*

Saudi Arabia is a third significant Middle East country that has perceptibly turned its focus to the East. Although long regarded as an ally of the United States, it is now hedging its bets. Saudi Arabia's re-orientation toward China and Russia is clear. In fact, the late King Abdullah adopted a 'look east' trade policy shortly after taking the throne in 2005 and was the first Saudi monarch to visit China. And in 2017, Abdullah's brother, King Salman, pointedly chose to make lavish official visits to China and Russia in the first year of the Trump presidency – although it had once been customary for a Saudi king to give priority to an official visit to a newly elected United States president at the

White House. When his son, Defence Minister Crown Prince Mohammed Bin Salman, visited Washington, he made it clear that Saudi Arabia was 'keeping all its options open'.

The Saudi relationship with China is warm and getting warmer. When the crown prince visited China in January 2020 – before the onset of the COVID-19 pandemic – he cited 'a 32 percent increase in bilateral trade last year' and remarked that future opportunities between the two countries 'are very big'. Saudi Arabia is China's largest trading partner in Western Asia; the two countries have a comprehensive strategic partnership and are important cooperation partners in building the BRI; both are looking at economic transformation, connecting the Middle East and Asia and aligning their respective regional visions – Saudi Arabia's '2030 Vision' and China's BRI; and both are investing heavily in each other's economies – in oil, energy, petrochemical and aluminium projects among others. One of the more symbolic projects is a Chinese-built monorail in Mecca for the transport of pilgrims. Another is a high-speed rail line connecting Jeddah with Mecca and Medina. And in telecommunications, Saudi Arabia has welcomed China's Huawei, which is partnering with a Saudi telecommunications company to build a 5G network – just as it has done in Bahrain, Egypt, Kuwait and the United Arab Emirates among others.

Oil ties have substantially strengthened as well. Saudi Arabia's oil exports to China – already its biggest customer – doubled in 2019. And as Saudi Arabia and Russia push the oil price lower – hitting the United States shale oil industry – and global demand plummets because of the pandemic, China will take more.

Military collaboration between China and Saudi Arabia is also deepening. In late 2019, the two countries conducted a three-week joint naval exercise codenamed 'Blue Sword' at King Faisal Naval Base. It preceded China's tripartite naval exercises with Russia and Iran. The Saudi hedge toward China, 'stemming from mounting doubts about the reliability of the United States as an ally', was showcased recently when China opened in Saudi Arabia its 'first overseas defence production facility for the manufacture of the CH-4 Caihong, or Rainbow drone'.

Like other monarchies and non-democratic countries in the Middle East, Saudi Arabia quietly prefers China's emphasis on 'development peace' rather than 'democratic peace', as well as China's professed model of international multi-polarity and non-interference. When King Salman visited China in 2017, he stated that 'Saudi Arabia is willing to work hard with China to promote global and regional peace, security and prosperity'. He also made clear that Saudi Arabia would welcome China taking an increased role in the Middle East. And unlike most Western powers, Saudia Arabia is one of thirty-seven states that have offered explicit support for China's 'de-radicalisation efforts' in Xinjiang, where China and Saudi Arabia share an interest in containing the threat of radical Islamic terrorism. Muslim extremism has a long and bloody history in western China – dating to the Qing empire's occupation of Xinjiang in 1759. Beijing's heavy-handed conduct toward the Uighurs is undoubtedly unacceptable by Western standards but it fears any modern repetition of the disastrous major outbreaks that occurred in the mid-nineteenth century.

As with China, so also with Russia – although the relationship became more complicated over oil in 2020. King Salman's visit to Russia in 2017 was the first ever by a Saudi monarch. While in Moscow, he announced that Saudi Arabia would purchase Russia's S-400 air defence missile system. When President Putin visited Riyadh late last year, defence discussions continued about the purchase of the Russian system and more than twenty separate agreements and bilateral deals worth more than $2 billion were announced. Riyadh may yet still acquire the US THAAD system but significantly, in London, the Saudi Ambassador to the United Kingdom, Prince Khalid bin Bandar bin Sultan, issued a deft diplomatic warning to the West. It was a reminder of the geopolitical and cultural reality of the Middle East:

> Russia is becoming an important player in the region –
> whether one likes it or not, it is a fact…The Russians do
> to a certain extent understand the East better than the
> West does.

Saudi Arabia's drift from the West is clear. But all of the Arab Gulf nations are moving in the same broad direction. All have launched eastward-facing campaigns. In 2019, heads of state, emirs, crown princes and political leaders from the Middle East beat a well-trodden path to Beijing, resulting in big contracts and ambitious memoranda of understanding. Every single member country of the Gulf Cooperation Council has declining trade with the United States, while their trade with Asia is 'surging'. In 2016, China became the 'largest extra-regional source of foreign direct investment in the Middle East and since then has only gotten bigger'. Arabic has become the fastest-growing language at Beijing's Foreign Studies University. Dubai now hosts branches of China's four largest banks, a currency swap centre that 'moved nearly $7 billion worth of transactions in Chinese yuan in 2018' and more than 4200 Chinese businesses. And Saudi Arabia – like Russia, China and Iran – has threatened to drop the US dollar as its default currency on oil trades. The 'petroyuan' is coming.

*

The drift to China across the Middle East also includes Egypt, where President Sisi, who took office in 2014, is deepening ties with Beijing while simultaneously reducing security and trade dependence on the West. Egypt and China have signed a comprehensive strategic partnership agreement. In President Sisi's view, China is 'the world's future political and security superpower' and Egypt's greatest mistake during the Mubarak era was to align itself solely with the West. At the time of writing, Sisi has visited China six times and met with Xi Jinping seven times. On his first trip, he signed twenty-five bilateral agreements and pledged to cooperate on the BRI. China has become an essential component of Egypt's future prosperity. Showcase projects such as the proposed new administrative capital and a new Suez Canal industrial zone are being built with Chinese financing and expertise, as are energy projects at Aswan, railway projects, infrastructure projects and several industrial zones.

The Suez Canal is a critical link in China's 21st Century Maritime Silk Road. On the other side of the Mediterranean, another key link is the 2500-year-old Greek port of Piraeus. While the United States is splashing defence dollars to increase its military presence in Greece – because of its Russia fears – China and Greece are collaborating on mutual economic advancement, working together to establish Piraeus as the largest port and container terminal in Europe. It has already become the largest in the Mediterranean region. The China Ocean Shipping Company (COSCO), which became the majority owner of the port in 2016, has invested almost $3 billion – raising turnover by a third, increasing profitability fourfold and paying dividends to the Greek state. During Xi Jinping's visit in November 2019, the two countries signed sixteen memoranda of cooperation, not limited to the port of Piraeus. They included plans for a major solar power station and the establishment of an Athens branch of the Industrial and Commercial Bank of China.

*

It is the same story in war-ravaged Iraq and Afghanistan, whose economies and infrastructure were decimated by Washington's pursuit of its foreign policy objectives. While the United States now seeks to extricate itself from those countries, China has become their largest investor and is helping to rebuild them. It is the number one trading partner for both Iraq and Afghanistan. China's investments in Iraq include oil but also extend to power plants, cement factories, water treatment facilities, engineering, construction and credit provision. When the Iraqi prime minister arrived in Beijing in September 2019 with a fifty-five-member delegation, he described his visit as heralding a 'quantum leap' in bilateral relations. The visit culminated in the signing of eight wide-ranging memoranda of understanding, a framework credit agreement and the announcement of plans for Iraq to join the BRI.

In Afghanistan, as the United States seeks a resolution to the war that it initiated, China has not only become the largest foreign investor but has increased its economic aid. Where Washington once sought to impose military solutions, China is providing telecom equipment, building fibre optic cables, purchasing mineral rights, developing copper mines and extracting oil. And it is contributing to the peace process, at one stage stepping in to revive the peace talks through its long-established contacts with the Taliban. The contrast with the United States could not be clearer. And it is not all because of President Bush's 2001 invasion. Presidents Carter and Reagan also intervened disastrously in Afghanistan, authorising the CIA to secretly train and arm the Mujahideen. Their efforts duly gave rise to 'a whole cadre of trained and motivated people who turned against' America, of whom Osama bin Laden was one.

South Asia

South Asia is another significant area for China's BRI. As always, it is a question of geography. Pakistan, in particular, has warmed to the embrace of China. Under Prime Minister Imran Khan, the former national cricket hero, Pakistan's relationship with China is close, and getting closer. Both countries are seeking to realise Pakistan's potential as a gateway to the Arabian Sea from Western China and Central Asia. The deep-water Pakistani port of Gwadar is the end point of the China–Pakistan Economic Corridor, which is 'the most operationalized element of the Belt and Road Initiative to date' and the flagship of the BRI. It is intended to provide a link to China's '21st Century Maritime Silk Road'.

Beijing and Islamabad have big plans for the China–Pakistan Economic Corridor. The Pakistani foreign minister said recently that it is his country's 'top priority'. Some – like US Ambassador Alice Wells – contend that the shine has come off the China–Pakistan Economic Corridor but many Pakistanis regard it as the 'best thing that has ever happened' to their country and more than 80 per cent of the population was recently said to have 'a favourable view of China'. The first phase, valued at $62 billion, consisted of a network of projects for the development of roads, railways, pipelines and energy undertakings – not to mention the Gwadar Port itself, with its adjoining 2282-acre free trade area leased to the China Overseas Port Holding Company. The most expensive component was the upgrade of the railway from Karachi to Peshawar. The second phase of the megaproject 'will focus on industrialization, agriculture, and socio-economic development, with a particular emphasis on special economic zones'. It will be delayed by the current global economic contraction but after the Pakistani president visited Beijing to show solidarity in late March 2020, the Pakistani foreign minister expressed confidence that the project 'will march forward and eventually benefit the whole region'.

Neither China nor Pakistan wants prohibitive debt to jeopardise the China–Pakistan Economic Corridor, especially given Washington's campaign to discredit the BRI and the growing awareness of issues of cost, debt and transparency. Imran Khan's government, like that of Malaysia, Kenya and many others, is conscious of these concerns. To help Pakistan 'get rid of the dollar burden' in bilateral trade, China and Pakistan have agreed to conduct their trade in yuan instead of US dollars. And although a forty-year lease for the operation of the port has been given to China Overseas Port Holding

Company, the finance minister explained on the sidelines of the 2020 World Economic Forum in Davos that:

> The port belongs to the people and government of
> Pakistan...this network of roads to the port will benefit
> Pakistani society. We are inviting foreign investment from
> every country, including the US. We are building this
> network of roads, ports and electricity plants not meant
> exclusively for the Chinese.

Given the region's strategic significance, the United States is working hard to re-set its relationship with Pakistan – after President Trump had initially tweeted angrily about Islamabad's 'lies and deceit' and suspended security assistance. But Pakistan's relationship with China will be more enduring. Like India, Pakistan is part of the Beijing-based Shanghai Cooperation Organisation, which covers two-thirds of the Eurasian landmass and embraces 'almost half the human race in a gigantic network'. And Imran Khan, like many Asian leaders, is wary of Washington's predilection for 'military solutions'. In fact, for some time, Washington regarded Khan as 'anti-American and pro-Taliban' simply because, as he explained in an interview at Davos in 2020:

> I, for one, have always opposed this military solution [in
> Afghanistan]. I always believed that the so-called war on
> terror was the wrong way to fight terrorism. I felt that
> it created more terrorism due to collateral damage...the
> more drone attacks, the more people got killed, the more
> people joined the militants. I was opposed to this, and for
> that I was considered anti-American and pro-Taliban...we

lost 70,000 people in the war on terror, and at the end,
we were held responsible for the US not succeeding...I am
a firm believer that military means are not a solution to
ending conflicts.

Khan is a realist however and recognises the deterrent value of
a strong military. Pakistan is, after all, a nuclear power. And
China and Pakistan are said to be 'iron brothers' with an 'all
weather friendship'. Their strategic partnership is decades long.
In fact, Pakistan was the first Muslim country to recognise the
People's Republic of China in 1950. And it is well known that
China transferred nuclear weapons and missile technology to
Pakistan in the 1980s and 1990s. Over the last ten years, the
Pakistani military has been 'increasingly inducting Chinese
platforms' into its army, navy and air force operations. And
China has far surpassed the United States as a supplier of
weapons and military equipment to Pakistan. The 'military
interoperability of the two nations – backed by the common
systems being used' has become a significant feature of their
relationship. In January 2020, China and Pakistan conducted
their sixth bilateral naval exercise. The PLA Navy has been
particularly busy. The joint naval exercise with Pakistan in
the Arabian Sea followed only weeks after China's joint naval
exercise with Saudi Arabia and its tripartite naval exercise with
Russia and Iran in the same region.

Beijing has also strengthened and deepened relations among
the smaller countries of South Asia – Bangladesh, Nepal,
Sri Lanka and the Maldives. It is a major investor in Bangladesh
and has upgraded bilateral ties to that of a strategic partnership.
It has also been successful in 'significantly expanding its
foothold' in Nepal, Sri Lanka and the Maldives. This has not

been without some controversy, although the levels of debt to China are not as great as some critics suggest. On balance, according to the United States Institute of Peace 'smaller South Asian countries have benefitted from China's growing economic and military engagement with them and the region. Chinese projects have helped increase connectivity within these countries as well as with external trading networks'. The institute's report added that smaller South Asian countries 'are increasingly aware of the potentially negative impacts and consequences of Chinese financing of development projects and they are weighing the economic benefits...against the potential strategic costs'.

India is a separate case. It is an economic behemoth in its own right, which is benefitting from the Asian growth story but it treads carefully with China. Its economic policy, once called 'Look East' and now called 'Act East', has resulted in bilateral trade with China approaching $100 billion and trade with ASEAN nations growing even faster – projected to double to $300 billion in the next five years, subject, of course, to the as yet unquantified economic consequences of the global contraction caused by the COVID-19 pandemic. Despite its strategic wariness, India is 'reluctant to be unnecessarily antagonistic' toward China and is 'seeking to develop a constructive narrative rather than sharpen antagonisms'. Along with Pakistan, it has joined the Shanghai Cooperation Organisation, although for economic reasons it has chosen not to join the Regional Comprehensive Economic Partnership.

At the same time, the United States is striving to cultivate India – including by the signing of a landmark communications compatibility and security agreement and a presidential visit in February 2020. Prime Minister Modi may do the unexpected but India historically prefers to be non-aligned and Russia is by far its largest arms supplier. It may well still be true to say that 'Delhi has looked to Moscow for support and partnership… rather than Washington, not just for years but for generations'.

Southeast Asia

Further to the east, Southeast Asia has emerged as a core pillar of Asia's future. With prolonged relative peace since the 1970s, epitomised by the end of America's conflict in Vietnam, the ASEAN nations have achieved remarkable levels of regional stability, integration, economic growth and mutual prosperity. The rise of Southeast Asia and the rise of China have been mutually reinforcing. In the not too distant future, the trade and transport corridors of the BRI – including the proposed high-speed rail network from Kunming in southern China through Laos, Thailand and Malaysia to Singapore – will knit China ever more closely to Southeast Asia.

China's Southeast Asian footprint is already substantial. Poorer ASEAN nations, such as Laos and Cambodia, have become firmly linked to China, whose state enterprises have large and sometimes controlling interests in everything from electricity to factories. Myanmar's position is similar. China supported the old military junta in Yangon, and even though the country has liberalised, it still dominates the trade and investment landscape. Vietnam, more than most other ASEAN nations, stands up pugnaciously for its sovereignty. But it wants a modus vivendi with China and has agreed to suspend some of its oil and gas exploration projects in the disputed waters of the South China Sea. Indonesia's bilateral ties with China are relatively stable due to a mutual desire to create a strong maritime partnership and cooperate on infrastructure development. And Thailand, while also being an alliance partner of the United States, is a key regional ally of China and is said to have a 'sibling' relationship with it. Like Malaysia, Thailand is a top cooperation partner in the BRI.

Singapore is wealthy, pragmatic and balanced. At the Shangri-La Dialogue in 2019, Prime Minister Lee Hsien Loong issued a warning to all countries, including the ASEAN nations, and perhaps more specifically the United States:

> The rest of the world too has to adjust to a larger role for China. Countries have to accept that China will continue to grow and strengthen, and that it is neither possible nor wise for them to prevent this from happening.

Malaysia and the Philippines, formerly staunch allies of the United States, have 'more recently tilted toward China'. Malaysia's elderly former Prime Minister Mahathir once criticised the BRI and renegotiated some projects but in 2019 he announced his 'full support' for the BRI. The most ambitious BRI initiative currently underway in Malaysia is the deep-water port at Malacca, whose key investors are China's State Power Investment Corporation and three provincial governments. In the Philippines, President Duterte 'like all other Asian leaders – prefers multidirectional alignment to reliance on the United States alone'. In 2020, he gave notice of the cancellation of the longstanding US–Philippines military cooperation agreement. Cambodia has also cancelled military drills with the United States and Australia but held them with China.

To date the ASEAN countries have been major beneficiaries of the BRI. According to a 2018 study by Oxford Economics and the CIMB ASEAN Research Institute, the investment in BRI projects in ASEAN countries amounted to more than $739 billion – of which Indonesia, Vietnam, Cambodia and Malaysia had been the largest beneficiaries. At the second BRI Forum in Beijing in 2019, all ASEAN leaders, except Joko Widodo, who was facing a presidential election, were enthusiastic attendees. But a few months later, seven out of ten ASEAN leaders absented themselves at the ASEAN–US summit in Bangkok, while a Washington representative read an invitation from President Trump to visit the United States for a separate 'special summit'. It was said to be an 'intentional effort to embarrass' President Trump. And in February 2020, in the midst of the COVID-19 crisis, the foreign ministers of all ASEAN nations came together with China in Vientiane, Laos in a show of cooperation to consider how best to deal with the pandemic. The ASEAN nations are going their own way.

Economic transitions in East Asia are multiple, interlocking and mutually reinforcing. The complementarities are 'creating a whole much greater than the sum of its parts'. The resilience of the economies of East Asia is such that the Western 'global financial crisis' of 2007–08, which originated in the United States, never really became an Asian crisis. Intra-Asian trade was 'so robust that it cushioned the shock of falling exports to the United States and European Union'. Less than a decade later, internal Asian trade had almost doubled. In Northeast Asia, the five main exporters – China, Taiwan, Hong Kong, Japan and South Korea – account for as much, if not more, than the whole of the European Union and North America combined; electronic products that were once exported mostly to the West are now increasingly supplied to an upwardly mobile Asia; and Southeast Asia is taking on the mantle of 'factory of the world' as Japanese, South Korean and even Chinese manufacturing firms outsource to the region.

The trend is growing. Asian nations are advancing their trade ties with one another while 'diminishing their dependence on exports to the United States and European Union'. In the process, a 'great diversion of capital' is underway. As Parag Khanna explained:

Asians' appetite for US Treasuries is waning as United States debt rises, and Asian trade within Asia and with Europe grows faster than that with the United States...Instead of underwriting the US dollar, Asians are increasingly investing in their own debt and capital markets...Many Asian governments are issuing large amounts of sovereign debt in their own currencies rather than US dollars. China accounts for about half of Asia's debt issuance...These moves have supported an enormous expansion in Asia's corporate bond markets.

The same trend is discernible in relation to security dependence. 'From Saudi Arabia to Japan', Asians are positioning themselves to rely less on America while 'pursuing greater strategic autonomy... building their own defence capacity so they can depend less on the United States'. Asian nations recognise the shifting winds, the changing balance of power. China 'now possesses the region's largest navy with more than 300 surface and underwater vessels compared with 187 vessels for the USA'. And according to a report by a leading United States Study Centre:

America no longer enjoys military primacy in the Indo-Pacific and its capacity to uphold a favourable balance

of power is increasingly uncertain...America has an
atrophying force that is no longer ready, equipped or
postured for great power competition in the Indo-Pacific.

Westad also remarked on America's loss of regional military
primacy in an article for *Foreign Affairs* in 2019:

Today, [China] has enough ground-based ballistic
missiles, aircraft and ships to plausibly contend that
it has achieved military superiority in its immediate
backyard. The Chinese missile force presents such a
challenge to US air bases and aircraft carriers in the
Pacific that Washington can no longer claim supremacy
in the region. The problem will only get worse, as
China's naval capabilities are set to grow massively
within the next few years...

Asians can see where the strength lies. Their growing
independence is pragmatic but its origins are also cultural
and economic. Stuart Gulliver, former head of the British
multinational bank, HSBC, observed that 'The American
dream of the 20th century is becoming the Asian dream of the
21st century...a house, a car, a smartphone, travel, banking
services, healthcare – the prospect of unfettered upward
social mobility...' Among Asians, there is a confidence and an
independence about their future, not to mention a growing
conviction that the American way may not be their way, at least
the 'America First' version of the American way. For some, the
appeal of American-style democracy, unregulated capitalism
and unsustainable consumerism is 'fading'. They believe that
the anchor of global order is not necessarily a single country or

set of values – neither Chinese nor American, neither Western nor Asian; and that the future of the world is a multi-polar, multi-civilisational order – a view, of course, which Washington regards as 'antithetical to US values and interests'.

Africa

Africa is another case of increasing orientation to the East. China–Africa relations prospered before the BRI – dating back to China's support for anti-colonial and anti-apartheid movements. Relations advanced further with a 1970s United Nations plan for cooperation among developing countries known as 'South-South cooperation'. But in the twenty-first century, a new era of Chinese–African economic collaboration has quietly got underway. Chinese interests in Africa, through strategic investments and project finance, have ballooned: 'Spindles of Chinese-paved roads have unfurled across the continent, along with huge bridges, new airports, dams and power plants'. As one commentator put it 'China is all over Africa these days, building railroads, bridges and ports, doing what European colonialists should have done a long-time ago'. And as another expressed it 'Chinese loans are building the continent'. It is little wonder that the title of a recent book by Howard French, the prizewinning foreign correspondent and former *New York Times* bureau chief in Africa, is *China's Second Continent: How a Million Migrants Are Building a New Empire in Africa.*

Much of China's investment and lending in Africa has related to ports, railways, oil and gas pipelines, and power plants – 'securing access to resources and using excess capacity in construction and transportation'. Many Chinese investments are concentrated in Nigeria and Angola and are closely linked to their oil industries. *The Washington Post* noted that between 2014 and 2018, Chinese companies invested twice as much money in Africa as American companies. A former US ambassador in Africa, David Shinn, remarked that 'American trade in Africa is falling off a cliff'. And according to Forbes:

> Since 2011, China has been the biggest player in Africa's infrastructure boom, claiming a 40 percent share that continues to rise. Meanwhile, the shares of other players are falling precipitously: Europe declined from 44 to 34 percent, while the presence of US contractors fell from 24 to just 6.7 percent.

The transformative presence of China on so many fronts in Africa has changed the continent. African governments 'have turned east almost in unison'. At least forty of Africa's fifty-four countries have signed up to the BRI. When Djibouti's foreign minister came to New York to seek a non-permanent seat on the United Nations Security Council, he put it simply: 'It was quite natural that we raise our partnership with China. Neither Europe nor America were ready to build the infrastructure we needed'.

Djibouti happens to be the site of one of China's most important strategic investments in Africa. Located on the Horn of Africa in the Gulf of Aden at the entrance to the Red Sea, Djibouti was once a place of contact and passage for Egyptians, Phoenicians, Romans, Greeks, Byzantines and Arabs. Today it lies at the crossroads of twenty-first century shipping lanes that link Europe, Asia and Africa – global arteries that carry much of the world maritime trade. Djibouti is now home to a Chinese-built multi-purpose deep-water port known as Doraleh; a Chinese-built free trade zone; and a Chinese naval base, which is currently China's only overseas military facility. From Djibouti, Chinese companies have financed and built a railway to Ethiopia and are constructing an undersea cable, connected to internet servers run by Chinese telecom companies, which will transmit data across a region that spans East Africa to the Arabian Peninsula.

The Doraleh port is a central node in China's 21st Century Maritime Silk Road, providing connections with other Chinese-built port clusters in the region – in the Suez Canal, at the Strait of Hormuz, at Gwadar in Pakistan, at Hambantota in Sri Lanka and eventually also at Malacca in Malaysia. But Djibouti is not alone. Throughout Africa, China has focused heavily on investment in the construction of ports and container terminals. In Namibia, on the west coast, the new container terminal at Walvis Bay is said to be one of China's 'most highly prized'. The Chinese ambassador called it 'the most brilliant pearl on the Atlantic coast of southwest Africa'. The port 'will connect southern Africa to [other] China Harbor Engineering Company ports and infrastructure in São Tomé and Príncipe, Cameroon, Nigeria, Ghana, the Ivory Coast and Guinea, as well as planned facilities in Gambia and Senegal'. One former United States intelligence officer identified 'at least 46 existing or planned port projects in sub-Saharan Africa with some Chinese involvement'. It is no coincidence that sub-Saharan Africa is expected to be the most populous area of the world by 2050.

Despite the potentially transformative benefits of large-scale infrastructure projects, and the enthusiasms of local African politicians, there is now a greater perception of sovereign risk – heightened by worldwide economic contraction and the looming global recession. Even before 2020, China had become 'more focussed on the viability' of some African projects and had renegotiated terms on some and 'put the brakes' on others. Among other pull-backs, it agreed with Ethiopia to write off interest on some loans and extended repayment on another from ten to thirty years. And although the flagship high-speed Kenyan railway line from Mombasa to Nairobi exceeded expectations for passenger and freight volumes, Beijing deferred the more problematic extension of the railway through to Uganda, involving a further $4.9 billion.

The investment by China in African ports, railways and energy infrastructure is only part of the picture. Before the 2020 pandemic, there was a noticeable shift in the pattern of Chinese investment toward manufacture and financial services – 'supporting Africa's efforts to diversify its economy and reduce its over-reliance on natural resources for growth'. More than a decade ago, China overtook the United States as Africa's largest trading partner. China–Africa trade grew from $10 billion in the year 2000 to $220 billion in 2014, and 'increased by 19.7 per cent' in 2018; more than forty African nations now have trade agreements with China; and more than 10,000 Chinese-owned firms are operating throughout Africa. The value of Chinese business in Africa 'since 2005 amounts to more than $2 trillion'. The mutual trade has been so extensive that, as one commentator observed, 'Crushing Africa in debt so that they cannot buy anything that the Chinese make simply does not make a lot of sense'.

There is also another dimension. The votes of Africa's fifty-four nations at the United Nations, the World Health Organisation, the International Monetary Fund and the

World Bank are important to China. That importance may be illustrated by the fact that in response to the COVID-19 pandemic, China's Jack Ma Foundation announced that it would donate to each of the fifty-four African countries '200,000 test kits, 100,000 masks and 1,000 medical use protective suits and face shields'. Meanwhile, China's military engagement in Africa has also deepened – as the top supplier of weapons and United Nations peacekeeping troops; by the training of African military officers; by entering into military cooperation agreements; and by the greater involvement of the PLA Navy in regional maritime security, counter-piracy and visits to African ports. Beijing's 2015 white paper on military strategy emphasises that 'great importance has to be attached to managing the seas and oceans and protecting maritime rights and interests'. A recent investigative report by the *Financial Times* was labelled 'How China Rules the Waves'.

The outlook for 2020 is uncertain, although there are some hopeful signs. Africa has considerable experience as a result of the Ebola and HIV Aids epidemics and the World Health Organisation is focused on the continent. Nonetheless, it may still be correct to say that it is 'only a matter of time before the epidemic spreads across African countries in full force and leads, in parallel to a public health crisis, to a severe economic crisis'. Some experts anticipate that sub-Saharan Africa, Central Asia and Eastern Europe will inevitably see a 'dip in BRI related activity, relative to Southeast Asia'. This has now become obvious. But America has long since ceased to be competitive with China in Africa. The US secretary of state was recently reduced to preaching that the only path to 'true liberation' in Africa is economic partnership with the United States. This caused *The Washington Post* Nairobi bureau chief to remark that the Trump administration 'has shifted US policy toward the rhetorical as opposed to the tangible'.

Latin America

Latin America is a similar story. Like Africa, it has turned to the East. The American economist Mark Weisbrot wrote that 'Latin America, and especially South America, has become independent of Washington', adding that Latin American nations have a 'strong political interest in…a multi-polar world and a greater role for the United Nations, developing countries and international law and diplomacy'. These goals do not sit comfortably with Washington. This may explain why Senator Rick Scott from Florida bizarrely warned that China's influence in Latin America is a 'threat to our way of life'.

In pursuit of its 'America First' policy, the Trump administration has adopted a policy of hostility – referring to Latin American nations as 'shithole countries'; imposing tariffs; deporting adults and minors; cutting off aid to countries that do not prevent migration to the United States; and declaring a national emergency in order to build a wall along the Mexican border – for which it has diverted billions of dollars of funds set aside for the Pentagon's defence construction projects. China's message has a different tone. Its stated policy toward Latin American and Caribbean countries – facilitated by lending and investment from China's state-owned or -funded institutions – is to establish 'a comprehensive and cooperative partnership featuring equality, mutual benefit and common development'.

The result is that China has become Latin America's largest lender, its major source of infrastructure investment and its second largest trade partner. In the ten years from

2008 to 2018, the volume of China's investment in South America rose a startling 480 per cent. And between 2007 and 2017, its official lending exceeded $150 billion – more than the World Bank and the Inter-American Development Bank. Nineteen countries in the region have joined the BRI and many of those that have not yet done so accept significant Chinese investment. Ecuador has become a full member of the AIIB and Argentina, Bolivia, Brazil, Chile, Peru, Uruguay and Venezuela are all prospective members.

According to Global Data's latest report, China's infrastructure participation in Latin America included fifty-nine large-scale projects. The projects are helping to provide transport, water, energy and sanitation systems to millions of people and have 'undoubtedly created jobs, furthered development and created a viable alternative strategic partnership'. The projects range from the San José hydroelectric plants in Bolivia; the Reventazón dam in Costa Rica; two nuclear power plants in Argentina's Patagonia region; the natural gas Martano power plant in Panama; an integrated iron ore mine, deep-water port and associated railway project in Bahia, Brazil; an oil drilling and exploration project in Ecuador; a water treatment plant in El Salvador; a subway project in Bogotá, Columbia; the Chaglla hydroelectric plant in Peru; hydroelectric plants and wind farms in Brazil; and oil production in the Orinoco Belt in Venezuela. Some have been criticised, such as the Coca Codo Sinclair dam in Ecuador, but most have contributed to a deepening of ties and strengthening of relations.

Latin America's leaders are naturally supportive. Even Brazil's Jair Bolsonaro has 'walked back his negative campaign rhetoric about China'. His government recently announced that it wants 'more Chinese investment in infrastructure projects as long as investors generate local jobs and abide by the country's rules'. And in March 2019, he stated that 'Our great economic partner is China. In second place, the United States'. Similar expressions of support have come from the leaders of Argentina, Bolivia, Chile, Ecuador, Peru, Mexico, Panama and Venezuela. Argentina's former president, Mauricio Macri, pointed to Chinese flexibility, saying that 'China is willing to revise agreements where we see errors and expand relations rather than reduce them...We are growing ever closer'.

This flexibility, partly in response to the constant warnings about 'debt-trap' diplomacy, has contributed to changes in China's investment model. The Inter-American Development Bank has worked with the China International Contractors Association to build a set of principles for sustainable infrastructure development in Latin America. And instead of 'going it alone on symbolic projects, a range of Chinese institutional investors now see benefits in operating more like their international counterparts, working in partnerships and seeking long-term returns'. Headline-grabbing turnkey contracts backed by China's state banks are being replaced by 'Chinese participation in consortia and increased equity investment'. The Bogotá subway project, in which China Harbour Engineering successfully joined with a Canadian company, is an example.

Once firmly in Europe's colonial orbit, then under the thumb of the United States, Latin America has undergone a fundamental re-orientation, without revolution. Its westward ties across the Pacific, to Asia and especially to China, have blossomed. China is displacing the United States in Latin America and outpacing it in infrastructure loans, investment, influence and goodwill. Its diplomatic rhetoric of cooperation and collaboration on development issues, and its willingness to fund critical infrastructure projects, are in marked contrast to Washington's approach. Professor Ellis from the US Army War College Strategic Studies Institute explained, 'It is not principally a military challenge, it is an erosion of the US strategic position...' It is, in truth, a loss of leadership. A case in point is the Panama Canal, where Chinese companies operate ports at the Pacific and Caribbean ends. Panama, El Salvador and the Dominican Republic were once 'considered very close to the United States' but when all three recently switched diplomatic recognition from Taiwan to Beijing, neither chose to consult Washington or provide any prior warning.

Europe

Europe, like Latin America and Africa, has benefitted from the rise of China and Asia. At the time of writing, the pandemic has closed borders and trade has been diminished but there is little question, it seems, that in the longer term 'Europe will prevail over the United States in the race to profit from Asia's rise' and that a 'declining United States [has] put Euro-Asian convergence front and centre'. Prior to 2020, China's trade with the European Union was '$500 billion more per year' than with the United States. Daily bilateral trade in goods amounted to '1.5 billion Euros'. Europe's trade with Asia was expected to reach $2.5 trillion by 2025, almost double the current trade between Europe and North America.

Asia's growth, as is the world's growth, will continue to be fuelled by China, while the United States is a diminishing global economic resource. The figures bear it out. The International

Monetary Fund projected that China's contribution to global growth would exceed 28 per cent by 2024 – while the contribution of the United States would fall to 9.2 per cent. By that date, India's contribution was expected to surpass America's by almost 70 per cent. A global recession resulting from the COVID-19 pandemic will alter the numbers but is unlikely to change the comparative position.

The trade between China and Europe works both ways – just as it did in the seventeenth century when the Dutch guilds first opened up the trade with China and Japan. Over land, freight trains have replaced camel trains. The growth in the overland trade with China has been facilitated by the 'launch of more than fifty new freight rail lines linking a dozen Asian countries to a dozen major European cities'. China's target in 2019 was 5000 westbound freight train movements per year. And that year, Denmark's Maersk, the largest container shipping company in the world, expected to double its volume of containers moved by freight train from China to Europe. The trade is not just coming from China. It has been partly fuelled by other Asian exporters who ship to China and tranship onto freight trains to Europe. And until the contraction in early 2020, the same containers headed to Asia were increasingly filled with European luxury goods, premium motor vehicles, foodstuffs, powdered milk and wine. Nestlé and Unilever now earn 'no more than 20 percent of their revenues in Europe'.

It is not only about trade. China has also been buying up Europe. It is not the biggest investor but in the last decade its advance into Europe through investments and acquisitions has been relentless. A comprehensive Bloomberg audit showed that over the past ten years China bought or invested in assets in Europe 'amounting to $318 billion…roughly 45 percent more than the US during this period'. Even this figure underestimates the true extent, because it excludes hundreds of mergers, investments, joint ventures, greenfield developments and stock-market transactions for which information is unavailable. Most people know about Volvo, Pirelli and Lotus in the automotive industry; Gieves and Hawkes, Kent and Curwen, and Bally in the fashion industry; and football teams such as AC Milan, West Bromwich Albion and Wolverhampton Wanderers to name a few. But many of China's European investments have been more strategic.

They include whole or partial interests in at least a dozen office towers in the City of London and Canary Wharf, of which the Lloyd's building is one; airports at Toulouse, Frankfurt and Tirana, and even Heathrow; seaports and container terminals at Zeebrugge, Rotterdam, Marseilles, Valencia, Bilbao, Trieste and Piraeus; oil rigs in the North Sea; wind farms in Scotland, Denmark, Spain and the North Sea; and the Hinkley nuclear power station in southern England. The Portuguese electricity grid is another. So is British Steel's Scunthorpe plant; the German robotics firm of Kuka; and the Swiss pesticide manufacturer Syngenta, whose $40 billion acquisition by China National Chemical Corporation was China's largest to date. And then there are the infrastructure and construction projects, just a few of which include a highway in Montenegro, a bridge and access roads in Croatia and an undersea tunnel between Finland and Estonia.

Some European leaders have been outspoken in their support. The Hungarian strongman, Prime Minister Viktor Orbán, said that 'the world economy's centre of gravity is shifting from west to east; while there is some denial of this in the western world, that denial does not seem to be reasonable', adding that the 'centre of gravity [is] shifting from the Atlantic region to the Pacific region. This is not my opinion – this is a fact'. And the former German foreign minister, Sigmar Gabriel, pointed out that 'China currently seems to be the only country in the world with any sort of genuinely global, geostrategic concept', adding that 'China is entitled to develop such a concept'.

Germany has been noticeably forward-leaning. It wants Beijing to allow more competition but has had thriving relations with China and other Asian nations. The transport hub of Duisburg in Germany has become China's overland gateway to Europe. Before the pandemic, it could be said that 'every week, around 30 Chinese trains arrive...from Chongqing, Wuhan or Yiwu, or...from Milan heading the other way'. China has replaced the United States as Germany's top trading partner and has been its largest source of imports for a decade; the German and Chinese cabinets meet annually for a joint session; and the German engineering giant Siemens has 'thrown its weight behind Belt and Road'. Significantly, despite Washington's objections, Germany, like the United Kingdom, chose to become a founding member of the China-led AIIB. And Germany may well open its door to Huawei's 5G technology as the Netherlands has done. Other European states are likely to follow, now that the European Commission has rebuffed American calls for a blanket ban and adopted a 'non-biased and fact-based approach'.

After a decade of expanding Chinese investment and trade, the European Union became cautiously assertive – seeking fairer competition through engagement and negotiation – but eschewing Washington's trade war and its ideological opposition. Brussels was 'keen to maintain cordial relations'.

A commission paper called for a 'flexible and pragmatic' response. It described China as 'a negotiating partner with whom the EU needs to find a balance of interests' and an 'economic competitor in the pursuit of technological leadership'. The paper also went on to refer to China as a 'systemic rival promoting alternative models of governance', which was more contentious, but 'reflected growing impatience in EU circles with China's failure to open its markets...in key sectors'. The underlying theme was the need to strengthen competition while recognising the importance of the mutual trading relationship. Brussels is searching for a mutually profitable modus vivendi with China.

The relationship took a different turn when the COVID-19 crisis took hold and the World Health Organisation declared Europe to be the new epicentre. Beijing sought to strengthen its ties with Europe by adopting a more muscular diplomatic and public relations approach – endeavouring to leverage its own successful response to the outbreak; presenting its governance model of control, confinement and surveillance in a favourable light; and promoting itself as a generous and responsible international actor. From mid-March 2020, Chinese aircraft started arriving at European airports with medical teams and equipment. The Silk Road trains that previously transported goods across continents began moving life-saving medical supplies. And the corridors, ports and logistic hubs of the BRI served to support Beijing's efforts to position itself as a global leader in healthcare and humanitarian aid. As one of the world's leading producers of pharmaceuticals, and 'a top contributor of funds and troops to the United Nations peacekeeping program', it may be well-placed to do so. Xi Jinping has called this extension of the BRI the 'Health Silk Road'.

A Chinese initiative that caused disquiet in Brussels even before the pandemic is a working group formerly known as the '16+1' cooperation framework. The name refers to the sixteen post-communist states of Central and Eastern Europe, including the Balkans and the Baltic states, plus China. When Greece joined the framework last year, the association became '17+1' and the dynamics changed. Unlike other members, Greece is neither a post-communist state nor a new or prospective member of the European Union. And significantly, Austria, Belarus and the Republic of Moldova have expressed an interest in joining as well. Only twelve of the seventeen are members of the European Union. And Beijing has now indicated that it will take a more hands-on approach in the future. In mid-March 2020, Chinese officials hosted a video conference with their 17+1 counterparts to share lessons about combating the coronavirus outbreak.

By late 2019, a map of Eastern and Central Europe showed an intimidating wave of countries that had signed up to the BRI, pushing up against the edges of Western Europe, and in the case of Italy, Greece and Portugal, extending deep into it. As one professional advisor described it, 'China's Belt & Road has now moved further west than Genghis Khan's armies'. While some European Union members have signed up to China's BRI, so have many European countries outside the union. And between the European Union and China sits the Russia-led Eurasian Economic Union, to which China is a free trade partner. It includes Armenia, Belarus, Kazakhstan, Kyrgyzstan and Russia. In Belarus, on Europe's eastern fringe, Chinese companies are building a second runway at Minsk international airport that is poised to facilitate the movement of more cargo into Europe. And a nearby industrial park is filling with Chinese manufacturers looking to the European market.

For those Europeans still living in the twentieth century, it might seem as if the barbarians are at the gate. But in the twenty-first century, wishing China away in Europe will be impossible. Trade and investment have slowed and BRI projects have been put on hold as global economies contract and the world comes to grips with the consequences of an unwanted pandemic. Before the crisis, Brussels proposed greater screening for foreign investments in critical sectors such as energy, ports and airports, communications, data, space and financial industries. Since the crisis, concerns about sovereignty and the need to diversify supply chains have become more prominent. The pandemic has given a boost to voices calling for less European dependency on China. France's President Macron and others have supported the addition of medical supplies to the list of strategic sectors where Europe needs greater sovereignty.

But Brussels is diplomatically cautious about its trading relationship with China. And in late April, it agreed to demands to substantially soften a report criticising a 'Chinese disinformation campaign about the pandemic'. In the view of one commentator: 'The implications are clear. It is to Eurasia that Europe should be looking, and in many cases is actively doing so'.

CONCLUSION

Since commencing this book, the world has been engulfed in a health and economic crisis that few anticipated. And the latter will be more significant and longer-lasting than the former. The looming global recession may well bring to an end the era of unsustainable credit-fuelled growth, not to mention the distorting effect of interest rates at 500-year lows that have enabled it. But China and most of the east Asian nations are positioned to fare better and recover faster than the rest of the world. We are entering what has been described as a 'post-American world'. Some have seen it coming. But few anticipated that it would be precipitated by the global spread of an infectious disease. And few foresaw that America would manage to make itself the global epicentre of the pandemic.

The former American diplomat Richard Haass, long-time president of the Council on Foreign Relations, explained: 'Long before COVID-19 ravaged the earth, there had already been a precipitous decline in the appeal of the American model'. Under the heading 'Post-American World', he wrote that a characteristic of the current crisis is 'a marked lack of US leadership'; that the United States has 'not rallied the world in a collective effort to confront either the virus or its economic effects'; and nor has it 'rallied the world to follow its lead in addressing the problem at home'. Haass concluded that if the shape of the world that follows this crisis is 'one in which the United States dominates less and less...It has been apparent for at least a decade'.

In fact, rather than leading, the United States has used the pandemic to advance its dangerous and self-interested semi-war with China. It has focused on apportioning blame – while overlooking that America was responsible for the last global financial crisis – and making baffling public statements calculated to provoke and offend Beijing. Among other things, Washington has criticised the World Health Organisation for being 'China-centric'; implied that the virus was manufactured, not naturally occurring; and hindered effective action in the G7 and the United Nations Security Council by pressing for resolutions that 'single out China for blame'. And while almost all of the world's leaders attended a virtual vaccine summit on 4 May 2020, the Trump administration refused to participate. The importance of effective international cooperation, leadership and goodwill seems lost on Washington. China has become its abiding obsession, which is, in turn, acting increasingly defensively. Distrust breeds distrust.

This is the most destabilising aspect of Washington's twenty-first century world view – its relentless and unwavering anti-China conviction. It has some adherents in the corridors of power in Whitehall, Ottawa and Canberra but less elsewhere. It is far from a universal view. Singapore's prime minister, Lee Hsien Loong, spoke for many when he told an audience of foreign and defence ministers at the 2019 Shangri-La Dialogue: 'This negative view of China has permeated the US establishment. It is not confined to the White House or the Administration, but is shared widely by Congress, the military, the media, academics and NGOs too'. He added: 'Those inclined to a more positive view of China have been marginalised'.

Washington's negative view is fuelled by a nativist fear that 'a new world is coming into being...one being shaped in distant lands and by foreign people'; that American leadership is under threat; and that the United States will cease to be the dominant force it once was. All of those things will happen. But fear is a corrosive that searches for blame and results in denial. Strategic distrust of China has become an American national security and defence policy, just as strategic distrust of Soviet Russia prevailed during the Cold War. China is regarded not merely as a competitor, but as a 'revisionist power', a strategic adversary, an enemy. It is a dire, dyspeptic view, one that advocates that America 'must draw the battle lines...and engage in a great Manichean struggle that will define the next century'.

But as the Cold War scholar and China specialist Odd Arne Westad has reminded us, there is no irreconcilable ideological divide between China and the United States, as there once was with Moscow. Soviet ideology was inherently opposed to any long-term coexistence with the West. By contrast, Chinese society 'is more similar to American society than Soviet society ever was'. China wants to trade with America, and with the rest of the world. And for the vast majority of Chinese, 'communism is simply a name for the ruling party rather than an ideal to seek'. The Chinese people are 'interested above all in getting ahead in their competitive, market oriented society'. They recognise that globalisation is a reality, not a choice; an opportunity, not a loss of sovereignty.

Prime Minister Lee Hsien Loong made the same point:

China may be communist in political structure, but
it has adopted market principles in many areas. The
Soviets sought to overturn the world order. But China

has benefitted from, and by and large worked within,
the framework of existing multilateral institutions.
During the Cold War, the Communist bloc sought to
export Communism to the world. But China today is not
attempting to turn other countries Communist.

And unlike the former Soviet Union, China is more integrated
and connected with the world, including the United States,
than almost any other country. Soviet Russia's economic links
outside the Soviet bloc were negligible; it refused to join the
world economy. By contrast, China is the engine of the world
economy. And it will continue to be the largest contributor to the
world's GDP growth by a substantial margin, notwithstanding
its enforced contraction resulting from the pandemic. The
United States is still China's largest trading partner. And all of
the United States 'allies' in the Asia-Pacific, 'including Japan,
South Korea, the Philippines, Thailand and Australia, as well
as many of its friends and partners, including Singapore, have
China as their largest trading partner'.

Slaying the dragon will not work. John Lee, senior fellow at
the US Studies Centre and Hudson Institute in Washington DC,
explained that 'efforts to economically distance from China...
will prove unnecessary, self-defeating or else impossible'. Westad
commented to the same effect: 'Attempting to disentangle the
United States' economy from China's through political means,
such as travel restrictions, technology bans and trade barriers,
will not work, unless a de facto state of war makes economic
interaction impossible'.

There is no doubt that China seeks to advance its commercial
interests, to preserve its security and maintain economic
dominance. And it considers, not entirely unreasonably, that

the presence of the United States in the Asia-Pacific is an historical anomaly, which is why it has substantially increased its maritime force in the South China Sea. But China's last foreign military intervention was a brief border war in Vietnam in 1979 that lasted three weeks. And its last major conflict, the Korean War, ended almost seventy years ago. It has enjoyed forty years of peace and unparalleled prosperity. Unlike Washington, Beijing understands the disadvantages of war and the value of peace. Admittedly, China goes too far in pursuit of its security, exemplified by the heavy-handed crackdowns at Tiananmen Square in 1989, against the Uighurs in Xinjiang and perhaps now in Hong Kong. But commentators refer to Beijing's outlook as being 'nationalist rather than internationalist'.

This is controversial for some. There is no shortage of sceptics and China hawks who hold strong views; who readily resort to characterising those with different opinions as 'appeasers'. But it is difficult to deny the truth of the aphorism that for China, 'economics trumps politics'. The best predictions can be confounded by future events, but analysis suggests that China aspires to be a 'global commercial hegemon' – not a military, political or ideological hegemon, as Napoleonic France, Wilhelmine Germany, Imperial Japan or Nazi Germany all were. On this view, the China model is more like the Dutch commercial and trading empire of the sixteenth and seventeenth centuries. For that reason, it is said, China 'does not truly challenge the existing order in terms of political values, ideological norms or regime types'. Its actions are largely guided by 'pecuniary self-interest and profit maximisation', and trade with any country irrespective of its political system.

It is also clear that, unlike the former Soviet Union and Washington establishments past and present, China does not see the world in zero-sum terms: capitalism and democracy versus its own model of socialism with capitalist features. Nor does it believe that 'the United States or its system of government has to be defeated in order to achieve' its goals. Beijing regards Washington as an obstacle, not as an existential or ideological threat. A 'clash of civilisations' – or worse, of races – is the language of a former US state department official, not of China. Anti-China sentiment may be at its highest since Tiananmen Square, but China is not going to war – unless the United States overreacts or pushes Beijing to intolerable limits.

Those limits may be tested as the pandemic inexorably causes the United States to suffer 'the democratic recession that has been evident for the past 15 years' – inciting even greater political desperation and roiling internal unrest. In the dystopian British television drama, *Years and Years*, starring Emma Thompson, a weak and expedient US president launches a nuclear strike on an artificial island in the South China Sea. This may be the future that awaits us. But although a populist American foreign policy based on opposing China may have domestic appeal, it is hardly a responsible and reasonable answer to the challenges that shape today's world. Washington's failure of leadership means that the pandemic will 'accelerate history rather than re-shape it' – amplifying the decline of American power and facilitating greater opportunities for China to advance its influence and interests.

Seventy-five years after the heady days of 1945, the United States has become what was once predicted: 'a nation drifting dangerously amidst a global chaos it cannot control'. The deserved respect in which America was once held is rapidly evaporating, while the rest of the world has moved on. Fintan O'Toole, renowned columnist for *The Irish Times*, was punishingly direct in a recent piece about Washington's handling of the COVID-19 pandemic, writing that 'The world has loved, hated and envied the US. Now, for the first time, we pity it'.

Well-intentioned American aspirations of yesteryear seem like a faint and distant dream, remote from today's reality. High-sounding principles that were once recognisable as a canon of American policy, now seem foreign and disconnected. Consider the following statements, for example:

> No nation's security and well-being can be lastingly achieved in isolation but only in effective cooperation with fellow nations.
> Any nation's right to a form of government and an economic system of its own choosing is *inalienable*.
> Any nation's attempt to dictate to other nations their form of government is *indefensible*.
> A nation's hope of lasting peace cannot be firmly based upon any race in armaments but rather upon just relations and honest understanding with all other nations.

These are not the words of Ghandi, Mandela, Martin Luther King or even Xi Jinping but of President Dwight Eisenhower in early 1953, in the first hopeful months of his presidency. Eisenhower's early noble intentions never really aligned with the priorities, values and actions of the defence and security establishment. A military cast of mind still dominates in Washington. It is now supplemented by an 'America First' attitude – through which a thick vein of anxiety and insecurity runs deep. The distinguished American historian Alfred McCoy described what passes for 'insider wisdom in Washington' as a 'world view of stunning insularity'. It has long been reflected in Washington's intolerance for political and economic systems, beliefs and cultures that do not reflect its values and interests.

With the possible exception of sheer military hardware – killing capacity – there has been a shift in the global distribution of power; a movement away from American dominance across 'every other dimension – industrial, financial, social, cultural... economics and business, ideas and art'. The world has moved 'from anti-Americanism to post-Americanism'. It is a world defined by the rise of the rest, as much as by the decline of the United States. And it represents the third great power shift in modern history – from Europe to America and now to Asia, led by China.

It is appropriate to recall a few words of President Reagan. He told the American people that the history of the world teaches us that 'the freer the flow of world trade, the stronger the tides of human progress and peace among nations'. It also teaches us that pandemics have been the inevitable attendants of economic progress; and that interconnected trade networks and teeming cities have made societies both richer and more vulnerable. The most successful cities in history – Alexandria, Lisbon, Malacca, Canton and New York among many others – have been those that opened their doors to trade and immigration, resulting in diverse, prosperous and often tolerant entrepôts.

Ronald Reagan also explained that 'The expansion of the international economy is not a foreign invasion. It is an American triumph'. How things have changed in an 'America First' world. Washington's determination to isolate itself and to 'fight' with China on almost every level leaves it on the wrong side of history. The United States will not change. But the rest of the world has the opportunity to work with China, not fight with China. And we should be sceptical of Washington's populist declamatory rhetoric. It is time to heed the advice of the late Senator William Fulbright that we should 'accept the world as it is, with all its existing nations and ideologies, with all its existing qualities and shortcomings'.

NOTES

PREFACE & INTRODUCTION

Page 2 **lunging red arrows** James Curran, 'Our China Panic is Stepping into the World of Paranoia', 10 December 2019, *Financial Review*: https://www.afr.com/policy/foreign-affairs/our-china-panic-is-stepping-into-the-world-of-paranoia-20191210-p53ijz, accessed 1/4/2020

Page 5 **undeterred by rules and procedures** Simon Chesterman and Michael Byers, 'Has US Power Destroyed the UN?', *The London Review of Books*, Vol. 21, No. 9, pp. 29–30, 29 April 1999: https://www.lrb.co.uk/v21/n09/simon-chesterman/has-us-power-destroyed-the-un, accessed 1/4/2020

Page 5 **more and more to contravene** Chris Patten, *Not Quite the Diplomat: Home Truths About World Affairs*, Penguin, 2006, p. 302

Page 5 **survey of 67,806 respondents** Eric Zuesse, 'Polls: US Is "the Greatest Threat to Peace in the World Today"', *Strategic Culture Foundation*, 7 August 2017: https://www.strategic-culture.org/news/2017/08/07/polls-us-greatest-threat-to-peace-world-today/, accessed 4/2/2020

Page 5 **What worries me most** 'Remarks by President Donald Tusk before the G7 summit in Charlevoix, Canada', European Council, 8 June 2018: https://www.consilium.europa.eu/en/press/press-releases/2018/06/08/remarks-by-president-donald-tusk-before-the-g7-summit-in-charlevoix-canada/, accessed 11/3/2020

Page 5 **We are in danger of losing America** Thomas Friedman, 'Restoring Our Honor', *The New York Times*, 6 May 2004: https://www.nytimes.com/2004/05/06/opinion/restoring-our-honor.html, accessed 9/11/2019

Page 6 **higher than that trodden by the crowd** Justice Benjamin N Cardozo, *Meinhard v. Salmon*, 164 NE 545 (NY 1928): https://www.nycourts.gov/reporter/archives/meinhard_salmon.htm, accessed 8/3/2019

Page 6 **We cannot commend our society** Tom Bingham, *The Rule of Law*, Penguin Books, 2011, p. 136

Page 7 **to lead, save, liberate** Andrew J Bacevich, *Washington Rules: America's Path to Permanent War*, Metropolitan Books, 2010, p. 12

Page 7 **short American Century** Andrew J Bacevich (ed.), *The Short American Century: A Postmortem*, Harvard University Press, 2012

Page 7 **little more than half a century** George Packer, 'The End of the American Century', *The Atlantic*, May 2019: https://www.theatlantic.com/magazine/archive/2019/05/george-packer-pax-americana-richard-holbrooke/586042/, accessed 11/6/2019

Page 7 **worldwide democracy – victory for all mankind** Dean Rusk, *Winning a Worldwide Victory for Freedom*, The Department of State, 1962, pp. 1–9

Page 7 **a world leader that nobody follows** Immanuel Wallerstein, 'The Eagle Has Crash Landed', *Foreign Policy*, 11 November 2009: https://foreignpolicy.com/2009/11/11/the-eagle-has-crash-landed/, accessed 9/11/2019

Page 9 **So what? Of course. That's China.** 'How Should Australia handle its trade relationship with Beijing', ABC RN Breakfast, 22 November 2019: https://www.abc.net.au/radionational/programs/breakfast/how-should-australia-handle-its-trade-relationship-with-beijing/11727990, accessed 4/2/2020

Page 10 **the biggest populations and armies** Parag Khanna, 'Welcome to the Asian Country', *The Globe and Mail*, 2 February 2019: https://www.theglobeandmail.com/opinion/article-welcome-to-the-asian-century/, accessed 11/6/2019

Page 10 **flailing about** Kishore Mahbubani, *Has the West Lost It?*, Penguin, 2018, p. 7

CHAPTER 1 Exceptionalism

Page 14 **Justice was triumphant at Nuremberg** Henry T King, 35 Case W. Res J. Int'l L. 263 (2003)

Page 14 **not enough that we restore peace** Robert H Jackson, 'The Rule of Law Among Nations', *American Bar Association Journal*, 31 ABAJ 290 (1945): https://www.roberthjackson.org/wp-content/uploads/2015/01/Rule_of_Law_Among_Nations.pdf, accessed 11/6/2019

Page 14 **much hinges on acceptance** Jackson, 'The Rule of Law Among Nations'

Page 15 **futile to think.** Jackson, 'The Rule of Law Among Nations'

Page 15 **worst settlement of international disputes** Jackson, 'The Rule of Law Among Nations'

Page 15 **the most dispassionate** Robert H Jackson, Opening Statement before the International Military Tribunal, Second Day, Wednesday, 11/21/1945, Part 04, in Trial of the Major War Criminals before the International Military Tribunal, Volume II, Proceedings: 11/14/1945-11/30/1945: https://www.roberthjackson.org/speech-and-writing/opening-statement-before-the-international-military-tribunal/, accessed 13/2/2019

Page 15 **great effort to make the peace** Jackson, Opening Statement

Page 16 **whatever grievances** Jackson, Opening Statement

Page 16 **Any resort to war** Jackson, Opening Statement

Page 16 **How did it come about** Jackson, Opening Statement

Page 17 **If certain acts in violation of treaties** Robert H Jackson, *Minutes of Conference Session of July 23, 1945*, International Conference on Military

Trials: https://www.loc.gov/rr/frd/Military_Law/pdf/jackson-rpt-military-trials.pdf, accessed 13/2/2019

Page 17 **We must never forget** Jackson, Opening Statement

Page 17 **end of history** Francis Fukuyama, *The End of History and the Last Man*, Free Press, 1992

Page 17 **divine mission** Jeffrey D Sachs, *A New Foreign Policy: Beyond American Exceptionalism*, Columbia University Press, 2018, p. 23

Page 17 **deeply set in American culture** Sachs, *A New Foreign Policy*, p. 21

Page 18 **destiny and duty** Godfrey Hodgson, *The Myth of American Exceptionalism*, Yale University Press, 2009, p. 10

Page 18 **an imagined order** Yuval Noah Harari, *Sapiens: A Brief History of Humankind*, Random House, 2014, p. 127

Page 18 **encapsulated the curious** Bernard-Henri Lévy, *The Empire and the Five Kings: America's Abdication and the fate of the World*, Henry Holt, 2019, pp. 47–49

Page 18 **the Brits believe in British exceptionalism** Barack Obama, 'News Conference by President Obama', *The White House*, 4 April 2009: https://obamawhitehouse.archives.gov/the-press-office/news-conference-president-obama-4042009, accessed 7/2/2019

Page 18 **God has created us** Robert A Klein, *Sovereign equality among states: The history of an idea*, University of Toronto Press, 1974, p. 51

Page 18 **the first race in the world.** Klein, *Sovereign equality among states*, p. 51

Page 19 **greatest sermon of the millennium** Hodgson, *The Myth of American Exceptionalism*, p. 1

Page 19 **The ideal of America** George W Bush, 'President's Remarks to the Nation', *The White House*, 11 September 2002: https://georgewbush-whitehouse.archives.gov/news/releases/2002/09/20020911-3.html, accessed 7/2/2019

Page 20 **world's best hope** Thomas Jefferson, 'First Inaugural Address', *The Avalon Project Yale Law School*, 4 March 1801: https://avalon.law.yale.edu/19th_century/jefinau1.asp, accessed 14/3/2020

Page 20 **last, best hope on earth** Abraham Lincoln, 'Second Annual Message to Congress', *National Archives*, 1 December 1862: https://www.archives.gov/legislative/features/sotu/lincoln.html, accessed 14/3/2020

Page 20 **There can be no slavery in a free land** Arthur Phillip, HRNSW, Vol. 1, Part 2, p. 53

Page 20 **manifest destiny to overspread** John L O'Sullivan, 'Manifest Destiny', *New York Morning News*, 27 December 1845

Page 21 **Christianize the heathens** Interview with President William McKinley in *The Christian Advocate*, 22 January 1903, p. 17

Page 21 **Philippines are ours forever** Albert Beveridge, 'America's Destiny (1900)': http://www.historymuse.net/readings/beveridge.html, accessed 11/6/2019

Page 21 **for the elevation of the spirit** George McLean Harper (ed.), *President Wilson's Addresses*, Henry Holt, 1918: https://archive.org/stream/

wilsonsaddress00harprich/wilsonsaddress00harprich_djvu.txt, accessed 9/11/2019

Page 22 **make the world safe for democracy** Harper (ed.), *President Wilson's Addresses*

Page 22 **responsibility to protect** Tony Smith, 'An Interview with Tony Smith, author of Why Wilson Matters: The Origin of American Liberal Internationalism and Its Crisis Today': https://press.princeton.edu/interviews/qa-10840, accessed 11/2/2019

Page 22 **America might have led the world** Ivo H Daalder and James M Lindsay, *The Empty Throne: America's Abdication of Global Leadership*, Hachette, 2018, p. 15

Page 23 **all his strength, character and cleverness** Lévy, *The Empire and the Five Kings*, p. 45

Page 23 **the first America First movement** Lévy, *The Empire and the Five Kings*, p. 45

Page 23 **five thousand Allied sailors died** Odd Arne Westad, *The Cold War: A World History*, Penguin, 2017, p. 48

Page 23 **if the United States had not helped us** Sergei Khrushchev, *Memoirs of Nikita Khrushchev, Volume 1, Commissar [1918–1945]*, Pennsylvania State University Press, 2004, p. 639

Page 23 **give Americans a messianic desire** Stephen Kinzer, *Overthrow: America's Century of Regime Change from Hawaii to Iraq*, Henry Holt, 2006, p. 319

Page 24 **moral imperative** Harari, *Sapiens*, pp. 221–2

Page 24 **encouraging the State Department** Paul Kennedy, *The Parliament of Man: The United Nations and the Quest for World Government*, Allen Lane, 2006, p. 25

Page 25 **right to feel** Andrew Glass, 'Churchill, FDR meet off Newfoundland, Aug. 9, 1941', *Politico*, 8 September 2017: https://www.politico.com/story/2017/08/09/churchill-fdr-meet-off-newfoundland-aug-9-1941-241372, accessed 12/6/2019

Page 25 **wider and permanent system** *Atlantic Charter*, 14 August 1941: http://cdn.un.org/unyearbook/yun/pdf/1946-47/1946-47_37.pdf, accessed 11/2/2019

Page 25 **the right of all peoples to choose** *Atlantic Charter*, 14 August 1941

Page 26 **program of purposes and principles** *Declaration by the United Nations*, 1 January 1942: http://cdn.un.org/unyearbook/yun/pdf/1946-47/1946-47_36.pdf, accessed 11/2/2019

Page 27 **recognize the necessity** *The Moscow Declaration on General Security*, 30 October 1943: http://cdn.un.org/unyearbook/yun/pdf/1946-47/1946-47_38.pdf, accessed 11/2/2019

Page 27 **Ten thousand men a day** Westad, *The Cold War: A World History*, p. 49

Page 27 **principle of sovereign equality** *The Formation of the United Nations*, 1945: https://history.state.gov/milestones/1937-1945/un, accessed 14/3/2020

Page 28 **refrain from the threat or use of force** *Charter of the United Nations*,

1945: https://www.un.org/en/sections/un-charter/un-charter-full-text/, accessed 14/3/2020

Page 29 **the twin ideas** Daalder and Lindsay, *The Empty Throne*, p. 18

Page 29 **Regime change might be a consequence** Bingham, *The Rule of Law*, p. 122

Page 30 **To expect every country** Lee Hsien Loong, Keynote Address, 'The 18th IISS Shangri-La Dialogue', International Institute for Strategic Studies (IIS), 31 May 2019: https://www.pmo.gov.sg/Newsroom/PM-Lee-Hsien-Loong-at-the-IISS-Shangri-La-Dialogue-2019, accessed 4/2/2020

Page 30 **a true 'Parliament of Man'** Kennedy, *The Parliament of Man* 'A Note on the Title', pp. ix–x

Page 32 **perfectly adamant...absolutely no** George Monbiot, 'Keynes is innocent: the toxic spawn of Bretton Woods was no plan of his', *The Guardian*, 18 November 2018: https://www.theguardian.com/commentisfree/2008/nov/18/lord-keynes-international-monetary-fund, accessed 11/2/2019

Page 32 **Lord Keynes was right** Monbiot, *The Guardian*, 18 November 2018

Page 33 **work better for the United States** Westad, *The Cold War: A World History*, p. 66

CHAPTER 2 Ideology

Page 34 **little in common with Roosevelt** Oliver Stone and Peter Kuznick, *The Untold History of the United States*, Random House, 2013, p. 118

Page 34 **not a deep thinker** Daalder and Lindsay, *The Empty Throne*, p. 15

Page 34 **charisma, political suaveness** Westad, *The Cold War: A World History*, p. 57

Page 35 **Missouri County court-house calibre** Peter G Boyle, 'The British Foreign Office View of Soviet–American Relations 1945–46', *Diplomatic History*, Vol. 3, Issue 3, July 1979: https://doi.org/10.1111/j.1467-7709.1979.tb00317.x

Page 35 **If we see that Germany is winning** Alden Whitman, 'Harry S. Truman: Decisive President', *The New York Times*, 27 December 1972: https://www.nytimes.com/1972/12/27/archives/harry-s-truman-decisive-president-the-lightning-strikes-in-war.html, accessed 15/11/2019

Page 35 **The chief lesson that I have learned** 'Memorandum from Henry L. Stimson to Harry S. Truman', 11 September 1945: https://www.trumanlibrary.org/whistlestop/study_collections/bomb/large/documents/index.php?documentid=22&pagenumber=5, accessed 28/3/2019

Page 36 **exert upon the world** Henry R Luce, 'The American Century', *Life*, Vol. 10, No. 7, 17 February 1941, p. 63

Page 36 **Some have spoken of the 'American Century'** Henry A Wallace, *The Century of the Common Man*, 8 May 1942: https://www.americanrhetoric.com/speeches/henrywallacefreeworldassoc.htm, accessed 13/2/2019

Page 37 **The only kind of competition** Henry A Wallace, 12 April 1946, cited in Stone and Kuznick, *The Untold History of the United States*, p. 194

Page 37 **too innocent and idealistic** Anthony Cave Brown 'C': *The Secret Life of Sir Stewart Graham Menzies*, MacMillan, NY, 1987, pp 481–4

Page 37 **We may not like what Russia does** Henry A. Wallace, *The Price of Vision: The Diary of Henry A. Wallace, 1942–1946*, Houghton Mifflin, 1973, p. 666

Page 38 **Under friendly peaceful competition** Wallace, *The Price of Vision*, p. 666

Page 38 **Your courageous intervention** Albert Einstein letter to Henry Wallace, Secretary of Commerce, 18 September 1946: http://digital.lib.uiowa.edu/cdm/ref/collection/wallace/id/40083, accessed 22/2/2019

Page 38 **a pacifist one hundred percent** 'Typed Note of President Harry S. Truman', 19 September 1946, President's Secretary's Files: https://www.trumanlibrary.gov/library/truman-papers/longhand-notes-presidential-file-1944-1953/september-19-1946, accessed 25/5/2020

Page 39 **the last chance to avert the Cold War** Stone and Kuznick, *The Untold History of the United States*, p. 204

Page 39 **language of military power** Clark Clifford, *American Relations with the Soviet Union*, 24 September 1946, Conway Files, Truman Papers, 'Clifford-Elsey Report': https://www.trumanlibrary.gov/library/research-files/report-american-relations-soviet-union-clark-clifford-clifford-elsey-report, accessed 25/5/2020

Page 39 **black and white analysis** Melvyn P Leffler, *A Preponderance of Power: National Security, the Truman Administration, and the Cold War*, Stanford University Press, 1992, p. 133

Page 39 **no real background** Tim Weiner, *Legacy of Ashes: History of the CIA*, Anchor Books, 2008, pp. 616–17

Page 39 **would not provoke the next war** Weiner, *Legacy of Ashes*, p. 617

Page 39 **Winning the peace** Wallace, 20 September 1946, in *The Price of Vision*, p. 630

Page 40 **most of them emphasised reform** Westad, *The Cold War: A World History*, p. 11

Page 42 **murder, rape, pillage** Ole Hanson, *Americanism Versus Bolshevism*, Doubleday, 1920, p. viii

Page 43 **If it had not been for capitalism** Westad, *The Cold War: A World History*, p. 35

Page 43 **neither was ever fully replicated** Westad, *The Cold War: A World History*, pp. 7–8

Page 43 **hierarchy, authenticity, empathy** Westad, *The Cold War: A World History*, p. 23

Page 43 **felt their destiny was to forge** Westad, *The Cold War: A World History*, p. 22

Page 44 **they alone were set to fulfil God's plan** Westad, *The Cold War: A World History*, p. 16

Page 44 **sentimental relationship with Stalin** Westad, *The Cold War: A World History*, p. 64

Page 44 **Roosevelt has died but** Tsuyoshi Hasegawa, *Racing the Enemy: Stalin, Truman and the Surrender of Japan*, Harvard University Press, 2005, p. 57

Page 45 **turned into a wasteland** President John F Kennedy, 'Commencement Address at American University, Washington D.C.', 10 June 1963: https://www.jfklibrary.org/archives/other-resources/john-f-kennedy-speeches/american-university-19630610, accessed 26/2/2019

Page 45 **crisis of capitalism has manifested** Ivo Banac (ed.), *The Diary of Georgi Dimitrov: 1933–1949*, Yale University Press, 2003, p. 358

Page 45 **best I can do for Poland** Declaration on Poland, 10 February 1945: http://www.fdrlibraryvirtualtour.org/graphics/07-37/7.4_FDR_at_Yalta.pdf, accessed 28/3/2019

Page 46 **Everyone imposes his own system** Milovan Djilas, *Conversations with Stalin*, Penguin, 1969, p. 90

Page 46 **create democratic institutions** Yalta Conference Agreement, Declaration of Liberated Europe, 11 February 1945: https://digitalarchive.wilsoncenter.org/document/116176.pdf?v=66b99cbbf4a1b8de1

Page 46 **not of that kind** Westad, *The Cold War: A World History*, p. 52

Page 46 **Leahy...after the understanding at Yalta** Harry S Truman, *Memoirs of Harry S. Truman: Year of Decisions*, Vol. 1, Da Capo Press, 1986, p. 78

Page 46 **Stimson... Russians perhaps...more realistic** Truman, *Memoirs*, p. 78

Page 47 **imperious tone** Feliks I Chuev, Vyacheslav M Molotov and Albert Resis, *Molotov Remembers: Inside Kremlin Politics: Conversations with Feliz Chuev*, I R Dee, 1993, p. 55

Page 47 **I let him have it** John L Gaddis, *The United States and the Origins of the Cold War, 1941–1947*, Columbia University Press, 2000, p. 205

Page 47 **carried high the banners of hope** Westad, *The Cold War: A World History*, p. 74

Page 47 **In many parts of Europe** Westad, *The Cold War: A World History*, pp. 54–5

Page 48 **Groves... the most terrible** Henry L Stimson and McGeorge Bundy, *On Active Service in Peace and War: Volume 2*, Harper, 1948, p. 635

Page 49 **You realize of course** J. Rotblat, *The Nuclear Issue After the Posture Review*, INESAP, Bulletin 20, August 2002: http://www.inesap.org/sites/default/files/inesap_old/bulletin20/bul20art27.htm, accessed 21/2/2019

Page 49 **Groves... never...any illusion** United States Atomic Energy Commission: In the Matter of J. Robert Oppenheimer, Transcript of Hearing Before Personnel Security Board, Washington DC, 12 April 1954 to 6 May 1954, p. 173: https://archive.org/stream/unitedstatesatom007206mbp/unitedstatesatom007206mbp_djvu.txt, accessed 21/2/2019

Page 49 **position to dictate our own terms** Truman, *Memoirs*, p. 87

Page 49 **Mr Byrnes did not argue** Gar Alperovitz, *The Decision to Use the Atomic Bomb*, Fontana Press, 1996, p. 147

Page 50 **Japan now, officially** 'Russo–Japanese Relations (13–20 July 1945)', Publication of Pacific Strategic Intelligence Section, Commander-In-Chief

United States Fleet and Chief of Naval Operations, 21 July 1945, SRH-085, Record Group 457, Modern Military Branch, National Archives, cited in Stone and Kuznick, *The Untold History of the United States*, p. 162

Page 50 **I went to Potsdam** Allen W Dulles, *The Secret Surrender*, Harper and Row, 1966, pp. 255–6

Page 50 **telegram from the Jap Emperor** 'Diary entry of Harry S. Truman', 18 July 1945, Nuclear Files, http://www.nuclearfiles.org/menu/library/correspondence/truman-harry/corr_diary_truman.htm, accessed 25/5/2020

Page 50 **incredible pressure to get it done** United States Atomic Energy Commission hearing, p. 31: https://archive.org/stream/unitedstatesatom007206mbp/unitedstatesatom007206mbp_djvu.txt, accessed 21/2/2019

Page 50 **tremendously pepped up** Henry Stimson's Diary, 21 July 1945: https://nsarchive2.gwu.edu/nukevault/ebb525-The-Atomic-Bomb-and-the-End-of-World-War-II/documents/048.pdf, accessed 25/3/2019

Page 50 **a changed man** Stimson Diary, 22 July 1945: https://nsarchive2.gwu.edu/nukevault/ebb525-The-Atomic-Bomb-and-the-End-of-World-War-II/documents/048.pdf, accessed 25/3/2019

Page 51 **hoping for time** Walter Brown's Diary, 24 July 1945: https://nsarchive2.gwu.edu/nukevault/ebb525-The-Atomic-Bomb-and-the-End-of-World-War-II/documents/049.pdf, accessed 25/3/2019

Page 51 **Believe Japs will fold up** 'Diary entry of Harry S. Truman', 18 July 1945, Nuclear Files, http://www.nuclearfiles.org/menu/library/correspondence/truman-harry/corr_diary_truman.htm, accessed 25/5/2020

Page 51 **It is quite clear that the United States** Alperovitz, *The Decision to Use the Atomic Bomb*, p. 271

Page 52 **fate of the Korean peninsula** Sheila Miyoshi Jager, *Brothers at War: The Unending Conflict in Korea*, WW Norton & Company, 2013, p. 18

Page 52 **Six of the United States' seven star officers** Stone and Kuznick, *The Untold History of the United States*, p. 177

Page 52 **completely unnecessary** Dorris Clayton James, *The Years of MacArthur: 1941–1945*, Houghton Mifflin, 1975, p. 775

Page 52 **no material assistance** William Leahy, *I Was There: The Personal Story of the Chief of Staff to Presidents Roosevelt and Truman: Based on His Notes and Diaries Made at the Time*, Arcole Publishing, 2017, p. 441

Page 53 **Even without the atomic bomb** 'Giles Would Rule Japan a Century', *The New York Times*, 21 September 1945: https://www.nytimes.com/1945/09/21/archives/giles-would-rule-japan-a-century-air-general-says-undefeated.html, accessed 27/3/2019

Page 53 **unnecessary experiment** Alperovitz, *The Decision to Use the Atomic Bomb*, p. 331

Page 53 **I was against it on two counts** 'Ike on Ike', *Newsweek*, 11 November 1963

Page 53 **Dorothy, we will regret** Alperovitz, *The Decision to Use the Atomic Bomb*, p. 326

Page 53 **forever be on the conscience** Alperovitz, *The Decision to Use the Atomic Bomb*, p. 358

Page 53 **Dulles...Luce** Alperovitz, *The Decision to Use the Atomic Bomb*, p. 635

Page 53 **Soviet government interpreted** Ralph B Levering, Vladimir O. Pechatnov, Verena Botzenhart-Viehe and C Earl Edmonson, *Debating the Origins of the Cold War: American and Russian Perspectives*, Rowman & Littlefield Publishers, 2001, p. 105

Page 54 **It was clear already** Georgii Konstantinovich Zhukov, *The Memoirs of Marshal Zhukov*, Cape, 1971, p. 675

Page 54 **greatest thing in history** Truman, *Memoirs*, p. 421

Page 54 **blood on my hands...snivelling** Kai Bird and Martin J Sherwin, *American Prometheus: The Triumph and Tragedy of J. Robert Oppenheimer*, A. Knopf, 2005, p. 332; Rexford Guy Tugwell, *Off Course: From Truman to Nixon*, Praeger, 1971, p. 172

Page 55 **overreacted to Stalin,** Dean Acheson, *Present at the Creation: My Years in the State Department*, Hamish Hamilton, 1970, p. 753

Page 55 **looking for a means** Westad, *The Cold War: A World History*, p. 92

Page 55 **the very existence of the Greek state** Address of the President Before a Joint Session of Congress, *The Avalon Project*, Yale Law School, 12 March 1947: https://avalon.law.yale.edu/20th_century/trudoc.asp, accessed 16/3/2020

Page 55 **support free peoples** Address of the President, 12 March 1947

Page 55 **tantamount to a declaration** Lawrence S Wittner, *Cold War America: From Hiroshima to Watergate*, Holt, Reinhart and Winston, 1978, p. 34

Page 55 **two halves of the same walnut** Arnold A Offner, *Another Such Victory: President Truman and the Cold War, 1945–1953;* Stanford University Press, 2002, p. 461

Page 56 **crusade against Communism** Zhdanov on the Founding of the Cominform, September 1947 in Jussi M Hanhimakiand and Odd Arne Westad, (eds.) *The Cold War: A History in Documents and Eyewitness Accounts*, OUP, 2003, pp. 51–2

Page 56 **'Plan Broiler'** Jeffrey G Barlow, *From Hot War to Cold: The US Navy and National Security Affairs, 1945–1955*, Stanford University Press, 2009, p. 116

Page 57 **any serious plans** Steven Pinker, *Enlightenment Now: The Case for Reason, Science, Humanism and Progress*, Penguin, 2018, p. 312

Page 57 **with dramatic suddenness** P Grose, 'The Boss of Occupied Germany: General Lucius D. Clay', *Foreign Affairs*, Vol. 77, No. 4, July–Aug 1998, p. 179

Page 57 **worldwide counter offensive** 'National Security Council Directive on Office of Special Projects: NSC 10/2', *FRUS*, 1945–1950, 713, 18 June 1948: https://history.state.gov/historicaldocuments/frus1945-50Intel/pg_713, accessed 16/11/2019

Page 57 **overreacted in the most deplorable way** George F Kennan, *Memoirs 1925–1950*, Pantheon Books, NY, 1967, p. 400

Page 58 **seemingly benign Marshall Plan** Stone and Kuznick, *The Untold History of the United States*, p. 213; Weiner, *Legacy of Ashes*, p. 624

Page 58 **...Nightingale** Stone and Kuznick, *The Untold History of the United States*, p. 214

Page 59 **vast tragedy of unforeseeable consequences** 'The Tragedy of China', *The New York Times*, 24 January 1949, https://www.nytimes.com/1949/01/24/ archives/the-tragedy-of-china.html, accessed 27/3/2019

Page 59 **demonstrated capacity** Westad, *The Cold War: A World History*, p. 99

Page 59 **As soon as men decide** Christopher Dawson, *The Judgment of the Nations*, Sheed & Ward, 1942, p. 13

Page 59 **the greatest danger that can befall us** 'George Kennan's 'Long Telegram', 22 February 1946: https://digitalarchive.wilsoncenter.org/document/116178. pdf, accessed 16/11/2019; see also Thomas Bodenheimer and Robert Gould, *Rollback! Right-wing Power in U.S. Foreign Policy*, Second End Press, 1989, p. 13

Page 59 **Not only did the United States** Alfred W McCoy, 'You Must Follow International Law (Unless You're America)', *The Nation*, 24 February 2015, https://www.thenation.com/article/you-must-follow-international-law-unless-youre-america/, accessed 27/3/2019

Page 60 **Whatever we may choose to say** 'Memorandum of Discussion at the 229th Meeting of the National Security Council', *FRUS*, 1952–1954, 2:838, 21 December 1954: https://history.state.gov/historicaldocuments/frus1952-54v02p1/pg_838, accessed 16/11/2019

CHAPTER 3 Compromise

Page 64 **the sacred principles** 'George HW Bush, Speech before the UN General Assembly', *Security Council Report*, 31 January 1992: https:// www.securitycouncilreport.org/atf/cf/%7B65BFCF9B-6D27-4E9C-8CD3-CF6E4FF96FF9%7D/RO%20SPV%203046.pdf, accessed 24/11/2019

Page 64 **seventy-two attempts** Lindsey A O'Rourke, 'The U.S. tried to change other countries' governments 72 times during the Cold War', *The Washington Post*, 23 December 2016: https://www.washingtonpost.com/news/monkey-cage/wp/2016/12/23/the-cia-says-russia-hacked-the-u-s-election-here-are-6-things-to-learn-from-cold-war-attempts-to-change-regimes/?utm_term=.2596a4782bd1, accessed 29/5/2019

Page 64 **American military interventions of all types** Monica Duffy Toft, 'Why is America Addicted to Foreign Interventions', *The National Interest*, 10 December 2017: https://nationalinterest.org/print/feature/why-america-addicted-foreign-interventions-23582, accessed 13/9/2019

Page 64 **Whereas the target** Major D H Berger, 'The Use of Covert Paramilitary Activity as a Policy Tool: An Analysis of Operations Conducted by the United States Central Intelligence Agency, 1949–1951', Marine Corps Command and

Staff College (U.S.), 5 February 1995: https://fas.org/irp/eprint/berger.htm, accessed 29/5/2019

Page 65 **correlate and evaluate intelligence,** Section 102(d)(3), *National Security Act*, 1947

Page 65 **no evidence in the debates** Berger, The Use of Covert Paramilitary Activity as a Policy Tool

Page 65 **never considered** Walter L Pforzheimer quoted in Berger, The Use of Covert Paramilitary Activity as a Policy Tool

Page 65 **such other functions and duties,** Section 102(d)(5), *National Security Act*, 1947

Page 65 **Who is there left to object?** Berger, The Use of Covert Paramilitary Activity as a Policy Tool

Page 65 **no legislative authority** Berger, The Use of Covert Paramilitary Activity as a Policy Tool

Page 66 **reach into every corner** James Srodes, *Allen Dulles: Master of Spies*, Regnery Publishing, 1999, p. 439

Page 66 **so planned and executed** 'National Security Council Directive on Office of Special Projects – NSC 10/2', *FRUS*, 1945–1950, Emergence of the Intelligence Establishment, 18 June 1948: https://history.state.gov/historicaldocuments/frus1945-50Intel/pg_714, accessed 30/5/2019

Page 66 **moneys for which no voucher** 'War Report, Office of Strategic Services (OSS)', *The History Project*, U.S. Government Printing Office, July 1949, p. 84: https://stacks.stanford.edu/file/druid:yk502ct8920/OSS_war_report_v1_hq_organization.pdf, accessed 30/5/2019

Page 67 **We lied, we cheated** Michael R Pompeo, 'Why Diplomacy Matters', *U.S. Department of State,* 15 April 2019: https://www.state.gov/remarks-at-texas-am-wiley-lecture-series/, accessed 16/4/2020

Page 67 **Turkish government contend...** Tim Arango, 'Turks Can Agree on One Thing: US Was Behind Failed Coup', *The New York Times*, 3 August 2016: https://www.nytimes.com/2016/08/03/world/europe/turkey-coup-erdogan-fethullah-gulen-united-states.html, accessed 19/3/2020

Page 67 **Beijing allege** Andrew Higgins, 'China's Theory for Hong Kong Protests: Secret American Meddling', *The New York Times*, 8 August 2019: https://www.nytimes.com/2019/08/08/world/asia/hong-kong-black-hand.html, accessed 19/3/2020

Page 68 **covert operations that killed, wounded** Colman McCarthy, 'The Consequences of Covert Tactics', *The Washington Post*, 13 December 1987: https://www.washingtonpost.com/archive/lifestyle/1987/12/13/the-consequences-of-covert-tactics/0aed76c5-5517-4224-89c0-cab16948439c/?utm_term=.ad43daf1fd5b, accessed 1/4/2019; see also John Dower, *The Violent American Century: War and Terror Since World War II*, Haymarket Books, 2017, p. 52

Page 68 **Kent…clandestine operatives into** Robin W Winks, *Cloak and Gown: Scholars in the Secret War, 1939–1961*, Yale University Press, 1996, p. 451; see also Weiner, *Legacy of Ashes*, p. 626

Page 68 **America took off the gloves** James E Miller, 'Taking Off the Gloves: The United States and the Italian Elections of 1948', *Diplomatic History*, Vol. 7, No. 1, Winter 1983, p. 53

Page 68 **perilous new policy** Miller, p. 55

Page 69 **CIA Report** 'Consequences of Communist Accession to Power in Italy by Legal Means', *Central Intelligence Agency*, 5 March 1948: https://www.cia.gov/library/readingroom/docs/CIA-RDP78-01617A003100010001-5.pdf, accessed 19/3/2020

Page 69 **The estimate of funds** Weiner, *Legacy of Ashes*, p. 623

Page 69 **further American intervention abroad** Harry S Truman, *Public Papers of the Presidents*, 1948, pp 227–9 cited in Miller, p. 52

Page 71 **CIA Report** 'Consequences of Communist Accession to Power', *Central Intelligence Agency*, 1948

Page 71 **if [Mossadegh] were to be assassinated** 'Memorandum of Discussion at the 135th Meeting of the National Security Council', *FRUS*, 1952–1954, 10:693, 4 March 1953: https://history.state.gov/historicaldocuments/frus1952-54v10/pg_693, accessed 5/4/2019

Page 71 **create, extend and enhance public hostility** 'Appendix B, London Draft of the TPAJAX Operational Plan', p. 15: https://nsarchive2.gwu.edu/NSAEBB/NSAEBB28/appendix%20B.pdf, accessed 5/4/2019

Page 71 **members of parliament withdrew** Kinzer, *Overthrow*, p. 124

Page 72 **Gangs of thugs ran wildly** Kinzer, *Overthrow*, p. 127

Page 72 **military and police units,** Kinzer, *Overthrow*, p. 127

Page 73 **It is a reasonable argument** Mostafa T Zahrani, 'The Coup That Changed the Middle East: Mossadeq v. The CIA in Retrospect', *World Policy Journal*, Vol. 19, No. 2 (Summer 2002), p. 93

Page 74 **the original sin** Daniel Benjamin and Steven Simon, 'America's Great Satan: The 40-Year Obsession With Iran', *Foreign Affairs*, November/December 2019: https://www.foreignaffairs.com/articles/middle-east/2019-10-15/americas-great-satan, accessed 24/11/2019

Page 74 **free of such annoyances** Kinzer, *Overthrow*, p. 130

Page 75 **converting Guatemala** Jim Handy, *Gift of the Devil: A History of Guatemala*, South End Press, 1984, p. 115

Page 75 **Reds are in control** 'Excerpt from the Diary of James C. Hagerty, Press Secretary to the President', *FRUS*, 1952–1954, 4:1102, 26 April 1954: https://history.state.gov/historicaldocuments/frus1952-54v04/pg_1102, accessed 24/5/2019

Page 75 **Kremlin's design for world conquest** Kinzer, *Overthrow*, p. 135

Page 75 **based on our deep conviction** FRUS 1952–1954, 4:1106, 11 May 1954: https://history.state.gov/historicaldocuments/frus1952-54v04/pg_1106, accessed 7/5/2019

Page 76 **writing scripts or leaflets** 'Interview with Howard Hunt': https://nsarchive2.gwu.edu/coldwar/interviews/episode-18/hunt2.html, accessed 7/5/2019

Page 76 **demonic force called communism** Kinzer, *Overthrow*, p. 138

Page 76 **Those who expressed reservations** Bernard Gwertzman, 'U.S. Tells of '54 Guatemala Invasion', *The New York Times*, 4 January 1984: https://www.nytimes.com/1984/01/04/world/us-tells-of-54-guatemala-invasion.html, accessed 8/5/2019; and Kinzer, *Overthrow*, p. 140–1

Page 76 **department has no evidence** David M Barrett, 'Sterilizing a 'Red Infection' Congress, the CIA, and Guatemala, 1954', *CIA Library*: https://www.cia.gov/library/center-for-the-study-of-intelligence/kent-csi/vol44no5/html/v44i5a03p.htm, accessed 19/3/2020

Page 77 **regret to inform your Excellency** Stephen C Schlesinger and Stephen Kinzer, *Bitter Fruit: The Story of the American Coup in Guatemala*, Anchor Books, 1983, p. 183

Page 77 **the great ruse of Operation Success** Kinzer, *Overthrow*, p. 144

Page 77 **A cruel war** 'Arbenz' Resignation Speech', *CIA*, 1 May 1954: https://www.cia.gov/library/readingroom/docs/DOC_0000920952.pdf, accessed 9/5/2019

Page 77 **the biggest success** Max Paul Friedman, 'Fracas in Caracas: Latin American Diplomatic Resistance to United States Intervention in Guatemala in 1954', *Diplomacy and Statecraft*, Vol. 21, Issue 4, 2010, p. 681

Page 77 **extend a hand to the Soviets** 'Prime Minister Churchill to President Eisenhower', *FRUS*, 1952–1954, 6:973, 11 April 1953: https://history.state.gov/historicaldocuments/frus1952-54v06p1/pg_973, accessed 27/5/2019; see also Westad, *The Cold War: A World History*, p. 228

Page 78 **extremely heavy weather** Westad, *The Cold War: A World History*, p. 347; see also Max Friedman, 'Fracas in Caracas', p. 681

Page 78 **give them [the British] a lesson** Westad, *The Cold War: A World History*, p. 347

Page 78 **Not unless our automobiles collide** A. J. Langguth, *Our Vietnam: The War 1954–1975*, Simon & Schuster, 2000, p. 72

Page 79 **decided not to hold** Kinzer, *Overthrow*, p. 153; see also 'Dulles supports Diem's decision not to hold national election', *History*, updated 25/2/2019: https://www.history.com/this-day-in-history/dulles-supports-diems-decision-not-to-hold-national-election, accessed 27/5/2019

Page 79 **All men are created equal** Chi Minh Ho, *Selected Works*, Vol. 3, Foreign Languages Publishing House, 1961, p. 17

Page 80 **possibly eighty percent** Dwight David Eisenhower, *The White House Years: Mandate for Change: 1953–1956*, Vol. 1, Doubleday, 1963, p. 372

Page 80 **bound to lose** Westad, *The Cold War: A World History*, p. 314

Page 80 **Christ has gone to the South** Fredrik Logevall, *Embers of War: The Fall of an Empire and the Making of America's Vietnam*, Random House, 2012, p. 638

Page 80 **the Churchill of Southeast Asia** Stanley Karnow, *Vietnam: A History*, Viking, 1991, p. 214

Page 80 **the only boy we got there** Karnow, p. 230

Page 80 **plucked from a religious group** Kinzer, *Overthrow*, p. 155

Page 81 **all these soldiers...intensifying the conflict** Kinzer, *Overthrow*, p. 155

Page 81 **not want to be a protectorate** William Gibbons, *The U.S. Government and the Vietnam War: Executive and Legislative Roles and Relationships, Part II: 1961–1964*, Princeton University Press, 2014, p. 102

Page 81 **I am anti-communist** Kinzer, *Overthrow*, p. 156; see also 'American Experience', Vietnam Online, PBS: http://www.shoppbs.pbs.org/wgbh/amex/vietnam/series/pt_02.html, accessed 5/6/2019

Page 81 **no possibility** 'Telegram From the Embassy in Vietnam to the Department of State', *FRUS*, 1961–1963, 4:21, 29 August 1963: https://history.state.gov/historicaldocuments/frus1961-63v04/pg_21, accessed 5/6/2019

Page 81 **cannot tolerate a situation...Diem's replacement** 'Telegram From the Department of State to the Embassy in Vietnam', *FRUS*, 1961–1963, 3:628, 24 August 1963: https://history.state.gov/historicaldocuments/frus1961-63v03/pg_628, accessed 5/6/2019

Page 82 **We are launched on a course** 'Telegram From the Embassy in Vietnam to the Department of State', *FRUS*, 1961–1963, 4:21, 29 August 1963: https://history.state.gov/historicaldocuments/frus1961-63v04/pg_21, accessed 5/6/2019

Page 82 **Pentagon Papers** 'Evolution of the War, The Overthrow of Ngo Dinh Diem, May – November 1963', *The Pentagon Papers*, Vol. 2, Ch. 4: https://web.archive.org/web/20150926130012/http://media.nara.gov/research/pentagon-papers/Pentagon-Papers-Part-IV-B-5.pdf, accessed 5/9/2019

Page 83 **decision to get out honorably** 'Office of the Special Assistant for Counterinsurgency and Special Activities, Memorandum for the Record, Meeting at the State Department, 1100, 31 August 1963, Vietnam, 31 August 1963', *The Pentagon Papers*: https://www.mtholyoke.edu/acad/intrel/pentagon2/doc135.htm, accessed 5/6/2019

Page 83 **time to get out of Vietnam...hopelessly alien thought** Arthur M. Schlesinger Jr, *Robert Kennedy and His Times*, Mariner Books, 2002, p. 714

Page 83 **If I can do anything...please call me** 'Telegram From the Embassy in Vietnam to the Department of State', *FRUS*, 1961-1963, 4:513, 1 November 1963: https://history.state.gov/historicaldocuments/frus1961-63v04/pg_513, accessed 5/6/2019

Page 84 **preferred way to commit suicide** 'Memorandum for the Record of Discussion at the Daily White House Staff Meeting, Washington, November 4,

1963, 8.am', *FRUS*, 1961–1963, 4:556, 4 November 1963: https://history.state.gov/historicaldocuments/frus1961-63v04/pg_556, accessed 5/6/2019

Page 84 **complete and very profound review** Geoffrey C. Ward and Ken Burns, *The Vietnam War: An Intimate History*, Ebury Publishing, 2017, p. 93

Page 84 **mind their own business** Wilfried Mausbach, 'European Perspectives on the War in Vietnam', *GHI Bulletin*, No. 30, Spring 2002, p. 73: https://www.ghi-dc.org/fileadmin/user_upload/GHI_Washington/Publications/Bulletin30/71.pdf, accessed 7/6/2019

Page 84 **flaunted its inhumanity** Mark Atwood Lawrence, 'The Disaster that was the Vietnam War', *The New York Times*, 20 November 2018: https://www.nytimes.com/2018/11/20/books/review/max-hastings-vietnam.html, accessed 1/12/2019

Page 85 **red sandwich** Westad, *The Cold War: A World History*, p. 356

Page 85 **broad democratic tradition** Westad, *The Cold War: A World History*, p. 357

Page 85 **well on its way to modernity** Kinzer, *Overthrow*, p. 173

Page 85 **more than three thousand people** Westad, *The Cold War: A World History*, p. 357

Page 86 **the principle of legality** Salvador Allende, *First Speech to the Chilean parliament after his election:* https://www.marxists.org/archive/allende/1970/september/20.htm, accessed 28/5/2019; see also Westad, *The Cold War: A World History*, p. 355

Page 86 **some sort of communist government** Henry Kissinger, press briefing, 16 September 1970 in 'Hearings before the Select Committee to Study Governmental Operations with respect to Intelligence Activities, United States Senate', 94th Congress, 1st Session, Vol. 7, 4 and 5 December 1975, p. 174: https://www.intelligence.senate.gov/sites/default/files/94intelligence_activities_VII.pdf, accessed 28/5/2019

Page 86 **unacceptable** Hearings before the Select Committee p. 41: https://www.intelligence.senate.gov/sites/default/files/94intelligence_activities_VII.pdf, accessed 28/5/2019

Page 87 **intervention in the constitutional processes** Hearings before the Committee on Foreign Relations, United States Senate, 97th Congress on the Nomination of Alexander M Haig Jr to be Secretary of State, January 1981, p. 129: https://babel.hathitrust.org/cgi/pt?id=umn.31951002869633t&view=1up&seq=139, accessed 1/12/2019

Page 87 **errors we made in 1959-60** Kinzer, *Overthrow*, p. 180

Page 87 **patently a violation** 'Memorandum from Viron P. Vaky of the National Security Council Staff to the President's Assistant for National Security Affairs (Kissinger)', *FRUS*, 1969–1976, 21:239, 14 September 1970: https://history.state.gov/historicaldocuments/frus1969-76v21/pg_239, accessed 1/12/2019

Page 87 **son of a bitch** Seymour M. Hersh, 'The Price of Power, Kissinger, Nixon, and Chile', *The Atlantic*, December 1982: https://www.theatlantic.com/magazine/archive/1982/12/the-price-of-power/376309/

Page 87 **constant, constant pressure** Kinzer, *Overthrow*, p. 180

Page 87 **Sensitize feeling** Kinzer, *Overthrow*, p. 181

Page 87 **propaganda, black operations** 'Telegram from the Central Intelligence Agency to the Station in Chile', *FRUS*, 1969–1976, 21:374, 16 October 1970: https://history.state.gov/historicaldocuments/frus1969-76v21/pg_374, accessed 1/12/2019

Page 88 **provoke chaos in Chile** Kristian Gustafson, 'CIA Machinations in Chile in 1970', *CIA library*: https://www.cia.gov/library/center-for-the-study-of-intelligence/kent-csi/vol47no3/pdf/v47i3a03p.pdf, accessed 1/12/2019

Page 88 **credit to American ideals** Kinzer, *Overthrow*, p. 184

Page 88 **Two days after Allende's inauguration** 'Memorandum for the President from Henry A. Kissinger, NSC Meeting', 5 November 1970: https://nsarchive2.gwu.edu/NSAEBB/NSAEBB110/chile02.pdf, accessed 1/12/2019

Page 88 **bring him down** Kinzer, *Overthrow*, p. 184

Page 88 **all within our power** Hearing before the Subcommittee [of the Committee on the Judiciary], to Investigate Problems connected with Refugees and Escapees, United States Senate, 94th Congress, 2 October 1975: https://babel.hathitrust.org/cgi/pt?id=mdp.39015078639245&view=1up&seq=218

Page 88 **Viva Allende!** Robert Alden, 'Mr Allende follows outline of speech', *The New York Times*, 5 December 1972: https://www.nytimes.com/1972/12/05/archives/allende-at-un-charges-assault-by-us-interests-chilean-president.html, accessed 1/12/2019

Page 89 **forces that operate in the shadows** 'Salvador Allende speech to the United Nations', 4 December 1972: https://www.salvador-allende.cl/discursos/naciones-unidas/, accessed 1/12/2019

Page 89 **badge of honor** Dick Clark, 'That Helms "Badge Of Honor"', *The New York Times*, 13 November 1977: https://www.nytimes.com/1977/11/13/archives/that-helms-badge-of-honor.html, accessed 19/3/2020

Page 89 **renewed atmosphere of political unrest** Peter Kornbluh, *The Pinochet File: A Declassified Dossier on Atrocity and Accountability*, The New Press, 2016, p. 107

Page 89 **accelerated efforts** Kornbluh, pp. 108–9

Page 89 **bring our influence to bear** Kornbluh, pp. 108–9

Page 89 **Only way to remove Prats** Kinzer, *Overthrow*, p. 190

Page 90 **my sacrifice will not be in vain** 'Salvador Allende: Last Words to Nation', *Marxists*, 11 September 1973: https://www.marxists.org/archive/allende/1973/september/11.htm, accessed 19/3/2020

Page 90 **much more deadly than** Westad, *The Cold War: A World History*, p. 358

Page 91 **beginning of the end** David Kilcullen, *The Dragons and the Snakes*, Scribe, 2020, p. 219

Page 91 **on the agenda from the first days** Julian Borger, 'Bush decided to remove Saddam "on day one"', *The Guardian*, 12 January 2004: https://www.theguardian.com/world/2004/jan/12/usa.books, accessed 1/12/2019

Page 91 **about ten days after 9/11** General Wesley Clark and Amy Goodman, 'Global Warfare: We're Going to Take out 7 Countries in 5 Years: Iraq, Syria, Lebanon, Libya, Somalia, Sudan & Iran', *Global Research*, 2 March 2007: https://www.globalresearch.ca/we-re-going-to-take-out-7-countries-in-5-years-iraq-syria-lebanon-libya-somalia-sudan-iran/5166, accessed 1/12/2019

Page 91 **Donald Rumsfeld's disturbing note** 'U.S. Department of Defense Notes from Donald Rumsfeld, [Iraq War Planning], November 27, 2001', *The National Security Archive:* https://nsarchive2.gwu.edu/NSAEBB/NSAEBB326/doc08.pdf, accessed 7/6/2019

Page 92 **not in conformity** Ewen MacAskill and Julian Borger, 'Iraq War was illegal and breached UN charter, says Annan', *The Guardian*, 16 September 2004: https://www.theguardian.com/world/2004/sep/16/iraq.iraq, accessed 7/6/2019

Page 92 **International law…would have required** Oliver Burkeman and Julian Borger, 'War critics astonished as US hawk admits invasion was illegal', *The Guardian*, 20 November 2003: https://www.theguardian.com/uk/2003/nov/20/usa.iraq1, accessed 12/6/2019

Page 92 **Pope John Paul II** 'Address of His Holiness Pope John Paul II to the Diplomatic Corps', 13 January 2003: http://w2.vatican.va/content/john-paul-ii/en/speeches/2003/january/documents/hf_jp-ii_spe_20030113_diplomatic-corps.html, accessed 7/6/2019

Page 93 **discussion, not an enquiry** 'Chilcot report: What was Australia's role in the Iraq War and should we have had an inquiry?', 7 July 2016: https://www.abc.net.au/news/2016-07-07/chilcot-report-what-was-australias-role-in-the-iraq-war/7576604, accessed 7/6/2019

Page 93 **no basis in international law** 'Iraq invasion violated international law, Dutch inquiry finds', *The Guardian*, 13 January 2010: https://www.theguardian.com/world/2010/jan/12/iraq-invasion-violated-interational-law-dutch-inquiry-finds, accessed 7/6/2019

Page 94 **risible…fatuous…bad** Bingham, *The Rule of Law*, pp. 124 & 189

Page 94 **to defend itself** United Nations Security Council, 57th year, 4644th meeting, 8 November 2002, S/PV.4644, p. 3: http://www.globalissues.org/external/1441Speeches.pdf, accessed 7/6/2019

Page 94 **two problems…** Bingham, *The Rule of Law*, p. 124

Page 95 **Negroponte…further breach** United Nations Security Council, 57th year, 4644th meeting, 8 November 2002, S/PV.4644, p. 3: http://www.globalissues.org/external/1441Speeches.pdf, accessed 7/6/2019

Page 95 **Greenstock…no automaticity** United Nations Security Council, 57th year, 4644th meeting, 8 November 2002, S/PV.4644, p. 5: http://www.globalissues.org/external/1441Speeches.pdf, accessed 7/6/2019

Page 95 **Having been attacked by Al Qaeda** Richard A. Clarke, *Against All Enemies: Inside America's War on Terror*, Thorndike Press, 2004, p. 73

Page 95 **Iraq project was lunacy** Christopher D. O'Sullivan, *Colin Powell: American Power and Intervention From Vietnam to Iraq*, Rowman and Littlefield, 2009, p. 170; see also Kinzer, *Overthrow*, p. 290

Page 95 **scant evidence** Brent Scowcroft, 'Don't Attack Saddam', *Wall Street Journal*, 15 August 2002: https://www.wsj.com/articles/SB1029371773228069195, accessed 1/12/2019

Page 96 **fixed around the policy** 'The Secret Downing Street Memo, Iraq: Prime Minister's Meeting', 23 July 2002: https://nsarchive2.gwu.edu/NSAEBB/NSAEBB328/II-Doc14.pdf, accessed 1/12/2019

Page 96 **strategic obsession with Iraq** Nicholas Lemann, 'Remember the Alamo', *The New Yorker*, 18 October 2004: https://www.newyorker.com/magazine/2004/10/18/remember-the-alamo, accessed 1/12/2019

Page 96 **The US went in [to Iraq]** Annie Maccoby Berglof, 'Hans Blix – the diplomat with a disarming nature', *Financial Times*, 20 September 2014: https://www.ft.com/content/14d2eb98-39bb-11e4-83c4-00144feabdc0, accessed 1/12/2019

Page 96 **new generation of terrorist leaders** 'Declassified Key Judgments of the National Intelligence Estimate: Trends in Global Terrorism: Implications for the United States', April 2006: https://fas.org/irp/dni/trends.pdf, accessed 1/12/2019

CHAPTER 4 Criticism

Page 98 **high class muscle man** Federation of American Scientists, 'Smedley Butler on Interventionism': https://fas.org/man/smedley.htm, accessed 1/4/2020

Page 98 **informal and changing coalition** Carroll W. Pursell, *The Military-Industrial Complex*, Harper & Row Publishers, 1972, p. ix

Page 98 **Every gun...every warship** Dwight D. Eisenhower, Address 'The Chance for Peace' delivered before the American Society of Newspaper Editors, 16 April 1953: https://babel.hathitrust.org/cgi/pt?id=umn.31951d03597166h&view=1up&seq=1, accessed 23/7/2019

Page 99 **permanent war-based economy** See Charles J. Griffin 'New Light on Eisenhower's Farewell Address', *Presidential Studies Quarterly* 22, No. 3 (Summer 1992), pp. 469–79 referred to in Stephen Glain, *State vs. Defense*, Broadway Paperbacks, NY, p. 118

Page 100 **Eisenhower's Farewell Address** Dwight D. Eisenhower, 'Farewell Radio and Television Address to the American People', 17 January 1961: https://www.eisenhowerlibrary.gov/sites/default/files/all-about-ike/speeches/wav-files/farewell-address.mp3

Page 100 **militaristic and aggressive nation** David M. Shoup, 'The New American Militarism', *The Atlantic*, April 1969. United States of America Congressional Record, Proceedings and Debates of the 91st Congress, 1st Session, Vol. 115, Part 6, 20 March 1969 to 1 April 1969, p. 7972

Page 101 **born of the necessities of World War II** United States of America Congressional Record, Proceedings and Debates of the 91st Congress, 1st Session, Vol. 115, Part 6, 20 March 1969 to 1 April 1969, p. 7777

Page 101 **belief in military solutions** United States of America Congressional Record, 1969 hearing, p. 7777

Page 101 **relationship between** United States of America Congressional Record, 1969 hearing, p. 7973

Page 101 **influential nucleus** United States of America Congressional Record, 1969 hearing, p. 7776

Page 101 **kind of unwanted ideology** 'Present Situation in Vietnam', Hearing before the Committee on Foreign Relations United States Senate, 90th Congress, Second Session with General David M. Shoup, Former Commandant, United States Marine Corps, 20 March 1968, p. 46: https://babel.hathitrust.org/cgi/pt?id=uc1.$b643618&view=1up&seq=54, accessed 1/12/2019

Page 102 **knocking at the doors of Pearl Harbor** Shoup 1968 hearing, p. 3

Page 102 **the chance to determine their own fate** Shoup 1968 hearing, p. 6

Page 102 **dirty, bloody, dollar-crooked fingers** Shoup 1968 hearing, p. 47

Page 102 **encircled her with nuclear bombs and missiles** Shoup 1968 hearing, p. 48

Page 102 **The present actuality of nuclear bases** William Appleman Williams, *The Tragedy of American Diplomacy*, The World Publishing Company, NY, 1959, pp. 188–9

Page 103 **Americans were told** Glain, *State vs. Defense*, p. 408

Page 103 **Help people get things** Shoup 1968 hearing, p. 51

Page 103 **They just keep trying** 'General Shoup Derides US Stand on Vietnam', *Washington Post*, 19 December 1967

Page 104 **Some place up the line** Shoup 1968 hearing, p. 7

Page 104 **through the determined exercise** Andrew J. Bacevich, *The New American Militarism: How Americans Are Seduced by War*, Oxford University Press, 2013, p. 225

Page 104 **share the fate** Bacevich, *The New American Militarism*, p. 225

Page 105 **reckless or preposterous** Bacevich, *The New American Militarism*, p. 90

Page 105 **one true universal church** Bacevich, *The New American Militarism*, p. 78

Page 105 **final triumph of American ideals** Bacevich, *The New American Militarism*, p. 83

Page 105 **series of convictions...hostility toward realism** Bacevich, *The New American Militarism*, pp. 83–7

Page 105 **collective security is a mirage** Charles Krauthammer, 'The Anti-Superpower Fallacy', *Washington Post*, 10 April 1992

Page 106 **woolly-headed and fatuous** Bacevich, *The New American Militarism*, p. 84

Page 106 **guarantor of nothing** Charles Krauthammer, 'The Unipolar Moment', *Foreign Affairs*, Vol. 70, No. 1, 1990/91, p. 25

Page 106 **world chaos** William Kristol and Robert Kagan, 'Foreign Policy and the Republican Future (II)', *Weekly Standard*, 12 October 1998: https://www.weeklystandard.com/robert-kagan-and-william-kristol/foreign-policy-and-the-republican-future-ii, accessed 10/7/2019

Page 106 **brought into being by American might** Bacevich, *The New American Militarism*, p. 94

Page 106 **best democracy program ever invented** Bacevich, *The New American Militarism*, p. 85

Page 106 **incumbent on the Pentagon** Bacevich, *The New American Militarism*, p. 86

Page 106 **America must be able to fight** Frederick Kagan in Robert Kagan and William Kristol (ed.), *Present Dangers: Crisis and Opportunity in America Foreign and Defense Policy*, Encounter Books, 2000, p. 261

Page 106 **win any conflict, anywhere** Karen Paresh, 'Dempsey: Defense Budget Reflects Clear Strategic Choices', *Department of Defense News*, 26 January 2012: https://archive.defense.gov/News/NewsArticle.aspx?ID=66941, accessed 19/7/2019

Page 106 **however unwelcome** Bacevich, *The New American Militarism*, p. 233

Page 106 **proper aim of American statecraft** Bacevich, *Washington Rules*, p. 237

Page 107 **model freedom** Bacevich, *Washington Rules*, p. 234

Page 107 **demonstrating the feasibility** Bacevich, *Washington Rules*, p. 237

Page 107 **giant triplets** Bacevich, *Washington Rules*, p. 236

Page 107 **strident and aggressive American policy** J. William Fulbright, *The Arrogance of Power*, Vintage Books, 1966, p. x

Page 107 **force is the ultimate proof** Fulbright, *The Arrogance of Power*, p. 5

Page 107 **bigger, better, or stronger** Fulbright, *The Arrogance of Power*, p. 5

Page 108 **crusades...men with doctrines** Fulbright, *The Arrogance of Power*, p. 248

Page 108 **why did it take three of you?** Fulbright, *The Arrogance of Power*, pp. 12–13

Page 108 **not really cut out for the job** Fulbright, *The Arrogance of Power*, p. 14

Page 109 **'American empire'...romantic nonsense** Fulbright, *The Arrogance of Power*, p. 20

Page 109 **the idea...seems to be flattering** Fulbright, *The Arrogance of Power*, p. 19

Page 109 **struggling and striving** George Bernard Shaw, *Cashel Byron's Profession*, The Floating Press, 2011, p. 115; see also Fulbright, p. 19

Page 109 **not God's chosen saviour of mankind** Fulbright, *The Arrogance of Power*, p. 20

Page 109 **passing phase of Soviet communism** Fulbright, *The Arrogance of Power*, pp. 80–1

Page 110 **clauses are not ambiguous** Fulbright, *The Arrogance of Power*, p. 93

Page 110 **a matter of vital interest** Fulbright, *The Arrogance of Power*, p. 93

Page 111 **violate the law ourselves** Fulbright, *The Arrogance of Power*, p. 96

Page 111 **a pre-emptive war in defense of freedom** Fulbright, *The Arrogance of Power*, p. 154

Page 111 **humanism of Lincoln** Fulbright, *The Arrogance of Power*, p. 246

Page 111 **advanced level of civilization** Fulbright, *The Arrogance of Power*, p. 249

Page 111 **putting the world right** Fulbright, *The Arrogance of Power*, p. 255

Page 112 **a little more civilized** Fulbright, *The Arrogance of Power*, p. 255

Page 112 **unduly legalistic and moralistic** George F. Kennan, 'Morality and Foreign Policy', *Foreign Affairs*, Vol. 64, No. 2, Winter 1985, p. 205: https://www.law.upenn.edu/live/files/5139-kennanmoralityandforeignpolicyforeignaff airswinter, accessed 24/7/2019

Page 112 **moral impulses** Kennan, *Foreign Affairs*, p. 206

Page 112 **moral standards are theirs as well** Kennan, *Foreign Affairs*, p. 208

Page 112 **injurious to our interests** Kennan, *Foreign Affairs*, p. 209

Page 113 **men with doctrines** Kennan, *Foreign Affairs*, pp. 208–9

Page 113 **politically influential minority elements** Kennan, *Foreign Affairs*, p. 210

Page 113 **Practices or policies** Kennan, *Foreign Affairs*, p. 210

Page 113 **Democracy is a loose term** Kennan, *Foreign Affairs*, p. 209

Page 114 **Democracy, as Americans understand it** Kennan, *Foreign Affairs*, pp. 211–12

Page 114 **not everyone...responsible** Kennan, *Foreign Affairs*, p. 212

Page 114 **quick to allege** Kennan, *Foreign Affairs*, p. 210

Page 114 **seldom if ever...veto power** Kennan, *Foreign Affairs*, p. 210

Page 114 **avoidance of the worst** Kennan, *Foreign Affairs*, p. 212

Page 115 **example exerts a greater power** Kennan, *Foreign Affairs*, p. 216

Page 115 **devastating effect** Kennan, *Foreign Affairs*, p. 216

Page 115 **not to be confused with** Kennan, *Foreign Affairs*, p. 213

Page 115 **a regular and routine feature** Kennan, *Foreign Affairs*, p. 214

Page 115 **not in character** Kennan, *Foreign Affairs*, p. 214

Page 116 **exorbitant dreams of world influence** Kennan, *Foreign Affairs*, p. 216

Page 116 **living beyond its means** Kennan, *Foreign Affairs*, pp. 215–16

Page 116 **the duty of bringing** Kennan, *Foreign Affairs*, p. 215

Page 117 **destruction of civilization** Kennan, *Foreign Affairs*, p. 216

Page 117 **environmental and nuclear crises** Kennan, *Foreign Affairs*, p. 216

Page 117 **far smaller tragedy** Kennan, *Foreign Affairs*, pp. 216–17

Page 117 **whatever the nature** Kennan, *Foreign Affairs*, p. 217

Page 118 **possibilities of service** Kennan, *Foreign Affairs*, pp. 217–18

CHAPTER 5 Militarism

Page 121 **degree without precedent** Bacevich, *The New American Militarism*, p. 2

Page 121 **deeply entrenched** Bacevich, *Washington Rules*, p. 226

Page 121 **the truest measure of national greatness** Bacevich, *The New American Militarism*, p. 2

Page 121 **ideology and a set of practices** Pierre Guerlain, 'The Social and Economic Consequences of US Militarism', *Revue Lisa*, 2013: https://journals.openedition.org/lisa/5371, accessed 15/12/2019

Page 121 **cultural disease** Marc Pilisuk and Jennifer Achord Rountree, *The Hidden Structure of Violence: Who Benefits from Global Violence and War*, NYU Press, 2015; see also Molly S. Castelloe, 'Is Militarism a Disease?', *Psychology Today*, 12 April 2016: https://www.psychologytoday.com/us/blog/the-me-in-we/201604/is-militarism-disease?amp

Page 122 **hyper-militarisation** Louis Kreisberg, *Realizing Peace: A Constructive Conflict Approach*, Oxford University Press, 2015, p. 305

Page 122 **tempo of US military intervention** Bacevich, *The New American Militarism*, p. 19

Page 122 **Since the collapse of the Soviet Union** Glain, *State vs. Defense*, p. 407

Page 122 **wasting of strength** Eisenhower Address, *The Chance For Peace*, 16 April 1953

Page 122 **by diverting social capital** Andrew J. Bacevich, 'The Tyranny of Defense Inc.', *The Atlantic*, January/February 2011 Issue: https://www.theatlantic.com/magazine/archive/2011/01/the-tyranny-of-defense-inc/308342/, accessed 15/8/2019

Page 122 **every warship launched** Eisenhower Address, The Chance for Peace, 16 April 1953

Page 122 **more and more uneasiness** Dwight David Eisenhower, *Waging Peace: 1956–1961*, Doubleday, 1965, p. 614

Page 123 **cast of mind that defines** C. Wright Mills, *The Power Elite*, Oxford University Press, 2000, p. 222

Page 123 **revisionist powers of China and Russia** 'National Security Strategy of the United States of America, December 2017' (NSS), The White House, p. 25: https://www.whitehouse.gov/wp-content/uploads/2017/12/NSS-Final-12-18-2017-0905.pdf, accessed 15/8/2019

Page 123 **military overmatch** NSS, p. 28

Page 123 **ensure that American military superiority** NSS, p. 3

Page 124 **so that it remains pre-eminent** NSS, p. 4

Page 124 **we can and will defeat them** NSS, p. 28

Page 124 **build a more lethal force** 'Summary of the 2018 National Defense Strategy of the United States of America' (NDS), The Department of Defense, pp. 5–6: https://dod.defense.gov/Portals/1/Documents/pubs/2018-National-Defense-Strategy-Summary.pdf, accessed 15/8/2019

Page 124 **unmatched military advantages** NSS, pp. 3–4

Page 124 **warfighting domains** NDS, p. 6

Page 124 **own the undersea domain** Thomas L. Friedman, 'Parallel Parking in the Arctic Circle', *The New York Times*, 29 March 2014: https://www.nytimes.com/2014/03/30/opinion/sunday/friedman-parallel-parking-in-the-arctic-circle.html, accessed 14/8/2019

Page 124 **fetishize the military** Brett Rosenberg and Jake Sullivan, 'The Case for a National Security Budget: Why a Better American Foreign Policy Requires a New Way of Paying for It', *Foreign Affairs*, 19 November 2019: https://www. foreignaffairs.com/articles/2019-11-19/case-national-security-budget, accessed 12/12/20

Page 124 **manifesto of American militarism** Glain, *State vs. Defense*, p. 88

Page 125 **gratuitous, alarmist cant** Glain, *State vs. Defense*, p. 89

Page 125 **dramatization and magnification** Acheson, *Present at the Creation*, pp. 374–5

Page 125 **slave state…responsibility of world leadership** 'A Report to the National Security Council by the Executive Secretary (Lay) – NSC 68', *FRUS*, 1950, 1:234, 14 April 1950: https://history.state.gov/historicaldocuments/ frus1950v01/pg_234, accessed 20/8/2019

Page 125 **war-making capability in 1955** Glain, *State vs. Defense*, pp. 123–4; see also Gareth Porter, *Perils of Dominance: Imbalance of Power and the Road to War in Vietnam*, University of California Press, pp. 3–13

Page 126 **without losing a man to their defenses** Glain, *State vs. Defense*, p. 125

Page 126 **trembled with fear** William Taubman, *Khrushchev: His Life and Times*, WW Norton, 2003, p. 243; see also Glain, *State vs. Defense*, p. 125

Page 126 **great big target range** Taubman, *Khrushchev*, p. 243; see also Glain, *State vs. Defense*, p. 125

Page 126 **I see US missiles** Alex Abella, *Soldiers of Reason: The RAND Corporation and the Rise of the American Empire*, Houghton Mifflin Harcourt, 2008, p. 120; see also Glain, *State vs. Defense*, p. 125

Page 126 **a destructive capacity** Glain, *State vs. Defense*, p. 125

Page 126 **Fareed Zakaria**, 'The New China Scare: Why America Shouldn't Panic About Its Latest Challenger', *Foreign Affairs*, January/February 2020: https:// www.foreignaffairs.com/articles/china/2019-12-06/new-china-scare, accessed 3/2/2020

Page 126 **pre-emptive strike** Glain, *State vs. Defense*, pp. 124–5

Page 126 **diabolical plan for world domination** Glain, *State vs. Defense*, p. 126

Page 127 **'bomber gap' and a 'missile gap'** Bacevich, *The Atlantic*, January/ February 2011

Page 127 **fraudulent** Glain, *State vs. Defense*, p. 408

Page 127 **lucrative tradition of threat elevation** Glain, *State vs. Defense*, p. 128

Page 127 **hyping threats and exaggerating** Glain, *State vs. Defense*, p. 407

Page 127 **keep elevating the threat** Bacevich, *The Atlantic*, January/February 2011

Page 127 **from challenging our leadership** 'Extracts from 18 February 1992 Draft Defense Planning Guidance', National Security Council, 25 March 1992: https://www.archives.gov/files/declassification/iscap/pdf/2008-003-docs1-12. pdf, accessed 15/8/2019; see also 'US Strategy Plan Calls for Insuring No Rivals Develop: A One Superpower World', *The New York Times*, 8 March

1992: https://www.nytimes.com/1992/03/08/world/us-strategy-plan-calls-for-insuring-no-rivals-develop.html, accessed 15/8/2019

Page 127 **world order is ultimately backed** *The New York Times*, 8 March 1992: https://www.nytimes.com/1992/03/08/world/us-strategy-plan-calls-for-insuring-no-rivals-develop.html, accessed 15/8/2019

Page 128 **not a single square inch** Danny Sjursen, 'The United States is Militarizing the Globe', *The Nation*, 21 November 2018: https://www.thenation.com/article/pentagon-united-states-military-worldwide-global-war/, accessed 14/8/2019

Page 130 **most powerful men on Earth...commonly referred** Glain, *State vs. Defense*, p. 347; see also Sjursen, *The Nation*, 21 November 2018

Page 130 **had twenty ambassadors** Chalmers A. Johnson, *The Sorrows of Empire: Militarism, Secrecy and the End of the Republic*, Verso, 2004, p. 124

Page 131 **near total control** Glain, *State vs. Defense*, p. 347

Page 131 **kinetic diplomacy** Monica Duffy Toft, 'The Dangerous Rise of Kinetic Diplomacy', *War on the Rocks*, 14 May 2018: https://warontherocks.com/2018/05/the-dangerous-rise-of-kinetic-diplomacy/, accessed 3/2/2019

Page 131 **creeping militarization** 'Gates: Beware "Creeping Militarization"', *Military.com*, 21 July 2008: https://www.military.com/dodbuzz/2008/07/21/gates-beware-creeping-militarization, accessed 29/3/2020

Page 131 **migration of functions and authorities** Derek S. Reveron, *Exporting Security: International Engagement, Security Cooperation and the Changing Face of the U.S. Military*, Georgetown University Press, 2010, p. 56; see also Glain, *State vs. Defense*, p. 402

Page 131 **not by civilian medics** Glain, *State vs. Defense*, pp. 404–5

Page 131 **70 out of 188** Monica Duffy Toft, 'Fewer diplomats, more armed force defines US leadership today', *The Conversation*, 26 March 2018: https://theconversation.com/fewer-diplomats-more-armed-force-defines-us-leadership-today-92890, accessed 14/8/2019

Page 131 **fifty-two US ambassadorships** Roey Hadar, Gwen Ifill Fellow, and Sandy Petrykowski, 'Key U.S. ambassador posts remain vacant', *Washington Week*, 4 April 2019: https://www.pbs.org/weta/washingtonweek/blog-post/key-us-ambassador-posts-remain-vacant, accessed 21/8/2019

Page 131 **more than 25 per cent** Deborah Snow, 'China rising: Beijing has world's biggest network of diplomatic posts', *Sydney Morning Herald*, 27 November 2019: https://www.smh.com.au/politics/federal/china-rising-beijing-has-world-s-biggest-network-of-diplomatic-posts-20191126-p53eac.html, accessed 15/12/2019

Page 131 **China now boasts** Bonnie Bley, 'The New Geography of Global Diplomacy: China Advances as the United States Retreats', *Foreign Affairs*, 27 November 2019: https://www.foreignaffairs.com/articles/china/2019-11-27/new-geography-global-diplomacy, accessed 29/3/2020

Page 132 **White House regularly pushes** William J. Burns, 'The Demolition of U.S. Democracy: Not Since Joe McCarthy Has the State Department Suffered Such a Devastating Blow', *Foreign Affairs*, 14 October 2019: https://www.foreignaffairs.com/articles/2019-10-14/demolition-us-diplomacy, accessed 17/12/2019

Page 132 **more lawyers** Walter Pincus, 'Vast Number of Military Bands May Not be Music to Gates's Ears', *The Washington Post*, 24 August 2010: http://www.washingtonpost.com/wp-dyn/content/article/2010/08/23/AR2010082304711_pf.html, accessed 19/8/2019; Glain, *State vs. Defense*, p. 413; Kreisberg, *Realizing Peace*, p. 305

Page 132 **all but eclipsed** Glain, *State vs. Defense*, p. 2

Page 133 **Boy Scout Handbook** Ted Strickler, 'Working With the U.S. Military: 10 Things the Foreign Service Needs to Know', *The Foreign Service Journal*, October 2015: https://www.afsa.org/working-us-military-10-things-foreign-service-needs-know, accessed 20/8/2019

Page 133 **base structure report** Kreisberg, *Realizing Peace*, p. 305; see also Chalmers Johnson, '737 U.S. Military Bases = Global Empire', *The Asia-Pacific Journal, Japan Focus*, Vol. 5, Issue 2, 2 February 2007: https://apjjf.org/-Chalmers-Johnson/2358/article.pdf, accessed 19/8/2019

Page 133 **909 military facilities** Glain, *State vs. Defense*, p. 8

Page 133 **800 foreign bases** David Vine, *Base Nation: How U.S. Military Bases Abroad Harm America and the World*, Metropolitan Books, 2015, pp. 6–7

Page 133 **more bases in other people's lands** Vine, *Base Nation*, p. 3

Page 134 **throw a dart at a map** Michael Moran, 'GI Joe as Big Brother', MSNBC, 6 April 2001 referred to in Johnson, *The Sorrows of Empire*, p. 155 & 161

Page 134 **Original missions may become outdated** United States Security Agreements and Commitments Abroad, Committee on Foreign Relations, United States Senate, 91st Congress, Vol. 2, Parts 5–11, 21 December 1970, p. 2433: https://babel.hathitrust.org/cgi/pt?id=hvd.32044057377178&view=1up&seq=1319, accessed 29/3/2020

Page 135 **can actually make war** Vine, *Base Nation*, p. 12

Page 135 **major catalyst for anti-Americanism** Bradley L. Bowman, 'After Iraq: Future U.S. Military Posture in the Middle East', *The Washington Quarterly*, Vol. 31, No. 2, Spring 2008, p. 85

Page 135 **The American military presence in Saudi Arabia** Vine, *Base Nation*, p. 327; see also Stephen Glain, 'What Actually Motivated Osama bin Laden', *U.S. News and World Report*, 3 May 2011: https://www.usnews.com/opinion/blogs/stephen-glain/2011/05/03/what-actually-motivated-osama-bin-laden, accessed 14/8/2019

Page 135 **the interest (conscious or unconscious)** Vine, *Base Nation*, p. 327

Page 136 **get out of South Korea** Sam Roggeveen, 'North Korea's ICBMs, China's rise and the future of United States leadership in Asia', Address to the Royal United Services Institute on 28 August 2018, United Service 69(4) December 2018: https://www.rusinsw.org.au/Papers/20180828.pdf, accessed 3/2/2020

Page 136 **1,000 miles closer to Moscow** Peter Ricketts, 'How to fix Nato',
Financial Times, 7 December 2019: https://www.ft.com/content/7b447d92-
16a1-11ea-b869-0971bffac109, accessed 3/12/2019

Page 136 **inflame the nationalistic** John Glaser, 'NATO Expansion is Unwise.
Saying So Isn't Treasonous', Cato Institute, 17 March 2017: https://www.
cato.org/blog/nato-expansion-unwise-saying-so-isnt-treasonous, accessed
15/12/2019; see also George F. Kennan, 'A Fateful Error', *The New York
Times*, 5 February 1997: https://www.nytimes.com/1997/02/05/opinion/a-
fateful-error.html, accessed 29/3/2020

Page 136 **shows so little understanding** Thomas L. Friedman, 'Foreign Affairs;
Now a Word From X', *The New York Times*, 2 May 1998: https://www.
nytimes.com/1998/05/02/opinion/foreign-affairs-now-a-word-from-x.html,
accessed 15/12/2019

Page 136 **beginning of a new cold war** Friedman, *The New York Times*, 2 May 1998

Page 137 **convincing most Russians** Glaser, Cato Institute, 17 March 2017

Page 137 **working for Vladimir Putin** Glaser, Cato Institute, 17 March 2017

Page 137 **opposed expanding NATO** Thomas L. Friedman, 'Why Putin Doesn't
Respect Us', *The New York Times*, 4 March 2014: https://www.nytimes.
com/2014/03/05/opinion/friedman-why-putin-doesnt-respect-us.html, accessed
3/2/2020

Page 138 **fascism comes to America** 'Disguised Fascism Seen as a Menace; Prof.
Luccock Warns That It Will Bear the Misleading Label "Americanism"', *The
New York Times*, 12 September 1938: https://www.nytimes.com/1938/09/12/
archives/disguised-fascism-seen-as-a-menace-prof-luccock-warns-that-it-
will.html, accessed 14/8/2019; see also Sarah Churchwell, 'It will be called
Americanism: the U.S. writers who imagined a fascist future', *The Guardian*,
3 February 2017: https://www.theguardian.com/books/2017/feb/03/
americanism-us-writers-imagine-fascist-future-fiction, accessed 14/8/2019

Page 138 **Stockholm International Peace Research Institute** 'World Military
Expenditure Grows to $1.8 trillion in 2018', Sipri, 29 April 2019: https://
www.sipri.org/media/press-release/2019/world-military-expenditure-grows-18-
trillion-2018, accessed 29/3/2020

Page 139 **add several hundred billion** Glain, pp. 8–9; Lawrence J. Korb,
'What the FY 2020 Defense Budget Gets Wrong', Centre for American
Progress, 29 April 2019: https://www.americanprogress.org/issues/security/
reports/2019/04/29/469086/fy-2020-defense-budget-gets-wrong/, accessed
15/12/2019

Page 139 **2.7 million veterans since 2001** Neta C. Crawford, 'United States
Budgetary Costs of the Post-9/11 Wars Through FY2019: $5.9 Trillion Spent
and Obligated', Watson Institute, International and Public Affairs, Brown
University, 14 November 2018: https://watson.brown.edu/costsofwar/files/
cow/imce/papers/2018/Crawford_Costs%20of%20War%20Estimates%20
Through%20FY2019.pdf

Page 139 **more than $1 trillion** Crawford, Watson Institute, 14 November 2018

Page 140 **just the approximately $80 billion** William D. Hartung, 'How the Pentagon Devours the Budget', *Salon*, 28 February 2018: https://www.salon.com/2018/02/28/how-the-pentagon-devours-the-budget_partner/, accessed 3/2/2020

Page 140 **beautiful military equipment** Nina Elbagir, Salma Abdelaziz, Mohamed Abo El Gheit and Laura Smith-Spark, 'Sold to an ally, lost to an enemy', *CNN*, February 2019: https://edition.cnn.com/interactive/2019/02/middleeast/yemen-lost-us-arms/, accessed 3/2/2020

Page 140 **major beneficiaries of American weapons** 'Global arms trade: USA increases dominance; arms flows to the Middle East surge, says SIPRI', Sipri, 11 March 2019: https://www.sipri.org/media/press-release/2019/global-arms-trade-usa-increases-dominance-arms-flows-middle-east-surge-says-sipri, accessed 21/8/2019

Page 141 **161 out of 163 countries** 'Global Peace Index 2019, Measuring Peace in a Complex World', Institute for Economics & Peace, June 2019: http://visionofhumanity.org/app/uploads/2019/06/GPI-2019-web003.pdf, accessed 15/12/2019

Page 141 **no visible public outrage** William Hartung, 'Tomgram: William Hartung, The Pentagon Budget as Corporate Welfare for Weapons Makers', 27 February 2018 https://www.tomdispatch.com/blog/176391/tomgram%3A_william_hartung%2C_the_pentagon_budget_as_corporate_welfare_for_weapons_makers

Page 141 **enduring consensus.** Bacevich, *Washington Rules*, p. 15

Page 141 **Pentagon deserves whatever funding** Crawford, Watson Institute, 14 November 2018

Page 141 **cost of one modern heavy bomber** Eisenhower Address, The Chance for Peace, 16 April 1953

Page 142 **largest and most complex** SMP Strategic Management Plan, The Business of Defense, FY2014–FY2015, 1 July 2013: https://cmo.defense.gov/Portals/47/Documents/Publications/ASP/FY1415_SMP.pdf, accessed 15/12/2019

Page 143 **world's largest employer** Crawford, Watson Institute, 14 November 2018

Page 143 **1.4 million active duty personnel** Kimberly Amadeo, 'The Department of Defense and Its Effect on the Economy', *The Balance*, 25 June 2019: https://www.thebalance.com/department-of-defense-what-it-does-and-its-impact-3305982, accessed 20/8/2019

Page 143 **more office space than Manhattan** Amadeo, *The Balance*, 25 June 2019

Page 143 **With a quick infusion** Dana Priest and William M. Arkin, 'A Hidden World, Growing Beyond Control', *The Washington Post*, 19 July 2010: https://www.pulitzer.org/cms/sites/default/files/content/washpost_tsa_item1.pdf, accessed 20/8/2019

Page 143 **more than 1200 government** Priest and Arkin, *The Washington Post*, 19 July 2010

Page 144 **has become a measure of status** Priest and Arkin, *The Washington Post*, 19 July 2010

Page 144 **four times the size** Priest and Arkin, *The Washington Post*, 19 July 2010

Page 145 **overload of hourly** Priest and Arkin, *The Washington Post*, 19 July 2010

Page 145 **There's only one entity** Priest and Arkin, *The Washington Post*, 19 July 2010

Page 146 **consequence of this war funding** Linda J. Bilmes, 'The Credit Card Wars: Post 9/11 War Funding Policy in Historical Perspective', Watson Institute, International and Public Affairs, Brown University, 8 November 2017: https://watson.brown.edu/costsofwar/files/cow/imce/papers/2017/Linda%20J%20Bilmes%20_Credit%20Card%20Wars%20FINAL.pdf, accessed 21/8/2019

Page 146 **President Truman raised** Bilmes, Watson Institute, 8 November 2017

Page 146 **7-key plan to hold prices down** Alistair Walton, 'The Elephant in the Room: The US Deficit & Debt Outlook Over the Next 30 Years', ANU College of Business & Economics, 10 September 2019; see also Jacob Greber, 'Catastrophic conflict from US debt blowout', *Financial Review*, 11 September 2019: https://www.afr.com/world/north-america/catastrophic-conflict-from-us-debt-blowout-20190910-p52pr6

Page 147 **a cool $915,000** Peter Frankopan, *The New Silk Roads: The Present and the Future of the World*, Bloomsbury Publishing, 2018, p. 147

Page 147 **unlimited extravagance...flying mountain of gold** Kilcullen, *The Dragons and the Snakes*, p. 203

Page 147 **the first time in American history** 'Economic Consequences of War on the U.S. Economy', Institute For Economics and Peace, 2011: http://economicsandpeace.org/wp-content/uploads/2015/06/The-Economic-Consequences-of-War-on-US-Economy_0.pdf, accessed 29/8/2019

Page 147 **the credit card wars** Bilmes, Watson Institute, 8 November 2017

Page 148 **$4.9 trillion** Crawford, Watson Institute, 14 November 2018

Page 148 **except death and destruction** Richard Fontaine, 'The Nonintervention Delusion: Why Washington Cannot Abandon Military Intervention', *Foreign Affairs*, November/December 2019: https://www.foreignaffairs.com/articles/2019-10-15/nonintervention-delusion, accessed 3/2/2020

Page 148 **$5.9 trillion** Crawford, Watson Institute, 14 November 2018

Page 148 **likely be greater** Crawford, Watson Institute, 14 November 2018

Page 148 **the share of the interest** William Hartung, 'The Trillion Dollar National Security Budget', *TomDispatch*, 25 July 2017: http://www.tomdispatch.com/post/176311/tomgram%3A_william_hartung%2C_the_trillion-dollar_national_security_budget/, accessed 29/8/2019

Page 148 **of the more than $500 billion** William Hartung and Mandy Smithberger, 'America's Defense Budget Is Bigger Than You Think', *The Nation*, 7 May 2019: https://www.thenation.com/article/tom-dispatch-america-defense-budget-bigger-than-you-think/, accessed 29/8/2019

Page 148 **Pentagon devours the budget** Hartung, *Salon*, 28 February 2018

Page 149 **fundamental fiscal, debt** Walton, ANU College of Business & Economics, 10 September 2019

Page 149 **corporate welfare for weapons makers** William Hartung, 'Corporate Welfare for Weapons Makers, The Hidden Costs of Spending on Defense and Foreign Aid', Cato Institute, 12 August 1999: https://www.cato.org/ publications/policy-analysis/corporate-welfare-weapons-makers-hidden-costs-spending-defense-foreign-aid, accessed 29/8/2019

Page 149 **the sweat of its laborers,** Eisenhower address, 16 April 1953

Page 150 **relentlessly predatory effects** Guerlain, *Revue Lisa*, 2013

Page 150 **vampiristic effect** Seymour Melman, *The Permanent War Economy: American Capitalism in Decline*, Simon & Schuster, 1985, pp. 128–43

Page 150 **absence of economic functional usefulness** Melman, *The Permanent War Economy*, pp. 128–43

Page 150 **most economic models** Dean Baker, 'The Economic Impact of the Iraq War and Higher Military Spending', *Center for Economic and Policy Research,* May 2007: http://cepr.net/documents/publications/military_ spending_2007_05.pdf, accessed 15/12/2007; see also Guerlain, *Revue Lisa,* 2013

Page 150 **overgrown military establishments** George Washington, Farewell Address, 17 September 1796, Library of Congress: https://www.loc.gov/ resource/mgw2.024/?sp=235&st=text, accessed 3/2/2020

Page 151 **Of all the enemies** 'An Excerpt from "Political Observations" by James Madison', 20 April 1795: http://reclaimdemocracy.org/madison_perpetual_ war/, accessed 15/12/2019

Page 151 **between 480,000 and 507,000** Neta Crawford, 'Human Cost of the Post-9/11 Wars: Lethality and the Need for Transparency', Watson Institute, International and Public Affairs, Brown University, November 2018: https:// watson.brown.edu/costsofwar/files/cow/imce/papers/2018/Human%20 Costs%2C%20Nov%208%202018%20CoW.pdf, accessed 15/12/2019

Page 152 **human cost to the United States** Crawford, Watson Institute, November 2018

Page 152 **breeding a deep resentment** 'Declassified Key Judgements of National Intelligence Estimate "Trends in Global Terrorism: Implications for the United States"', April 2006: https://fas.org/irp/dni/trends.pdf, accessed 6/1/2020

Page 153 **It is curious that the Americans** Martin Luther King Jr. speech in New York on 4 April 1967, 'Beyond Vietnam', King Institute, Stanford University: https://kinginstitute.stanford.edu/king-papers/documents/beyond-vietnam, accessed 29/3/2020

CHAPTER 6 Unilateralism

Page 154 **new orthodoxy** David Gergen (flyleaf) in Clyde V. Prestowitz, *Rogue Nation: American Unilateralism and The Failure of Good Intentions,* Hachette, 2008

Page 155 **save the world** Niall Ferguson, *Colossus: The Rise and Fall of the American Empire*, Penguin, 2012, p. 80

Page 155 **willing to become citizens** Prestowitz, *Rogue Nation*, p. 177

Page 157 **alone among** Marie Wilken, 'US Aversion to International Human Rights Treaties', Global Justice Centre, 22 June 2017: http://globaljusticecenter.net/blog/773-u-s-aversion-to-international-human-rights-treaties, accessed 9/1/2020

Page 157 **freely determine their political status** Article 1, *International Covenant on Economic, Social and Cultural Rights*, 3 January 1976

Page 157 **objectionable to the United States** Ann M. Piccard, 'The United States' Failure to Ratify the International Covenant on Economic, Social and Cultural Rights: Must The Poor Be Always With Us?', *The Scholar*, Vol. 13, p. 249: https://core.ac.uk/download/pdf/47210061.pdf, accessed 3/2/2020

Page 157 **slammed the Trump administration** Carol Morello, 'US Withdraws from UN Human Rights Council over perceived bias against Israel', *The Washington Post*, 20 June 2018: https://www.washingtonpost.com/world/national-security/us-expected-to-back-away-from-un-human-rights-council/2018/06/19/a49c2d0c-733c-11e8-b4b7-308400242c2e_story.html, accessed 9/1/2020

Page 158 **Kenneth Roth...observed** Morello, *The Washington Post*, 20 June 2018

Page 158 **questioning the United States** Peter Beinert, 'Obama's Idealists: American Power in Theory and Practice', *Foreign Affairs*, November/December 2019: https://www.foreignaffairs.com/reviews/review-essay/2019-10-07/obamas-idealists, accessed 3/2/2020

Page 159 **strategy of the weak** 'The National Defense Strategy of the United States of America', Department of Defense, March 2005, p. 5: https://archive.defense.gov/news/Mar2005/d20050318nds1.pdf, accessed 31/3/2020

Page 159 **The court was puzzled** *Nicaragua v United States of America*, ICJ Reports, 1986, 14

Page 160 **decades-long trend** Scott Anderson, 'Walking Away from the World Court', *Lawfare*, 5 October 2019: https://www.lawfareblog.com/walking-away-world-court, accessed 4/11/2019

Page 160 **completing the move** Jeffrey D. Sachs, *A New Foreign Policy*, p. 180

Page 161 **sore loser kind of move** Adam Liptak, 'US Says It Has Withdrawn from World Judicial Body', *The New York Times*, 10 March 2005: https://www.nytimes.com/2005/03/10/politics/us-says-it-has-withdrawn-from-world-judicial-body.html, accessed 4/11/2019

Page 161 **less to do with Iran and the Palestinians** Scott Anderson, *Lawfare*, 5 October 2019

Page 162 **If the court comes after us** John Bolton, Speech to the Federalist Society, 'Protecting American Constitutionalism and Sovereignty from International Threats', *Lawfare*, 10 September 2018: https://www.lawfareblog.com/national-security-adviser-john-bolton-remarks-federalist-society, accessed 4/11/2019

Page 163 **unacceptable face** Simon Tisdall, 'Trump attack on ICC is the unacceptable face of US exceptionalism', *The Guardian*, 11 September 2018: https://www.theguardian.com/us-news/2018/sep/10/trump-attack-on-icc-is-the-unacceptable-face-of-us-exceptionalism, accessed 4/11/2019

Page 163 **The Bolton speech today** Ambassador David Scheffer, 'Ambass. David Scheffer on John Bolton's Announcement of 'Ugly and Dangerous' Punitive Actions against Judges, Prosecutors of Int'l Criminal Court', *Just Security*, 10 September 2019: https://www.justsecurity.org/60678/ambass-david-scheffer-john-boltons-announcement-ugly-dangerous-punitive-actions-judges-prosecutors-intl-criminal-court/, accessed 4/11/2019

Page 164 **American Service-Members' Protection Act** See Jennifer Elsea, 'US Policy Regarding the International Criminal Court', *CRS Report for Congress*, 29 August 2006: https://fas.org/sgp/crs/misc/RL31495.pdf, accessed 4/11/2019

Page 165 **doubled as a share of world GDP** Sait Akman, Shiro Armstrong et al., 'The Crisis in World Trade', T20 Japan 2019: https://t20japan.org/policy-brief-crisis-in-world-trade/, accessed 3/2/2020

Page 165 **economically wrong-headed** Alan Beattie, 'US Bullying On Trade Deals Undermines Global Rule Book', *Financial Times*, 5 March 2019: https://www.ft.com/content/79997886-3c44-11e9-b72b-2c7f526ca5d0, accessed 9/1/2020

Page 165 **one of the main drivers** Beattie, *Financial Times*, 5 March 2019

Page 165 **the most prolific user** William Alan Reinsch, Jack Caporal and Jonas Heering, 'Art.25: An Effective Way to Avert WTO Crisis?', *Center for Strategic and International Studies (CSIS)*, 24 January 2019: https://www.csis.org/analysis/article-25-effective-way-avert-wto-crisis, accessed 9/1/2020

Page 165 **batting average is .500** John Brinkley, 'White House's NAFTA Renegotiation Letter To Congress Is Surprisingly Rational', *Forbes*, 18 May 2017: https://www.forbes.com/sites/johnbrinkley/2017/05/18/ustr-lighthizers-nafta-notification-letter-to-congress-is-surprisingly-rational/#4733f3f57d43, accessed 9/1/2020

Page 166 **get more by throwing** Beattie, *Financial Times*, 5 March 2019

Page 166 **no longer accept any external judgment** Trevor Wilson, 'The Crisis In International Trade', *Australian Institute of International Affairs*, 3 December 2018: http://www.internationalaffairs.org.au/australianoutlook/crisis-finding-international-order-trade-commerce/, accessed 9/1/2020

Page 166 **strangling the WTO** Keith Johnson, 'How Trump May Finally Kill the WTO', *Foreign Policy*, 9 December 2019: https://foreignpolicy.com/2019/12/09/trump-may-kill-wto-finally-appellate-body-world-trade-organization/, accessed 9/1/2020

Page 166 **the systemic concerns** Tom Miles, 'World trade's top court close to breakdown as US blocks another judge', *Reuters*, 27 September 2018: https://www.reuters.com/article/us-usa-trade-wto-judge/world-trades-top-court-close-to-breakdown-as-us-blocks-another-judge-idUSKCN1M621Y, accessed 9/1/2020

Page 167 **Accordingly, once** William Alan Reinsch, Jack Caporal and Jonas Heering, *CSIS*, 24 January 2019

Page 167 **major buyer…largest holder** 'The 2019 Lowy Lecture: Prime Minister Scott Morrison', Lowy Institute, 3 October 2019: https://www.lowyinstitute. org/publications/2019-lowy-lecture-prime-minister-scott-morrison, accessed 10/1/2020

Page 168 **trashing…cannot normally discriminate** Shiro Armstrong, 'Are Trump's tariffs legal under the WTO? It seems not, and they are overturning 70 years of global leadership', *The Conversation*, 9 August 2019: https:// theconversation.com/are-trumps-tariffs-legal-under-the-wto-it-seems-not- and-they-are-overturning-70-years-of-global-leadership-121425, accessed 10/1/21020

Page 169 **If the US succeeds** 'The US–China Conflict Challenges the World', *The Irish Times*, 21 May 2019: https://www.irishtimes.com/business/economy/the- us-china-conflict-challenges-the-world-1.3899823, accessed 4/4/20

Page 169 **Trump wants to abandon** Robert Reich, 'Trump administration set to abandon fundamental WTO rules after devising bill called Fart Act', *Independent*, 2 July 2018: https://www.independent.co.uk/news/world/ americas/us-politics/trump-wto-fart-bill-abandon-steve-mnuchin-us-tariffs-eu- trade-war-a8426246.html, accessed 3/2/2020

Page 169 **The era of a rules-based trade** Armstrong, *The Conversation*, 9 August 2019

Page 170 **policy tool of choice** Richard Hass, 'Economic Sanctions: Too Much of a Bad Thing', *Brookings*, 1 June 1998: https://www.brookings.edu/research/ economic-sanctions-too-much-of-a-bad-thing/, accessed 9/1/2020

Page 170 **Many European officials worry** Ellie Geranmayeh and Manuel Lafont Rapnouil, 'Meeting the challenge of secondary sanctions', European Council on Foreign Relations, 25 June 2019: https://www.ecfr.eu/publications/ summary/meeting_the_challenge_of_secondary_sanctions, 9/1/2020

Page 170 **economic sanctions demonstrably** Alfred de Zayas, 'Unilateral Sanctions and International Law', Alfred de Zayas, 27 June 2019: https://dezayasalfred. wordpress.com/2019/06/30/unilateral-sanctions-and-international-law/, accessed 30/3/2020

Page 172 **glamorisation of socialism** William M. LeoGrande, 'Trump Declares Economic War on Cuba', *The Conversation*, 18 April 2019 https:// theconversation.com/trump-declares-economic-war-on-cuba-115672, accessed 9/1/2020

Page 172 **insane** 'An interview with George Shultz', Charlie Rose, 22 December 2005: https://charlierose.com/videos/15214, accessed 10/1/2020

Page 173 **Let's let Cuba be** Nicholas Kristof, 'The Embargo on Cuba Failed. Let's Move On', *The New York Times*, 23 January 2019: https://www.nytimes. com/2019/01/23/opinion/cuba-embargo.html, accessed 25/5/2020

Page 173 **the most robust** 'Challenges in Nuclear Verification', *IAEA*, 5 April 2019:
https://www.iaea.org/newscenter/statements/challenges-in-nuclear-verification,
accessed 10/1/2020

Page 173 **these activities did not advance** *IAEA*, 5 April 2019

Page 174 **judge with high confidence** 'Iran: Nuclear Intentions and Capabilities',
National Intelligence Estimate, November 2007: https://www.dni.gov/files/
documents/Newsroom/Reports%20and%20Pubs/20071203_release.pdf,
accessed 10/1/2020

Page 174 **verified 12 times** Saeed Kamali Dehghan and Julian Borger,
'International Court of Justice orders US to lift new Iran sanctions', *The
Guardian*, 3 October 2018: https://www.theguardian.com/world/2018/oct/03/
international-court-of-justice-orders-us-to-lift-new-iran-sanctions, accessed
10/1/2020

Page 174 **We continue to assess** Daniel R. Coats, 'Statement for the Record:
Worldwide Threat Assessment of the US Intelligence Community', Director
of National Intelligence, 29 January 2019: https://www.dni.gov/files/ODNI/
documents/2019-ATA-SFR---SSCI.pdf, accessed 10/1/2020

Page 175 **reductions are reversible** 'IAEA Report Confirms JCPOA Monitoring
Underway', *Financial Tribune*, 4 March 2020: https://financialtribune.com/
articles/national/102470/iaea-report-confirms-jcpoa-monitoring-underway,
accessed 30/3/2020

Page 175 **estimated fallout to European** Geranmayeh and Rapnouil, European
Council on Foreign Relations, 25 June 2019

Page 175 **Italian bank freezing** Najmeh Bozorgmehr, 'Italian football coach quits
Iran's Esteghlal in sanctions row', *Financial Times*, 13 December 2019: https://
www.ft.com/content/2c6111a4-1cb9-11ea-9186-7348c2f183af, accessed
3/2/2020

Page 176 **currency as a weapon** Stephen Bartholomeusz, 'Trump has a lot to learn
about how currencies work', *Sydney Morning Herald*, 21 November 2019:
https://www.smh.com.au/business/markets/trump-has-a-lot-to-learn-about-
how-currencies-work-20191120-p53cbe.html, accessed 10/1/2020

Page 177 **risk that sanctions overreach** 'Remarks of Secretary Lew on the
Evolution of Sanctions and Lessons for the Future', Carnegie Endowment for
International Peace, US Department of the Treasury, 30 March 2016: https://
www.treasury.gov/press-center/press-releases/pages/jl0398.aspx, accessed
10/1/2020

Page 178 **attempted to bypass** Geranmayeh and Rapnouil, European Council on
Foreign Relations, 25 June 2019

Page 178 **attach the utmost importance** 'Iran and INSTEX – Joint statement by
France, Germany and the United Kingdom', France Diplomatie, 30 November
2019: https://www.diplomatie.gouv.fr/en/country-files/iran/news/article/iran-
and-instex-joint-statement-by-france-germany-and-the-united-kingdom-30-
nov, accessed 3/2/2020

Page 178 **other wide-ranging recommendations** Geranmayeh and Rapnouil, European Council on Foreign Relations, 25 June 2019

Page 180 **Dethroning the dollar** 'Dethroning the dollar: America's aggressive use of sanctions endangers the dollar's reign', *The Economist*, 18 January 2020: https://www.economist.com/briefing/2020/01/18/americas-aggressive-use-of-sanctions-endangers-the-dollars-reign, accessed 3/2/2020

Page 180 **European countries are now beginning** Geranmayeh and Rapnouil, European Council on Foreign Relations, 25 June 2019

Page 180 **Carney...dollar-centric system won't hold** *The Economist*, 18 January 2020

Page 180 **Nabiullina...global shift in mood** *The Economist*, 18 January 2020

Page 180 **the more we condition** Lew, US Department of the Treasury, 30 March 2016

Page 180 **This strong-arming** Brett McGurk, 'The Cost of an Incoherent Foreign Policy: Trump's Iran Imbroglio Undermines US Priorities Everywhere Else', *Foreign Affairs*, 22 January 2020: https://www.foreignaffairs.com/articles/iran/2020-01-22/cost-incoherent-foreign-policy, accessed 3/2/2020

Page 182 **major reason for withdrawing** Pranay Vaddi, 'Leaving the INF Treaty Won't Help Trump Counter China', *Carnegie Endowment for International Peace*, 31 January 2019: https://carnegieendowment.org/2019/01/31/leaving-inf-treaty-won-t-help-trump-counter-china-pub-78262, accessed 10/1/2020

Page 183 **treaty a hindrance** 'US Withdrawal From the ABM Treaty: President Bush's Remarks and US Diplomatic Notes', *Arms Control Association*, 13 December 2001: https://www.armscontrol.org/act/2002-01/us-withdrawal-abm-treaty-president-bush%E2%80%99s-remarks-us-diplomatic-notes, accessed 3/2/2020

Page 183 **unsurprising consequence** Dave Majumdar, 'Russia's Nuclear Weapons Buildup Is Aimed at Beating US Missile Defenses, *The National Interest*, 1 March 2018: https://nationalinterest.org/blog/the-buzz/russias-nuclear-weapons-buildup-aimed-beating-us-missile-24716, accessed 3/2/2020

Page 183 **must greatly strengthen** 'The New US Nuclear Strategy is Flawed and Dangerous. Here's Why', *Arms Control Association*, Vol. 10, Issue 3, 15 February 2018: https://www.armscontrol.org/issue-briefs/2018-02/new-us-nuclear-strategy-flawed-dangerous-heres-why, accessed 3/2/2020

Page 183 **skyrocket** Kingston Reif, 'US Nuclear Budget Skyrockets', 18 March 2020: https://www.armscontrol.org/act/2020-03/news/us-nuclear-budget-skyrockets, accessed 30/3/2020

Page 184 **concrete and direct** Article 51, *Protocol Additional to the Geneva Conventions of 12 August 1949, and Relating to the Protection of Victims of International Armed conflicts (Protocol 1)*, June 1977

Page 186 **US withdrawal...wide-ranging adverse** 'Fiddling with Accounting', *ABC RN Breakfast*, 9 December 2019: https://www.abc.net.au/radionational/programs/breakfast/fiddling-with-accounting-how-australia-meets-its-paris-targets/11778696, accessed 3/2/20

Page 186 **a bit of a nightmare** Gabby Orr and Nancy Cook, 'Trump walks
into 'nightmare' G7', *Politico*, 23 August 2019: https://www.politico.com/
story/2019/08/23/donald-trump-g7-summit-america-first-1473385, accessed
3/2/2020

Page 187 **with Trump at odds** Peter Nicholas, 'America's Allies Seem to Be
Moving On Without Trump', *The Atlantic*, 26 August 2019: https://www.
theatlantic.com/international/archive/2019/08/trump-g7/596875/, accessed
3/2/2020

Page 187 **uneasy, awkward and lonely** Naaman Zhou, 'Australian Journalist
demolishes Trump at G20: "biggest threat to the west"', *The Guardian*, 9 July
2017: https://www.theguardian.com/us-news/2017/jul/09/biggest-threat-to-the-
west-australian-journalist-demolishes-trump-after-g20, accessed 3/2/2020

Page 187 **We're America, Bitch** Jeffrey Goldberg, 'A Senior White House Official
Defines the Trump Doctrine: "We're America, Bitch"', *The Atlantic*, 11
June 2018: https://www.theatlantic.com/politics/archive/2018/06/a-senior-
white-house-official-defines-the-trump-doctrine-were-america-bitch/562511/,
accessed 3/2/2020

Page 187 **Only three countries** Fareed Zakaria 'The Rise of the Rest', *Newsweek*,
12 May 2008: https://fareedzakaria.com/columns/2008/05/12/the-rise-of-the-
rest, accessed 25/5/2020

CHAPTER 7 Asia First

Page 191 **most warlike nation** David Brennan, 'Jimmy Carter Took Call About
China From Concerned Donald Trump: "China Has Not Wasted a Single
Penny on War"', *Newsweek*, 15 April 2019: https://www.newsweek.com/
donald-trump-jimmy-carter-china-war-infrastructure-economy-trade-war-
church-1396086, accessed 5/2/2020

Page 192 **China is the only major power** 'China', *Munk Debates*, 9 May 2019:
https://munkdebates.com/getmedia/df69fb94-60cf-48c0-999a-24f6373f9e87/
Munk-Debate-China-May-2019-Transcript.pdf.aspx, accessed 5/2/2020

Page 192 **[China] has not gone to war** Fareed Zakaria, 'The New China Scare:
Why America Shouldn't Panic About Its Latest Challenger', *Foreign Affairs*,
6 December 2019: https://www.foreignaffairs.com/articles/china/2019-12-06/
new-china-scare, accessed 5/2/2020

Page 192 **'flailing about'** Mahbubani, *Has the West Lost It?*, p. 7

Page 193 **Next year, in purchasing power** Wang Huiyao, 'In 2020, Asian
economies will become larger than the rest of the world combined – here's
how', *World Economic Forum*, 25 July 2019: https://www.weforum.org/
agenda/2019/07/the-dawn-of-the-asian-century/

Page 193 **provide a better measure** 'The Long View: How will the global economic
order change by 2050?', *PWC*, February 2017: https://www.pwc.com.au/
government/pwc-the-world-in-2050-full-report-feb-2017.pdf, accessed
9/2/2020

Page 193 **for eighteen of the last** Chris Patten, 'Why Europe is getting China so wrong', *Financial Times*, 26 September 2005: https://www.ft.com/content/ba7a7570-2df4-11da-aa88-00000e2511c8, accessed 5/2/2020

Page 194 **McKinsey chart** Mahbubani, *Has the West Lost It?*, p. 5

Page 194 **among other remarkable things** Simon Winchester, *Bomb, Book & Compass: Joseph Needham and the Great Secrets of China*, Penguin, 2008, appendix 1

Page 195 **principal civilisations of Asia** Andre Gunder Frank, *ReOrient: Global Economy in the Asian Age*, University of California Press, 1998 p. 12

Page 195 **carried much greater** Frank, *ReOrient*, p. 5

Page 195 **nowhere in the world** Joseph Needham and Colin A. Ronan, *The Shorter Science and Civilisation in China: Volume 3*, Cambridge University Press, 1978, p. 118

Page 195 **China is much richer** Adam Smith, *The Wealth of Nations: A Translation into Modern English*, Industrial Systems Research, 2015, p. 177

Page 195 **widest and the best description** Voltaire, Le Siècle de Louis XIV, *Catalogue de la plupart des écrivains francais qui ont paru dans le Siècle de Louis XIV, pour servir à l'histoire littéraire de ce temps*, 1751.

Page 195 **particular riches of every province** Frank, *ReOrient*, p. 10

Page 196 **'The Asian Century has arrived'** 'The Future of Asia: Asian flows and networks are defining the next phase of globalization', McKinsey Global Institute, September 2019 https://www.mckinsey.com/featured-insights/asia-pacific/the-future-of-asia-asian-flows-and-networks-are-defining-the-next-phase-of-globalization, accessed 5/2/2020

Page 196 **industrial capitalism, internal stability** Parag Khanna, *The Future is Asian: Global Order in the Twenty-first Century*, Hachette, 2019, p. 9

Page 196 **inevitable and unstoppable** Mahbubani, *Has the West Lost It?*, p. 4

Page 196 **Their populations** Mahbubani, *Has the West Lost It?*, p. 4

Page 197 **have been the Asian poor** Branko Milanovic, *Global Inequality: A New Approach for the Age of Globalization*, Harvard University Press, 2016, p. 20

Page 197 **At the heart of the problem** R. W. Johnson, 'Trump: Some Numbers', *London Review of Books*, Vol. 38, No. 21, 3 November 2016: https://www.lrb.co.uk/the-paper/v38/n21/r.w.-johnson/trump-some-numbers, accessed 14/3/2020

Page 197 **some 70 per cent of Americans**, Gillian Tett, 'Is the populist wave in the west here to stay?', *FT Weekend*, 14–15 September 2019

Page 197 **US market rose 307 percent** Stephen Bartholomeusz, 'Is the coronavirus the 'Black Swan' event that blows up the US market?', *Sydney Morning Hearld*, 24 February 2020: https://www.smh.com.au/business/markets/is-the-coronavirus-the-black-swan-event-that-blows-up-the-us-market-20200224-p543qh.html, accessed 24/2/20

Page 197 **there is nothing more difficult** Niccoló Machiavelli, *The Prince*, 1513, Chapter 6

Page 198 **world hunger would decline** John Norberg, 'Despite many obstacles, the world is getting better', *The Guardian*, 15 February 2017: https://www.theguardian.com/global-development-professionals-network/2017/feb/14/despite-many-obstacles-the-world-is-getting-better

Page 198 **Let China sleep** Napoleon Bonaparte, 1803: see generally https://www.napoleon.org/en/history-of-the-two-empires/articles/ava-gardner-china-and-napoleon/, accessed 25/5/2020

Page 198 **China, which once surpassed** Jonathan Spence, *To Change China*, Little Brown, 1969, p. 293

Page 199 **could be worth $42.4 trillion** '2017 Foreign Policy White Paper': https://www.dfat.gov.au/about-us/publications/Pages/2017-foreign-policy-white-paper, accessed 13/4/19

Page 199 **chart adopted by the *Financial Times*,** Martin Wolf, 'Seven charts that show how the developed world is losing its edge', *Financial Times*, 19 July 2017: https://www.ft.com/content/1c7270d2-6ae4-11e7-b9c7-15af748b60d0, accessed 30/3/2020

Page 199 **China's economic power** Odd Arne Westad, 'The Sources of Chinese Conduct', *Foreign Affairs*, September/October 2019, 2 August 2019

Page 200 **biggest act of strategic folly** Mahbubani, *Has the West Lost It?*, p. 81

Page 200 **nasty, authoritarian and communist** Paul Dibb, 'Between the Lines', 21 June 2018: https://www.abc.net.au/radionational/programs/betweenthelines/paul-dibb/9893720, accessed 19/3/2020

Page 200 **fundamentally evil** Hugh White, 'China's Power and the Future of Australia', China in the World (CIW) Annual Lecture, 11 April 2017: https://chinamatters.org.au/wp-content/uploads/2017/04/Hugh-White_CIW-Lecture-April-17-Publshed-Text-11-April-17.pdf, accessed 9/3/2020

Page 200 **American millennials...surging national pride** Khanna, *The Future is Asian*, p. 3–4

Page 201 **China's economic progress is good,** Chris Patten, *Not Quite the Diplomat*, p. 269

Page 201 **Lee Hsien Loong** Lee Hsien Loong keynote address, IISS Shangri-La Dialogue 2019, 31 May 2019

Page 201 **the largest increase** White, CIW Annual Lecture, 11 April 2017

Page 202 **Lowy Institute report** David Orsmond, 'China's Economic Choices', Lowy Institute, 17 December 2019: https://www.lowyinstitute.org/publications/china-s-economic-choices, accessed 9/3/2020

Page 202 **China is going to be a trendsetter** Lisa Murray and Michael Smith 'Scott Morrison's great and powerful friends', *Financial Review*, 28 June 2019: https://www.afr.com/policy/foreign-affairs/scott-morrison-s-great-and-powerful-friends-20190626-p521co, accessed 9/3/2020

Page 203 **McKinsey & Company report** 'The Asian Century has arrived', McKinsey & Company, November 2019: https://www.mckinsey.com/featured-insights/asia-pacific/the-asian-century-has-arrived, accessed 9/3/2020

Page 203 **now far exceeds** Khanna, *The Future is Asian*, p. 14

Page 203 **one of the most ambitious** Andrew Chatzky and James McBride, 'China's Massive Belt and Road Initiative', Council on Foreign Relations, 21 February 2019: https://www.wita.org/wp-content/uploads/2019/02/China%E2%80%99s-Massive-Belt-and-Road-Initiative-_-Council-on-Foreign-Relations.pdf, accessed 9/3/2020

Page 203 **project of the century** Charles Clover, Sherry Fei Ju and Lucy Hornby, 'China's Xi hails Belt and Road as "project of the century"', *Financial Times*, 14 May 2017: https://www.ft.com/content/88d584a2-385e-11e7-821a-6027b8a20f23, accessed 14/3/2020

Page 204 **more than 160 countries** Daniel Wagner, 'China's dreams of world leadership are fading as its belt and road projects start to sour', *South China Morning Post*, 5 February 2020: https://www.scmp.com/comment/opinion/article/3048762/chinas-dreams-world-leadership-are-fading-its-belt-and-road, accessed 9/3/2020

Page 204 **more than eighty countries** Frankopan, *The New Silk Roads*, p. 93

Page 204 **more than sixty countries** Chatzky and McBride, Council on Foreign Relations, 28 January 2020

Page 204 **six corridors of integration** Charles Kunaka, 'Six Corridors of integration: connectivity along the overland corridors of the Belt and Road Initiative', World Bank Blogs, 4 October 2018: https://blogs.worldbank.org/trade/six-corridors-integration-connectivity-along-overland-corridors-belt-and-road-initiative, accessed 14/3/2020

Page 204 **combined population of 4.4 billion** Frankopan, *The New Silk Roads*, p. 93

Page 205 **market-based** Khanna, *The Future is Asian*, p. 110

Page 205 **boost mutual understanding** President Xi Jinping keynote speech at the opening of the Belt and Road Forum for International Cooperation, *Xinhuanet*, 14 May 2017: http://www.xinhuanet.com/english/2017-05/14/c_136282982.htm, accessed 14/3/2020

Page 206 **Debt Sustainability Framework** 'Debt Sustainability Framework for Participating Countries of the Belt and Road Initiative', *Ministry of Finance of People's Republic of China*, 25 April 2019: http://m.mof.gov.cn/czxw/201904/P020190425513990982189.pdf, accessed 30/3/2020

Page 206 **numerous unilateral debt write-downs** Parag Khanna, 'China Couldn't Dominate Asia if It Wanted to', *Foreign Policy*, 3 February 2019: https://foreignpolicy.com/2019/02/03/china-couldnt-dominate-asia-if-it-wanted-to/, accessed 14/3/2020

Page 206 **no longer be in a position to shower** Plamen Tonchev 'The Belt and Road After COVID-19', *The Diplomat,* 7 April 2020: https://thediplomat.com/2020/04/the-belt-and-road-after-covid-19/, accessed 15/4/20

Page 206 **Work has stopped** Wade Shepard 'China's 'Health Silk Road' Gets a Boost from COVID-19', 27 March 2020, Forbes: https://www.forbes.com/

sites/wadeshepard/2020/03/27/chinas-health-silk-road-gets-a-boost-from-covid-19/amp/, accessed 24/4/20

Page 207 **went well beyond China** Umesh Moramudali, 'Is Sri Lanka Really a Victim of China's 'Debt Trap'?', *The Diplomat*, 14 May 2019: https://thediplomat.com/2019/05/is-sri-lanka-really-a-victim-of-chinas-debt-trap/, accessed 14/3/2020

Page 207 **project failures** Tonchev, *The Diplomat*, 7 April 2020

Page 207 **incrementally making progress** Vinod Anand, 'Vietnam Continues to be Wary of China's Belt and Road Initiative (BRI)', *Vifindia*, 29 May 2019: https://www.vifindia.org/2019/may/29/vietnam-continues-to-be-wary-of-chinas-belt-and-road-initiative-bri, accessed 14/3/2020

Page 208 **significant uptick** Chatzky and McBride, Council on Foreign Relations, 28 January 2020

CHAPTER 8 Shifting Alliances

Page 209 **trade, financial and policy** Khanna, *The Future is Asian*, p. 85

Page 209 **pivot to the East** Khanna, *The Future is Asian*, pp. 82–3

Page 210 **No relationship matters** Bobo Lo, 'Once more with feeling: Russia and the Asia-Pacific', *Lowy Institute*, 20 August 2019: https://www.lowyinstitute.org/publications/once-more-feeling-russia-and-asia-pacific, accessed 23/3/2020

Page 210 **unparalleled friendly ties** 'American isolationism is drawing China and Russia closer together', *South China Morning Post*, 8 December 2019: https://www.scmp.com/comment/opinion/article/3041163/american-isolationism-drawing-china-and-russia-closer-together, accessed 23/3/2020

Page 210 **almost 30 times** 'Press statements following Russian–Chinese talks', President of Russia, 5 June 2019: http://en.kremlin.ru/events/president/news/60672, accessed 25/3/2020

Page 210 **meets regularly** Khanna, *The Future is Asian*, p. 85

Page 210 **busy receiving China's highest** Khanna, *The Future is Asian*, p. 84

Page 210 **number one source** 'Russia Remains China's Largest Crude Oil Source for 3rd Year: Report', *Global Times*, 24 March 2019: http://www.globaltimes.cn/content/1143223.shtml, accessed 23/2/2020; see also Bobo Lo, Lowy Institute, 20 August 2019

Page 210 **earning more from grain exports** 'Russia on Track to Remain World's Biggest Grain Exporter', *The Moscow Times*, 15 May 2019: https://www.themoscowtimes.com/2019/05/15/russia-on-track-to-remain-worlds-biggest-grain-exporter-a65592, accessed 25/3/2020

Page 211 **boost two-way trade** Keegan Elmer, 'China, Russia set to double trade to US$200 billion by 2024 with help of soybeans', *South China Morning Post*, 18 September 2019: https://www.scmp.com/news/china/diplomacy/article/3027932/china-russia-set-double-trade-us200-billion-2024-help-soybeans, accessed 23/3/2020

Page 211 **ready to replace US** 'No US, No Problem! Russia–China Trade Set to Double & Reach $200 Billion Soon', *RT*, 11 June 2019: https://www.rt.com/business/461577-russia-china-trade-turnover/, accessed 26/3/2020

Page 211 **China is investing $7 billion** Khanna, *The Future is Asian*, p. 85

Page 212 **High-Tech Forum** Samuel Bendett and Elsa Kania, 'A new Sino-Russian high-tech partnership', Australian Strategic Policy Institute, 29 October 2019: https://www.aspi.org.au/report/new-sino-russian-high-tech-partnership, accessed 23/3/2020

Page 212 **all-embracing...new heights** Jacqueline Westermann, 'The Kremlin looking east: Russia's interests in the Asia-Pacific', *United Service* 69 (4) December 2018, p. 23

Page 212 **sanctions on the procurement** 'US imposes sanctions on China for buying Russian weapons', BBC News, 21 September 2018: https://www.bbc.com/news/world-us-canada-45596485, accessed 23/3/2020

Page 212 **more warships than the US** China Power, 'How is China Modernizing Its Navy', Centre for Strategic and International Studies, 25 January 2019: https://amti.csis.org/chinapower-how-is-china-modernizing-navy/, accessed 23/3/2020

Page 213 called it **unprecedented** Jesse Johnson, 'Chinese military to join 'unprecedented' Russian joint exercises for first time', *Japan Times*, 22 August 2018: https://www.japantimes.co.jp/news/2018/08/22/asia-pacific/chinese-military-join-unprecedented-russian-joint-exercises-first-time/#.Xnvk6lUzZhE, accessed 23/3/2020

Page 213 **first ever joint long-range** Franz-Stefan Gady, 'China Sends Strategic Bombers, Tanks and 1,600 Troops to Russia for Large Military Drill', *The Diplomat*, 17 September 2019: https://thediplomat.com/2019/09/china-sends-strategic-bombers-tanks-and-1600-troops-to-russia-for-large-military-drill/, accessed 23/3/2020

Page 213 **China is now capable** 'China's Sea Control is a Done Deal, "Short of War With the U.S."', *The New York Times*, 20 September 2018: https://www.nytimes.com/2018/09/20/world/asia/south-china-sea-navy.html, accessed 1/4/2020; see also Kathy Gilsinan, 'How the U.S. Could Lose a War With China', *The Atlantic*, 25 July 2019: https://www.theatlantic.com/politics/archive/2019/07/china-us-war/594793/, accessed 25/3/2020

Page 214 **spinning out of NATO's orbit** Bret Baier Interviews Secretary Esper at Reagan National Defense Forum, U.S. Department of Defense, 7 December 2019: https://www.defense.gov/Newsroom/Transcripts/Transcript/Article/2035050/bret-baier-interviews-secretary-esper-at-reagan-national-defense-forum/, accessed 25/3/2020

Page 214 **overtures to its Turkic brethren** Khanna, *The Future is Asian*, p. 92

Page 214 **memorandum of understanding** 'Turkey's Multilateral Transportation Policy', Republic of Turkey: http://www.mfa.gov.tr/turkey_s-multilateral-transportation-policy.en.mfa, accessed 25/3/2020

Page 214 **natural gas from Turkmenistan** Khanna, *The Future is Asian*, p. 92

Page 215 **$3.6 billion package** Ilan Berman, 'Erdogan's Chinese gamble', *The Diplomat*, 4 October 2019: https://thediplomat.com/2019/10/erdogans-chinese-gamble/, accessed 25/3/2020

Page 215 **building thousands of kilometres** Khanna, *The Future is Asian*, p. 93

Page 216 **Turkey and China have major** President of Turkey, 'Turkey, China share a vision for future', *Global Times*, 1 July 2019: http://www.globaltimes.cn/content/1156357.shtml, accessed 21/3/2020

Page 216 **one of the most important** Frankopan, *The New Silk Roads*, p. 189

Page 216 **The stronger Iran gets** Frankopan, *The New Silk Roads*, p. 189

Page 216 **unilateralism and bullying** Laura Zhou, 'China, Iran should stand together against "unilateralism and bullying"', *South China Morning Post*, 1 January 2020: https://www.scmp.com/news/china/diplomacy/article/3044149/china-iran-should-stand-together-against-unilateralism-and, accessed 21/3/2020

Page 217 **Iran has held a joint manoeuvre** 'Iran, Russia, China launch joint maritime drills in Indian Ocean, Sea of Oman', Press TV, 27 December 2019: https://www.presstv.com/detail/2019/12/27/614670/iran-russia-china-kickoff-joint-maritime-drills, accessed 25/3/2020

Page 217 **not only is the US pressure** Brett McGurk, 'The Cost of an Incoherent Foreign Policy', *Foreign Affairs*, 22 January 2020: https://www.foreignaffairs.com/articles/iran/2020-01-22/cost-incoherent-foreign-policy, accessed 21/3/2020

Page 218 **keeping all its options open** David Qualaalou, 'Saudi Arabia pivots toward China: The Rise of a New Global Order', *HuffPost*, 31 March 2017: https://www.huffpost.com/entry/saudi-arabia-pivots-toward-china-the-rise-of-a-new_b_58dea9a4e4b03c2b30f6a607, accessed 21/3/2020

Page 218 **a 32 percent increase** 'Future opportunities between Saudi Arabia and China are very big: crown prince', *Arab News*, 23 February 2019: https://www.arabnews.com/node/1456356/saudi-arabia, accessed 21/3/2020

Page 218 **Oil ties have substantially** Natasha Turak, 'Saudi Arabia dramatically changing oil exports to China and the US', *CNBC*, 15 August 2019: https://www.cnbc.com/2019/08/15/saudi-arabia-dramatically-changing-its-oil-exports-to-china-and-the-us.html, accessed 21/3/2020

Page 219 **stemming from mounting doubts** James M. Dorsey, 'Playing for higher stakes: Saudi takes on Russia', *Asia Times*, 18 March 2020: https://asiatimes.com/2020/03/playing-for-higher-stakes-saudi-takes-on-russia/, accessed 1/4/2020

Page 219 **Saudi...willing to work hard** Robbie Gramer, 'Saudi Arabia, China Sign Deals Worth Up to $65 Billion', *Foreign Policy*, 16 March 2017: https://foreignpolicy.com/2017/03/16/saudi-arabia-china-sign-deals-worth-65-billion-boost-trade-ties-oil-energy-one-belt-one-road-saudi-vision-2030/, accessed 1/4/2020, accessed 25/5/2020

Page 219 **de-radicalisation efforts** 'Saudi Arabia and Russia among 37 states backing China's Xinjiang policy', *Reuters*, 15 July 2019: https://www.reuters.com/article/us-china-xinjiang-rights-idUSKCN1U721X

Page 220 **More than twenty separate** Frank Gardner, 'Saudi Arabia warms to Russia's embrace', BBC News, 16 October 2019: https://www.bbc.com/news/world-middle-east-50054546, accessed 21/3/2020

Page 220 **Russia is becoming an important** 'Russia Savors U.S. Missteps in Syria, and Seizes Opportunity', *The New York Times*, 14 October 2019: https://www.nytimes.com/2019/10/14/world/europe/russia-savors-us-missteps-in-syria-and-seizes-opportunity.html, accessed 26/3/2020

Page 220 **heads of state, emirs, crown princes** Jonathan Fulton, 'China Is Becoming a Major Player in the Middle East', *Brink*, 19 September 2019: https://www.brinknews.com/china-is-becoming-a-major-player-in-the-middle-east/, accessed 21/3/2020

Page 220 **trade with Asia is 'surging'** Khanna, *The Future is Asian*, p. 102

Page 220 **largest extra-regional source** Khanna, *The Future is Asian*, p. 102

Page 220 **nearly $7 billion worth** Fulton, *Brink*, 19 September 2019

Page 221 **threatened to drop the US dollar** Irina Slav, 'Saudi Arabia Threatens To Drop Dollar For Oil Trades', Oil Price, 5 April 2019: https://oilprice.com/Energy/Crude-Oil/Saudi-Arabia-Threatens-To-Drop-Dollar-For-Oil-Trades.html, accessed 21/3/2020

Page 221 **world's future political** Haisam Hassanein, 'Egypt Takes Another Step Toward China', The Washington Institute, 19 August 2019: https://www.washingtoninstitute.org/policy-analysis/view/egypt-takes-another-step-toward-china, accessed 21/3/2020

Page 222 **quantum leap** John Calabrese, 'China–Iraq Relations: Poised for a 'Quantum Leap'? Middle East Institute, 8 October 2019: https://www.mei.edu/publications/china-iraq-relations-poised-quantum-leap, accessed 21/3/2020

Page 223 **contributing to the peace process,** 'China steps into revive Afghanistan peace talks', *South China Morning Post*, 23 October 2019: https://www.scmp.com/news/china/diplomacy/article/3034179/china-steps-revive-afghanistan-peace-talks, accessed 21/3/2020

Page 223 **whole cadre of trained** Jason Burke, 'Frankenstein the CIA Created', *The Guardian*, 17 January 1999: https://www.theguardian.com/world/1999/jan/17/yemen.islam, accessed 21/3/2020

Page 223 **most operationalized element** Michael Kugelman, 'Pakistan's High Stakes CPEC Reboot', *Foreign Policy*, 19 December 2019: https://foreignpolicy.com/2019/12/19/pakistan-china-cpec-belt-road-initiative/, accessed 21/3/2020

Page 224 **top priority** Kugelman, *Foreign Policy*, 19 December 2019

Page 224 **best thing...favourable view** 'A Conversation with Ambassador Alice Wells China–Pakistan Economic Corridor', *U.S. Department of State*, 21 November 2019: https://www.state.gov/a-conversation-with-ambassador-alice-wells-on-the-china-pakistan-economic-corridor/, accessed 26/3/2020; see also Khanna, *The Future is Asian*, p. 114

Page 224 **will focus on industrialization** Khanna, *The Future is Asian*, p. 114

Page 224 **will march forward** 'CPEC to go ahead despite corona pandemic', *The News*, 21 March 2020: https://www.thenews.com.pk/print/632243-cpec-to-go-ahead-despite-corona-pandemic-qureshi, accessed 15/4/20

Page 224 **rid of the dollar burden** 'Pakistan, China agree to trade in yuan', *AA*, 5 November 2018: https://www.aa.com.tr/en/economy/pakistan-china-agree-to-trade-in-yuan/1303426, accessed 25/3/2020

Page 225 **The port belongs** Jonathan Tepperman, 'Imran Khan on Trump, Modi and Why He Won't Criticize China', *Foreign Policy*, 22 January 2020: https://foreignpolicy.com/2020/01/22/imran-khan-trump-modi-china/, accessed 23/3/2020

Page 225 **lies and deceit** Haroon Janjua, 'Nothing but lies and deceit: Trump launches Twitter attack on Pakistan', *The Guardian*, 1 January 2018: https://www.theguardian.com/world/2018/jan/01/lies-and-deceit-trump-launches-attack-on-pakistan-tweet, accessed 1/4/2020

Page 225 **almost half the human race** David Howell, 'Take the Shanghai Cooperation Organization seriously', *The Japan Times*, 7 June 2018: https://www.japantimes.co.jp/opinion/2018/06/07/commentary/world-commentary/take-shanghai-cooperation-organization-seriously/#.XnxEh1UzZhE, accessed 21/3/2020

Page 225 **I, for one, have always opposed** Tepperman, *Foreign Policy*, 22 January 2020

Page 226 **military interoperability** Manu Pubby, 'China backs iron brother Pakistan', *The Economic Times*, 15 March 2019: https://economictimes.indiatimes.com/news/defence/china-backs-iron-brother-pakistan-with-primary-weapons-and-complex-exercises/articleshow/68418192.cms, accessed 21/3/2020

Page 226 **joint naval exercise with Pakistan** Rajewwari Pillai Rajagopalan, 'China–Pakistan Naval Drills: More Than Just Symbolism', *The Diplomat*, 10 January 2020: https://thediplomat.com/2020/01/china-pakistan-naval-drills-more-than-just-symbolism/, accessed 23/3/2020

Page 226 **significantly expanding its foothold** Sanjeev Kumar, 'China's South Asia Policy in the New Era', *India Quarterly: A Journal of International Affairs*, Vol., 75, Issue 2, 2019: https://journals.sagepub.com/doi/10.1177/0974928419841769

Page 226 **not as great as some critics suggest** Moramudali, *The Diplomat*, 14 May 2019

Page 227 **smaller...countries have benefitted** Nilanthi Samaranayake, 'China's Engagement with Smaller South Asian Countries', United States Institute of Peace, 10 April 2019: https://www.usip.org/publications/2019/04/chinas-engagement-smaller-south-asian-countries, accessed 23/3/2020

Page 227 **are increasingly aware** Samaranayake, United States Institute of Peace, 10 April 2019

Page 227 **grow to $100 billion in 2019** 'India–China trade to cross USD 100 billion this year: Envoy', *Economic Times*, 6 June 2019: https://economictimes. indiatimes.com/news/economy/foreign-trade/india-china-trade-to-cross-usd-100-billion-this-year-envoy/articleshow/69676323.cms?from=mdr, accessed 23/3/2020

Page 227 **double to $300 billion** 'India–Asean bilateral trade may double by 2025 to $300 billion: Study', *Business Standard*, 12 November 2019: https://www. business-standard.com/article/economy-policy/india-asean-bilateral-trade-may-double-by-2025-to-300-billion-study-119111200547_1.html, accessed 23/3/2020

Page 227 **reluctant to be unnecessarily** Frankopan, *The New Silk Roads*, p. 180

Page 228 **Delhi has looked to Moscow** Frankopan, *The New Silk Roads*, p. 177

Page 228 **regional stability...prosperity** Muthiah Alagappa, 'International Peace in Asia: Will it Endure?', Carnegie Endowment for International Peace, 19 December 2014: https://carnegieendowment.org/2014/12/19/international-peace-in-asia-will-it-endure-pub-57588, accessed 23/3/2020

Page 228 **wants a modus vivendi** Bill Hayton, 'South China Sea: Vietnam "scraps new oil project"', BBC News, 23 March 2018: https://www.bbc.com/news/world-asia-43507448, accessed 23/3/2020

Page 228 **Indonesia's bilateral ties with China** Hongyi Lai, 'Indonesia: The Belt and Road Initiative and relations with China', *Asia Dialogue*, 4 October 2019: https://theasiadialogue.com/2019/10/04/belt-and-road-initiative-in-indonesia-and-relations-with-china/, accessed 23/3/2020

Page 229 **sibling' relationship** Pongphisoot Busbarat, 'Family making in SinoThai relations', *Kyoto Review*, January 2016: https://kyotoreview.org/yav/family-sino-thai-relations/, accessed 23/3/2020

Page 229 **The rest of the world too** Lee Hsien Loong, Keynote Address, IISS Shangri-La Dialogue 2019, 31 May 2019

Page 229 **more recently tilted** Khanna, *The Future is Asian*, p. 123

Page 229 **full support for the BRI** Chatzky and McBride, Council on Foreign Relations, 28 January 2020

Page 229 **like all other Asian leaders** Khanna, *The Future is Asian*, p. 123

Page 230 **more than $739 billion** Phidel Vineles, 'Making the Belt and Road work for Southeast Asia', *East Asia Forum*, 13 July 2019: https://www. eastasiaforum.org/2019/07/13/making-the-belt-and-road-work-for-southeast-asia/, accessed 23/3/2020

Page 230 **seven out of ten ASEAN leaders** 'Seven Asean members skip summit with US after Trump misses Bangkok meet', *Business Standard*, 4 November 2019: https://www.business-standard.com/article/news-ani/seven-of-10-asean-leaders-skip-summit-with-us-after-top-american-leaders-skip-event-119110400947_1.html, accessed 26/3/2020

Page 230 **intentional effort to embarrass** Natnicha Chuwiruch and Philip Heijmans, 'Asean Leaders Snub U.S. Summit After Trump Skips Bangkok

Meeting', *Bloomberg*, 4 November 2019: https://www.bloomberg.com/news/articles/2019-11-04/asean-leaders-snub-u-s-summit-after-trump-skips-bangkok-meeting, accessed 26/3/2020

Page 230 **creating a whole** Khanna, *The Future is Asian*, p. 151

Page 230 **so robust that** Khanna, *The Future is Asian*, pp. 151–2

Page 230 **factory of the world** Khanna, *The Future is Asian*, p. 153

Page 231 **diminishing their dependence** Khanna, *The Future is Asian*, p. 152

Page 231 **Asians' appetite for US Treasuries** Khanna, *The Future is Asian*, pp. 164–6

Page 231 **From Saudi Arabia to Japan** Khanna, *The Future is Asian*, p. 138

Page 231 **now possesses the region's largest** Deborah Welch Larson, 'Can China Change the International System? The Role of Moral Leadership', *The Chinese Journal of International Politics*, 27 February 2020: https://academic.oup.com/cjip/article/doi/10.1093/cjip/poaa002/5762630, accessed 24/4/20

Page 231 **America no longer enjoys** Ashley Townshend, Brendan Thomas-Noone and Matilda Steward, 'Averting Crisis: American Strategy, Military Spending and Collective Defence in the Indo-Pacific', United States Studies Centre, 19 August 2019: https://www.ussc.edu.au/analysis/averting-crisis-american-strategy-military-spending-and-collective-defence-in-the-indo-pacific, accessed 21/3/2020

Page 232 **enough ground-based ballistic missiles** Westad, *Foreign Affairs*, 2 August 2019

Page 232 **American dream of the 20th century** Stuart T. Gulliver, 'Seizing the Asian Opportunity', Speech at the Asian Business Insights Conference, Duesseldorf, 7 February 2017 referred to in Khanna, *The Future is Asian*, pp. 148–9

Page 232 **fading** Khanna, *The Future is Asian*, p. 23

Page 233 **South-South cooperation** Alicia Garica-Herrero and Jianwei Xu, 'China's investment in Africa: What the data really says, and the implications for Europe', *Bruegel*, 22 July 2019: https://www.bruegel.org/2019/07/chinas-investment-in-africa-what-the-data-really-says-and-the-implications-for-europe/, accessed 21/3/2020

Page 233 **Spindles of Chinese-paved** Max Bearak, 'In strategic Djibouti, a microcosm of China's growing foothold in Africa', *The Washington Post*, 30 December 2019: https://www.washingtonpost.com/world/africa/in-strategic-djibouti-a-microcosm-of-chinas-growing-foothold-in-africa/2019/12/29/a6e664ea-beab-11e9-a8b0-7ed8a0d5dc5d_story.html, accessed 21/3/2020

Page 233 **all over Africa** Panos Mourdoukoutas, 'Why is China Building Africa?', *Forbes*, 21 September 2019: https://www.forbes.com/sites/panosmourdoukoutas/2019/09/21/why-is-china-building-africa/#59a2e016502c, accessed 21/3/2020

Page 233 **building the continent** Janet Eom, '"China Inc" Becomes China the Builder in Africa', *The Diplomat*, 29 September 2016

Page 233 **securing access to resources** Garica-Herrero and Xu, *Bruegel*, 22 July 2019

Page 234 **The *Washington Post* noted** Bearak, *The Washington Post*, 30 December 2019

Page 234 **falling off a cliff** Bearak, *The Washington Post*, 30 December 2019

Page 234 **biggest player in Africa's infrastructure** Wade Shepard, 'What China Is Really Up to In Africa', *Forbes*, 3 October 2019: https://www.forbes.com/sites/wadeshepard/2019/10/03/what-china-is-really-up-to-in-africa/#1079ff1e5930, accessed 21/3/2020

Page 234 **turned east almost in unison** Bearak, *The Washington Post*, 30 December 2019

Page 234 **It was quite natural** Bearak, *The Washington Post*, 30 December 2019

Page 235 **The Doraleh port is** James Kyne, Chris Campbell, Amy Kazmin and Farhan Bokhari, 'How China rules the waves', *Financial Times*, 13 January 2017: https://ig.ft.com/sites/china-ports/, accessed 21/3/2020

Page 235 **most brilliant pearl...will connect** Paul Nantulya, 'Chinese Hard Power Supports Its Growing Strategic Interests in Africa', Africa Centre for Strategic Studies, 17 January 2019: https://africacenter.org/spotlight/chinese-hard-power-supports-its-growing-strategic-interests-in-africa/, accessed 21/3/2020

Page 236 **more focussed on the viability** Silja Frohlich, 'Africa: China's Belt and Road Forum – Does Africa Need New Funding Options?', *All Africa*, 26 April 2019: https://allafrica.com/stories/201904290002.html, accessed 21/3/2020; David Herbling and Dandan Li, 'China's Built a Railroad to Nowhere in Kenya', *Bloomberg*, 19 July 2019: https://www.bloomberg.com/news/features/2019-07-19/china-s-belt-and-road-leaves-kenya-with-a-railroad-to-nowhere, accessed 21/3/2020

Page 236 **supporting Africa's efforts to diversify** Baker McKenzie, 'The Impact of COVID-19 on China's Belt and Road Initiatives in Africa', 31 March 2020: https://www.bakermckenzie.com/en/newsroom/2020/03/bri-africa, accessed 15/4/20

Page 236 **increased by 19.7 per cent** Baker McKenzie, 31 March 2020

Page 236 **Crushing Africa in debt** Frohlich, *All Africa*, 26 April 2019

Page 236 **amounts to more than $2 trillion** Shepard, *Forbes*, 3 October 2019

Page 237 **200,000 test kits, 100,000 masks** Joe Penney, 'As the US blames China for the coronavirus pandemic, the rest of the world asks China for help', 19 March 2020, *The Intercept*: https://theintercept.com/2020/03/18/coronavirus-china-world-power/, accessed 22/3/20

Page 237 **military cooperation agreements;** Nantulya, Africa Centre for Strategic Studies, 17 January 2019

Page 237 **Beijing's 2015 white paper** Dennis J. Balsko, 'The 2015 Chinese Defense White Paper on Strategy in Perspective: Maritime Missions Require a Change in PLA Mindset', The Jamestown Foundation, 19 June 2015: https://jamestown.org/program/the-2015-chinese-defense-white-paper-on-strategy-in-perspective-maritime-missions-require-a-change-in-the-pla-mindset/, accessed 1/4/2020

Page 237 **recent investigative report** Kyne, Campbell, Kazmin and Bokhari, *Financial Times*, 13 January 2017

Page 237 **only a matter of time** Tonchev, *The Diplomat*, 7 April 2020

Page 237 **dip in BRI related** Baker McKenzie, 31 March 2020

Page 238 **has shifted US policy** Max Bearak, 'Promising 'true liberation', Pompeo contrasts US role in Africa with China's', *Washington Post*, 19 February 2020: https://www.inquirer.com/news/nation-world/pompeo-ends-africa-visit-warns-authoritarianism-promotes-us-partnership-20200219.html, accessed 26/3/2020

Page 238 **Latin America...independent of Washington** Mark Weisbrot, 'US foreign policy in Latin America leaves an open door for China', *The Guardian*, 1 February 2014: https://www.theguardian.com/commentisfree/2014/jan/31/latin-america-china-us-foreign-policy-reserve, accessed 26/3/2020

Page 238 **threat to our way of life** Rick Scott, 'Sen. Rick Scott: China's growing influence in Latin America is a threat to our way of life', *CNBC*, 11 June 2019: https://www.cnbc.com/2019/06/11/sen-rick-scott-chinas-growing-influence-in-latin-america-is-a-threat-to-us.html, accessed 26/3/2020

Page 238 **shithole countries** 'US Pentagon transfers another $3.8 billion to building Trump's Mexico border wall', *France 24*, 13 February 2020: https://www.france24.com/en/20200213-pentagon-shifts-3-8-billion-towards-building-mexico-border-wall, accessed 26/3/2020

Page 238 **comprehensive and cooperative** Haibin Niu, 'Building Development Partnership: Engagement Between China and Latin America', *China Research Centre*: https://www.chinacenter.net/2020/china_currents/19-1/building-development-partnership-engagement-between-china-and-latin-america/, accessed 1/4/2020

Page 238 **The result is that China** Andre Dabus, Meghna Dabus and Leon Yao, 'China's Belt and Road Reaches Latin America', *Brink*, 27 May 2019: https://www.brinknews.com/chinas-belt-and-road-reaches-latin-america/, accessed 26/3/2020

Page 239 **fifty-nine large-scale projects** 'Latin America continues to strengthen its economic ties with China through infrastructure investment, says GlobalData', *Global Data*, 18 November 2019: https://www.globaldata.com/latin-america-continues-to-strengthen-its-economic-ties-with-china-through-infrastructure-investment-says-globaldata/, accessed 26/3/2020

Page 239 **undoubtedly created jobs** Wenyuan Wu, 'The Missing Link in China's Economic Ambitions in Latin America', *The Diplomat*, 25 February 2020: https://thediplomat.com/2020/02/the-missing-link-in-chinas-economic-ambitions-in-latin-america/, accessed 26/3/2020

Page 239 **Bolsonaro...walked back** Max Nathanson, 'How to Respond to Chinese Investment in Latin America', *Foreign Policy*, 28 November 2018: https://foreignpolicy.com/2018/11/28/how-to-respond-to-chinese-investment-in-latin-america/, accessed 26/3/2020

Page 240 **more Chinese investment** *Global Data*, 18 November 2019

Page 240 **great economic partner is China** Emilie Sweigart, 'China–Latin America Relations – How Governments Are Playing It', *Americas Quarterly*: https://www.americasquarterly.org/content/china-latin-america-relations, accessed 26/3/2020

Page 240 **China is willing** Sweigart, *Americas Quarterly*

Page 240 **going it alone...consortia** Robert Soutar, 'How China Is Courting New Latin American Partners', *Americas Quarterly*, 14 January 2020: https://www.americasquarterly.org/content/how-chinas-investment-approach-changing-and-courting-new-latin-american-partners, accessed 26/3/2020

Page 241 **It is not principally** Michael Walsh, 'China's appeal grows in Latin America, where 'America First' is winning Donald Trump few friends', ABC News, 4 December 2018: https://www.abc.net.au/news/2018-12-04/chinas-appeal-grows-in-latin-america-as-america-first-falls-flat/10557418, accessed 27/3/2020

Page 241 **considered very close** Walsh, ABC News, 4 December 2018

Page 241 **Europe will prevail** Khanna, *The Future is Asian*, pp. 241

Page 241 **$500 billion more per year** Khanna, *Foreign Policy*, 3 February 2019

Page 241 **amounted to 1.5 billion Euros** Khanna, *Foreign Policy*, 3 February 2019

Page 241 **reach $2.5 trillion,** Khanna, *The Future is Asian*, p. 241

Page 241 **International Monetary Fund projected** Alexandre Tanzi and Wei Lu, 'These 20 Countries will Dominate Global Growth in 2024', *Bloomberg*, 19 October 2019: https://www.bloomberg.com/news/articles/2019-10-19/which-20-countries-will-dominate-global-growth-in-2024, accessed 27/3/2020

Page 242 **launch of more than fifty** Khanna, *The Future is Asian*, p. 243

Page 242 **5000 westbound freight** Keith Wallis, 'Maersk aims to double Asia–Europe rail volume', *JOC*, 20 November 2018: https://www.joc.com/rail-intermodal/international-rail/maersk-aims-double-its-asia-europe-rail-volume_20181120.html, accessed 27/3/2020

Page 242 **no more than 20 percent** Khanna, *The Future is Asian*, p. 244

Page 242 **amounting to $318 billion** Andre Tartar, Mira Rojanasakul and Jeremy Scott Diamond, 'How China Is Buying Its Way Into Europe', *Bloomberg*, 23 April 2018: https://www.bloomberg.com/graphics/2018-china-business-in-europe/, accessed 27/3/2020

Page 243 **world economy's centre of gravity** Viktor Orbán's speech, China–CEE Political Parties Dialogue, Budapest, 6 October, 2016: https://www.kormany.hu/en/the-prime-minister/the-prime-minister-s-speeches/viktor-orban-s-speech-at-the-conference-china-cee-political-parties-dialogue

Page 244 **China currently seems** Federal Foreign Office of Germany, 'Speech by Foreign Minister Sigmar Gabriel at Munich Security Conference', 17 February 2018: https://www.auswaertiges-amt.de/en/newsroom/news/rede-muenchner-sicherheitskonferenz/1602662

Page 244 **every week, around 30** Philip Oltermann, 'Germany's 'China City': how Duisburg became Xi Jinping's gateway to Europe', *The Guardian*, 1 August

2018: https://www.theguardian.com/cities/2018/aug/01/germanys-china-city-duisburg-became-xi-jinping-gateway-europe, accessed 27/3/2020

Page 244 **thrown its weight** Khanna, *The Future is Asian*, p. 242

Page 244 **non-biased and fact-based** 'EU issues strict 5G rules, stops short at Huawei ban', France 24, 29 January 2020: https://www.france24.com/en/20200129-eu-issues-strict-5g-rules-stops-short-at-huawei-ban, accessed 27/3/2020; see also Eric Brattberg and Philippe Le Corre, 'The EU and China in 2020: More Competition Ahead', Carnegie Endowment for International Peace, 19 February 2020: https://carnegieendowment.org/2020/02/19/eu-and-china-in-2020-more-competition-ahead-pub-81096, accessed 27/3/2020

Page 244 **keen to maintain cordial...systemic rival** Brattberg and Le Corre, Carnegie Endowment for International Peace, 19 February 2020

Page 245 **a top contributor** Lucy Best, 'What Motivates Chinese Peacekeeping', Council on Foreign Relations, 7 January 2020: https://www.cfr.org/blog/what-motivates-chinese-peacekeeping, accessed 24/4/20

Page 246 **more hands-on approach** Horia Ciurtin, 'The '16+1' becomes the '17+1': Greece Joins China's Dwindling Cooperation Framework in Central and Eastern Europe', The Jamestown Foundation, 29 May 2019: https://jamestown.org/program/the-161-becomes-the-171-greece-joins-chinas-dwindling-cooperation-framework-in-central-and-eastern-europe/, accessed 1/4/2020

Page 246 **further west than Genghis Khan** Chris Devonshire-Ellis, 'China's Moves Into Europe As Belt & Road Initiative Migrates West', *Silk Road Briefing*, 23 August 2019: https://www.silkroadbriefing.com/news/2019/08/23/chinas-moves-europe-belt-road-initiative-migrates-west/, accessed 1/4/2020

Page 247 **Chinese disinformation campaign** Matt Apuzzo, 'Pressured by China, EU Softens Report on Covid-19 Disinformation, *The New York Times*, 24 April 2020: https://www.nytimes.com/2020/04/24/world/europe/disinformation-china-eu-coronavirus.html, accessed 30/4/20

Page 247 **implications are clear** Devonshire-Ellis, *Silk Road Briefing*, 23 August 2019

CONCLUSION

Page 249 **Long before COVID-19** Richard Haass, 'The Pandemic Will Accelerate History Rather Than Reshape It', *Foreign Affairs*, 7 April 2020: https://www.foreignaffairs.com/articles/united-states/2020-04-07/pandemic-will-accelerate-history-rather-reshape-it, accessed 14/4/20

Page 250 **single out China for blame** Michael H Fuchs, 'The US-China Coronavirus Blame Game is Undermining Diplomacy', *The Guardian*, 31 March 2020: https://www.theguardian.com/commentisfree/2020/mar/31/us-china-coronavirus-diplomacy, accessed 14/4/20

Page 250 **This negative view** Lee Hsien Loong, Keynote Address, IISS Shangri-La Dialogue 2019, 31 May 2019

Page 251 **a new world is coming** Zakaria '*Newsweek*, 12 May 2008

Page 251 **must draw the battle lines** Zakaria '*Newsweek*, 12 May 2008

Page 251 **is more similar...interested above all** Westad, *Foreign Affairs*, 12 August 2019

Page 251 **China may be communist...largest trading partner** Lee Hsien Loong, Keynote Address, IISS Shangri-La Dialogue 2019, 31 May 2019

Page 252 **efforts to economically distance** John Lee 'Slaying the Dragon Won't Work', *The Weekend Australian*, 2-3 May 2020

Page 252 **Attempting to disentangle** Westad, *Foreign Affairs*, 12 August 2019

Page 253 **nationalist rather than internationalist** Westad, *Foreign Affairs*, 12 August 2019

Page 253 **economics trumps politics** Fareed Zakaria, 'Economics Trumps Politics' in RK Betts (Ed.) *Conflict after the Cold War*, fourth edition, 2013, Routledge

Page 253 **global commercial hegemon...profit maximisation** Lukas Danner, 'China's Hegemonic Intentions and Trajectory', *Asia and the Pacific Policy Studies*, Volume 6, Issue 2, 18 April 2019: https://onlinelibrary.wiley.com/doi/full/10.1002/app5.273, accessed 25/5/2020

Page 254 **the United States or its system** Westad, *Foreign Affairs*, 12 August 2019

Page 254 **A 'clash of civilisations' – or worse** Peter Harris, 'Conflict with China is not about a Clash of Civilizations', *The National Interest*, 3 June 2019: https://nationalinterest.org/feature/conflict-china-not-about-clash-civilizations-60877, accessed 25/5/2020

Page 254 **the democratic recession...accelerate history** Haass, *Foreign Affairs,* 7 April, 2020

Page 254 **a nation drifting** Wallerstein, *Foreign Policy*, 11 November 2009

Page 255 **The world has loved** Fintan O'Toole, 'Donald Trump Has Destroyed the Country He Promised to Make Great Again', *The Irish Times*, 25 April 2020: https://www.irishtimes.com/opinion/fintan-o-toole-donald-trump-has-destroyed-the-country-he-promised-to-make-great-again-1.4235928, accessed 30/4/20

Page 255 **No nation's security** Eisenhower, The Chance for Peace, 16 April 1953

Page 255 **insider wisdom in Washington** Alfred McCoy, *In the Shadows of the American Century*, Oneworld Publications, 2018, p. 27

Page 256 **every other dimension** Zakaria, *Newsweek*, 12 May 2008

Page 256 **from anti-Americanism** Zakaria, *Newsweek*, 12 May 2008

Page 256 **the freer the flow** Daniel Griswold 'Reagan Embraced Free Trade and Immigration', CATO Institute, 24 June 2004: https://www.cato.org/publications/commentary/reagan-embraced-free-trade-immigration, accessed 4/5/20

Page 256 **The expansion of the international** New York Public Radio WNYC, 9 June 2018: http://www.marketplace.org/shows/marketplace/06082018, accessed 4/5/20

Page 257 **accept the world** Fulbright, *The Arrogance of Power*, p. 255

INDEX

Ho Chi Minh 79, 80
Hong Kong
  CIA activities 67
  unrest (2019) 67
'How China Rules the Waves' by the
  Financial Times 237
*How Everything Became War and the
  Military Became Everything* by
  Professor Rosa Brooks 128
Huawei
  in European countries 244
  expansion into Russia 212
  in Saudi Arabia 218
Human Rights Watch 158
Hussein, President Saddam (Iraq) 92,
  95, 127
Hutchings, Robert 96
hyper-militarism 122

Ibn Battuta
  on China's wealth 195
ICBC Turkey 215
'Ice Silk Road' 211
Imran Khan, Prime Minister (Pakistan)
  223, 226
  US mistrust 225–6
India
  Chinese relations 227
  contribution to world growth 242
  economic growth 227
  economic history 193–5
  Russia's historical ties 227–8
  US relations 227–8
Indonesia
  Chinese relations 228–9
Industrial and Commercial Bank of
  China (ICBC)
  in Athens 222
  buys Turkey's Tekstilbank 215
Institute for Economics and Peace
  on US defence funding 147
Inter-American Development Bank
  and Chinese investment 240
Intermediate-Range Nuclear Forces
  (INF) Treaty
  US withdraws 181–2

International Atomic Energy Agency
  (ITAEA)
  on Iran's nuclear capability 173–4
International Bank for Reconstruction
  and Development 32
International Commission of Jurists
  on the Iraq invasion 93
International Court of Justice 30,
  158–9
  Iran vs USA 160–1
  Nicaragua vs USA 159
  Palestine vs USA 161
  Robert Jackson's vision 14–15
International Criminal Court 158
  US opposition 161–2
International Military Tribunal
  (Nuremberg)
  US leadership 13–17
International Monetary Fund
  African influence 236–7
  on China's contribution to growth
  242
  establishment 32
Iran
  CIA intervention (1953) 69–74
  compliance with the JCPOA 174
  effects of sanctions 174
  legacy of intervention 73–4
  military support from China and
  Russia 217
  nuclear capability 173–4
  revolution (1979) 73–4
  ties to China 216–17
  ties with Turkey 216
  US sanctions 173–5
Iraq
  Chinese investment 222
  joins the BRI 222
  opposition to US invasion 92
  US invasion (2003) 6, 90–6
isolationism in the USA 22–3
Italian general election (1948)
  CIA intervention 68–9

Jack Ma 210
  aid to Africa 237
Jackson, Robert 14–17

ACKNOWLEDGEMENTS

As this book has followed hard on the heels of my previous book on Korea, much of the research has overlapped and many of the same debts of gratitude have accumulated. During the last four years, while writing two books, I have had the benefit of the same assiduous research assistance from Kim Khong, the same sage advice from my Australian publisher, Pam Brewster, and the same continuous valuable input from friends and scholars. I am grateful to them all, especially to Kim, who has been indefatigable.

I owe a special debt to two institutions – the Institute for Advanced Study at Princeton and Wolfson College in the University of Cambridge. My time at Princeton – in the first year of the Trump presidency – was both revelatory and moving. I walked in the steps of George Kennan and Albert Einstein and was befriended by the late, legendary Freeman Dyson. I could clearly see then how much America had changed in the almost five decades since my first visit as an impressionable young man given the honour of ringing the bell at the New York Stock Exchange. Cambridge provided serenity and research facilities but it also introduced me to the world-renowned historian Sir Richard Evans, from whose approach and example I have gained valuable insights.

Given the nature of this book however, my principal debt must be to the thinkers, philosophers, historians, journalists and social scientists who have preceded me – who have had the courage to challenge orthodoxies, stand up for principle and call out hypocrisy, hubris and expedience, and whose writings have provided so much food for thought. My debts to Senator William Fulbright, George Kennan and Andrew Bacevich are apparent from what I have written but there are many others. I also owe a debt to AC Grayling, who encouraged me, and a general debt to Simon Winchester, who inspired me.

Closer to home, I must thank and acknowledge Deonie Fiford, who undertook the copy-editing with intelligence and sensitivity; Pam Brewster, whose deft suggestions, were always valuable; my loving wife Gillian, whose concern with tone and repetition was always welcome and whose patience and understanding were a constant source of comfort; and Captain John Sutton, who contributed a valuable defence perspective whenever called for. Finally, however, all errors, infelicities and miscalculations are mine and mine alone.

Michael Pembroke was born in Sydney in 1955. He is the author of *Arthur Phillip: Sailor, Mercenary, Governor, Spy* (2013), which was shortlisted for the Prime Minister's Literary Awards, and *Korea: Where the American Century Began* (2018), which was shortlisted for the Queensland Literary Awards and the NSW Premier's History Awards. He was educated at the Universities of Sydney and Cambridge and was a Director's Visitor in 2017 at the Institute for Advanced Study, Princeton, NJ. Pembroke is a former Supreme Court judge (2010–20) and is now the Chairman of Red Room Poetry.